AMERICAN WOMEN WRITERS ON VIETNAM: UNHEARD VOICES

GARLAND REFERENCE LIBRARY
OF THE HUMANITIES
(VOL. 1278)

AMERICAN WOMEN WRITERS ON VIETNAM: UNHEARD VOICES
A Selected Annotated Bibliography

Deborah A. Butler

GARLAND PUBLISHING, INC. • NEW YORK & LONDON
1990

Library of Congress Cataloging-in-Publication Data

Butler, Deborah A.
   American women writers on Vietnam : unheard voices : a selected
annotated bibliography / Deborah A. Butler.
      p.   cm. — (Garland reference library of the humanities; vol.
1278)
   Includes index
   ISBN 0–8240–3528–3 (alk. paper)
      1. Vietnamese Conflict, 1961–1975—Literature and the conflict—
Bibliography.   2. American literature—Women authors—Bibliography.
3. American literature—20th century—Bibliography.   5. Vietnamese Conflict,
1961–1975—United States—Bibliography.   6. Women and literature—
United States—Bibliography.   7. War in literature—Bibliography.
I. Title.   II. Series.
Z1227.B88   1990
[PS228.V5]
016.8109'358—dc20   89–11963
                                                                      CIP
                                                                      Rev.

Printed on acid-free, 250-year-life paper
Manufactured in the United States of America

Dedication

This book has its roots in two veterans' lives--

My father's, Carson Butler, Jr., whose love of the American military and lifelong service to it through two wars became imprinted on me, and

My husband's, Thomas Dickinson, whose passion as a Vietnam era veteran for the war's literature and history in no small way prompted the idea for this book.

Between them, they made war seem very close and inescapably real to me.

It is also dedicated to three women--

My mother, Mary Butler, who always encouraged me to believe in my own voice, and

My two daughters, Cortney Wilson and Kathleen Dickinson ... may your voices always be heard.

Table of Contents

Acknowledgments

The list of those who made this book possible
runs long. Of all those at Wabash College who were
instrumental to my work, two people must be generously
thanked. I especially thank Debbie Polley in
interlibrary loans, whose long and tireless searching
brought many works to light which otherwise would have
remained "unheard." I also wish to thank David
Reiring, my research assistant for two summers, who
helped me unfailingly in those early days even as I
groped my way toward the idea for this book. Many
others in the Wabash library donated their support,
time, and expertise, too: Larry Frye, Eileen Simmons,
and Bruce Brinkley are among those who helped.

Wabash College as a whole was generous with its
research support, but I owe a special thanks to Paul
McKinney, Dean of the College, as well as Peter
Frederick, Don Herring, and Aus Brooks, Division
Chairs of Social Sciences, Humanities, and Sciences
respectively. They not only funded my numerous
requests for travel to library collections in Colorado
and to the Library of Congress, but their continued
interest in the project often boosted my own energies.

I am grateful, too, for research support given by
the PICAS program sponsored by the Great Lakes
Colleges Association and the University of Michigan at
Ann Arbor. Many faculty, librarians, and staff
offered good advice and important leads during my work
there; in particular, Deb Biggs of the Center for
Continuing Education for Women, and Cheryl Malone,
librarian, made my work there much more fruitful.

Others with special interest in the literature on
Vietnam helped, too. John Newman and his staff at the
Colorado State University Library welcomed my project
and me with open arms and made the unique Vietnam War
Literature Collection there available without
qualification for my work.

As the spectre of editing approached, both Julia
Rosenberg and Tom Dickinson read drafts and offered
important criticisms and insights. I am especially
indebted to Tom for his excellent and diligent work on
the author, title, and subject indexes. Phyllis
Korper, senior editor at Garland Publishing, offered
valuable encouragement and guidance during these final
months, too. Finally, I would also like to thank both

Bill Doemel and Vanessa Fuson at Wabash College, whose expertise with computers helped me through not a few frustrating editing and printing sessions.

I would like to acknowledge at last the many members of my family who came to my aid during my numerous cross-country trips to libraries and universities: Dennis, Nancy, and Stacey Dickinson in Vienna, Virgina; Shirley and Katie Dickinson in Newport News, Virginia; Richard and Susan Butler, and Judith and Burr Porter, both in Colorado Springs. They always made me feel at home away from home.

Preface

Background and Rationale

This search for American women's writing on
Vietnam grew out of my own obsessive reading of this
war's literature during the last ten years. Only a
few years ago, I was struck by the invisibility of
women's perspectives and writings on this conflict.
With a few notable exceptions, most well-known fiction
and non-fiction works were authored by men. I knew of
Bernard Fall's **Street Without Joy**, Stanley Karnow's
Vietnam: A History, and David Halberstam's **One Very
Hot Day**, for instance, but had not heard of Ellen
Hammer's **Vietnam: Yesterday and Today** or Marguerite
Higgins' **Our Vietnam Nightmare.**

My observation prompted a number of questions.
What were women writing about Vietnam from 1954 to
1975? Or about the war's aftermath? What subjects
about the country, its people, or the war itself did
women consider important? What roles had women played
in this war? How did those serving in Vietnam or
living on the homefront perceive the war?

I found myself particularly intrigued by the
image of women in the war's fiction. How did authors,
either men or women, develop female characters? How
does women's war fiction contribute to unique insights
about contemporary women's identities? In either the
fiction or non-fiction, is women's language itself
unique from men's?

All these questions begged then for exploration
as they do still. Examining any of them demanded a
search for everything available on what women wrote on
Vietnam during the period of the American war there as
well as after it ended.

Initial research turned up an abundance of
women's writing in many genres. Personal accounts by
women, such as Kathryn Marshall's oral history **In the
Combat Zone**, were only the most recent in a long line
of oral histories and personal accounts written or
edited by women since the 1960's. The periodical
literature abounded with women who worked with Vietnam
veterans and their PTSD symptoms, with women
describing the lives of other women, both American and
Vietnamese, who waited out the war at home, and with
accounts by women who lived near combat zones. In
other pieces, women examined the social and moral
turmoil in America during and after the war.

Too, it became increasingly clear that women
poets, novelists, and dramatists long ago attempted to
translate the human mysteries of this war into the

imaginative realm. In fact, the sheer volume of works
written for children and adolescents, both imaginative
and non-fiction, strongly suggests that it is women
writers who have served and are serving as the chief
translators of the war's experience for the Vietnam
generation's offspring. When women writers are not
recreating the human effects of the war for children,
they are often exploring the emotional and social
fallout from the conflict, or seeking to understand
the Vietnamese woman's brand of independence, or even
struggling to crawl inside the combat soldier's skin
and experience vicariously the heat and surge of
battle and death.

Indeed, women have been **very** vocal about their
views and experiences of Vietnam during the war, and
they have written about them in their often unique
styles. But their voices have been unheard, their
writing largely unread. This selected, annotated
bibliography of American women's writing on Vietnam
and the war may help make women's writing much more
visible. As women, and women veterans in particular,
begin to speak out more in the 1980's about their own
lives during the Vietnam War, a resource such as this
is needed increasingly in the academic world--as a
database for scholars wishing to read and write more
about women and this war, or for literature and social
science teachers wishing to develop thorough courses
including content by and about women.

Scope of the Work

The idea behind this reference work was not only
to highlight women's writing on the Vietnam War
itself, but to make clear the ideas, events, and
personalities that women focused on, even if these
were not always about the female experience nor even
the Vietnam War directly. Yet, women's experiences of
this war as well as their writing on it are two
underlying threads determining the parameters of the
book.

In searching, then selecting, and organizing the
women's writing that appears here, a number of
decisions had to be made. All of the writing included
here was published between 1954 and 1987, even though
older books by such writers as Virginia Thompson and
Ellen Hammer exist and offer much information on
Vietnamese politics and culture. Selections are
limited to those by Americans because of my own

limitations with the French and Vietnamese languages. Included, however, as a comparative perspective, is a brief section of non-American women's writing on the Vietnam War which had been translated into English during 1954-1987. These women often made interesting comments about similar issues of concern to American women. The section is not meant to represent an exhaustive search into comparative works, however.

Only published works in print appear here because of an assumption that women's written artifacts themselves would prove to be unique in style, voice, and tone. So, the bibliography includes women's books, articles, chapters, dissertations, and a couple of theses, but not film, photography, music, or other works of visual art. Newspaper articles are the exception to this "print only" guideline; while there are articles here selected from an occasional news-weekly, daily newspaper articles are not represented since by-lines do not always appear on the stories. Book reviews were excluded, too, unless the author provided a significant analysis or background so that the piece bordered on literary criticism or a historical or biographical treatise.

Because both the content and the structure of the bibliography itself reveal insights about American women and Vietnam, only those works in print I was able to read and annotate myself appear in it. Unfortunately, there were many articles and books that were unobtainable, and which may have been very interesting additions to this collection.

All the works here are by women authors, co-authors, editors, compilers, or translators. Women whose partners were men are included here also, but with only a few exceptions, works with multiple authors (three or more) were not included. The exceptions occur when most of the multiple authors were women writers. It was, again, important not to include works in which women's voices were not significant or were overwhelmed by others. Of course, such a decision meant that men's writing on women's Vietnam experiences are not included, works like Keith Walker's excellent oral history of women and Vietnam, **Pieces of My Heart**. Indeed, men, too, have been vocal about both American and Vietnamese women's war experiences, but those works are not represented.

Arrangement of Entries

The annotations themselves are descriptive of each work rather than evaluative. They are all organized into three major sections which divide women's writing by type of discourse. Within each of those sections, subcategories of imaginative, personal, and factual writing comprise the whole. Author, subject, and title indexes appear at the end of the book. The terms for the subject index were arrived at by noting throughout the research phase certain common themes underlying much of the women's writing regardless of the genre.

Each subcategory is organized alphabetically, but chronologically by decade. The structure of this work reveals possible patterns in the experience behind women's writing in the 1950's, 60's, 70's, and 80's, so all entries are grouped together by these decades within each topical division. One then notes easily what general themes concerned women of each decade and whether or not women's concerns, in general, change or remain stable over time.

Finally, readers will notice variations in spellings of common terms from entry to entry or in common phrases (e.g., Viet Cong or Vietcong, Viet Nam or Vietnam, Conflict or War). Where possible, the variation used is one that the author preferred and used in her work. Beyond this, there may be errors in usage of some terms and perhaps in information. Readers' comments, corrections, and suggestions which make this work more useable are more than welcome. Especially welcome are notices of important writing left unheard since my own interest in the breadth of women's writing on Vietnam continues to grow.

List of Abbreviations

AAAS	American Association for Advancement of Science
AFSC	American Friends Service Committee
ARVN	Army of the Republic of Vietnam
ASEAN	Association of Southeast Asian Nations
DEROS	Date of Expected Return from Overseas
DOD	Department of Defense
DRV	Democratic Republic of Vietnam
GVN	Government of Vietnam
ICCS	International Commission of Control and Supervision
KIA	Killed In Action
MACV	Military Assistance Command, Vietnam
MIA	Missing In Action
NLF	National Liberation Front
NVA	North Vietnamese Army
POW	Prisoner of War
PRG	Provisional Revolutionary Government
PTSD	Post-traumatic Stress Disorder
UPI	United Press International
U.S. AID	U.S. Agency for International Development
USOM	United States Operations Mission
VA	Veterans Administration
VVAW	Vietnam Veterans Against the War

VVMF   Vietnam Veterans Memorial
                       Fund

WAC   Women's Army Corps
W.H.O.   World Health Organization

American Women Writers on
Vietnam: Unheard Voices

WOMEN, LITERATURE, AND VIETNAM

Novels

1960-1969

1. Carroll, Gladys Hasty. **The Light Here Kindled**. Boston: Little, Brown and Co., 1967. South Yarmouth, Mass.: J. Curley, 1983.

   The novel concerns family and personal relationships in the Vietnam era. The lives of several people and their families are interwoven, and through the course of the novel's plot, Carroll develops the themes of growth and generational differences. Each character's life crosses the others, and finally, the whole group buys a single dwelling. Vietnam and the war pervade the novel as Carroll creates a backdrop against the war protest and the Vietnam service of the young men in these families.

2. Dean, Nell. **Nurse in Vietnam**. New York: Julian Messner, 1969.

   The novel's main character, Lisa Blake, is a nurse on a surgical team at Clark Air Force Base. Because her lover, a pilot, was killed in Vietnam, she herself volunteers for service there. While in Vietnam, she meets a Green Beret and falls in love. The novel was billed at publication as "A Career Romance for Young Moderns."

3. Dunn, Mary Lois. **The Man in the Box: A Story from Vietnam**. New York: McGraw-Hill Bk. Co., 1968.

   A very young boy undertakes an adult-like moral quest when he tries to liberate an American prisoner from a box where the soldier is kept in the boy's village. The boy leaves his home to help the American return to his own territory. After the hardships they face, they develop a strong attachment. When the two are separated on the journey to DaNang, the boy endures great fear, but is later reunited with the soldier. The novel is written in a style that suggests it is a children's book, but its events are nightmarish.

4. Field, Della. **Vietnam Nurse**. New York: Avon Bks., 1966.

   This is a novel about a young nurse, Natalie, who joins the Navy in order to continue searching for her fiance who has been missing in Vietnam for over a year. As she searches, she begins to gain confidence in her own competencies. Finally, she realizes she has a mission beyond her own needs. Through a Vietnamese friend, she learns of her fiance's death, but because of her own feelings of mission, she remains in Vietnam even though she has a new romance with a soldier who has returned home.

5. Roberts, Suzanne. **Vietnam Nurse**. New York: Ace Bks., 1966.

   The novel is one of the earliest nurse novels of Vietnam. It is a romance set in a field hospital. The main character, Katie, finds herself fulfilling a long family tradition of combat nursing, and she also finds two men, opposites in personality, both of whom she loves. For much of the plot, she bobs back and forth from one to the other, finally ending up with a future husband.

6. Shepard, Elaine. **The Doom Pussy**. New York: Trident Press, 1967.

   Shepard, a journalist in Vietnam, writes of her time spent with the pilots who flew combat missions over the North at night. The book's title comes from an emblem the pilots wore. The work is actually quasi-fiction and fact because Shepard artistically shapes experiences into a near-novel form.

1970-1979

7. Browne, Corinne. **Body Shop: Recuperating from
    Vietnam**. New York: Stein and Day, 1973.

    Browne tells the story of six or seven men
    who are recuperating from wounds in a hospital
    and rest center for traumatically injured war
    veterans. The account, while based on fact,
    shades into fiction since Browne shows patient
    interrelationships using freely created
    dialogue. The book is a jolting account of men
    who must adjust to themselves and to a new life
    as crippled men re-entering "the world," trying
    to maintain or begin personal relationships
    again.

8. Clark, Ann Nolan. **To Stand Against the Wind**.
    New York: Viking Press, 1978.

    A young Vietnamese boy, Em, prays to his
    ancestors on an important ancestral day. He and
    the remainder of his family now live in America,
    and they rely on him as the head of household.
    As Em spends his day in meditation, he remembers
    his family's past personal history. Through
    flashbacks, his life in a small village, the
    departure of the French and the coming of the
    Americans, and the slow, painful deterioration
    of normal life over the war years, wash over
    him, revealing his inner reality. Em finds he
    is able to withstand the pain and even draw
    strength from remembering his family's past.

9. Davidson, Sara. **Loose Change, Three Women of
    the Sixties**. Garden City, N.Y.: Doubleday
    and Co., 1977.

    Davidson reclaims the 1960's by interweaving
    the story of three friends' lives during the
    late 1960's and early 1970's. For all the
    women, but especially Susie, the Vietnam War
    protest colors their lives. For years, Susie's
    life centers on her husband's and her war
    resistance. In one section, she actually visits
    South Vietnam, and takes a Vietnamese lover as
    part of her quest for identity.

10. Graham, Gail. **Cross-fire: A Vietnam Novel**.
     New York: Pantheon Bks., 1972.

          An American soldier awakens in the jungle to
     find that he is wounded and alone; his platoon
     is nowhere to be found. He stumbles upon four
     Vietnamese children who have just been orphaned
     by Americans bombing their village. The
     Vietnamese and the American soldier cannot
     understand each other, but because the author
     presents each side's feelings and thoughts in
     alternating chapters, the reader knows the
     story, feelings, and needs of each. Although
     their goals are at cross-purposes, gradually the
     soldier and one of the children establish an
     unspoken friendship and begin to protect each
     other. In spite of the growing hope of all the
     characters, they are killed and become anonymous
     victims of the war.

11. Karl, Terry, Gail Dolgin, Martha Williams, Rob
          Kessler, and Sarah Dandridge. **Children of
          the Dragon**. San Francisco: People's Press,
          1974.

          The book is a short children's book, a
     fiction version of the end of the war in 1973
     told from the North Vietnamese point of view. A
     young child Tri, who has been sent by his
     parents in Hanoi to his family in the
     countryside, lives with his cousin Hoa until it
     is safe to return to the city. In the country,
     he learns the old legends about independence
     from his grandmother, works in the village, and
     celebrates Vietnam's coming independence. He
     returns to Hanoi after the 1973 ceasefire having
     made new friends and having realized more about
     the richness of his country's heritage.

12. King, Annette. **The Magic Tortoise Ranch**. New
          York: Crown Pubs., 1972.

          This is a novel about a group of young people
     who live together on a farm in California. One
     character, Kenny, is a veteran, and a chapter in
     the novel is an account of his Vietnam
     experiences. The "family," an unaccepted
     phenomenon in the county, is driven out, leaving
     Kenny and several others dead. The novel ends

on a more hopeful note as the remaining members
of the family attempt to start a new life.

13. Moore, Robin, with June Collins. **The Khaki
     Mafia**. New York: Crown Pubs., 1971. New
     York: Avon Bks., 1972.

     The "khaki mafia" is a group of Army men who
design a money-making venture at the expense of
the Army: each makes a profit from swindled
goods in military clubs. The central plot
occurs in Vietnam during the American phase of
the war. Collins' experiences as an entertainer
in Vietnam seem to be developed in the plot
through the main character, Jody O'Neal, whose
exploits in Vietnam involve her intimately with
the "mafia." Eventually, she assists in the
lengthy government investigations designed to
break up the criminal activity.

14. Sanders, Pamela. **Miranda**. Boston: Little,
     Brown and Co., 1978. London: H. Hamilton,
     1979.

     Sanders uses Laos, Vietnam, and other
Southeast Asian countries as backgrounds for her
main character, the journalist Miranda, and her
romantic intrigues. The frame of the novel is a
sailing trip around the world with Miranda and
her domineering father. Much of the plot uses
flashbacks to develop the events of the novel.
These are usually daring journalistic escapades
spiced with sexual activity.

15. Silver, Joan, and Linda Gottlieb. **Limbo**. New
     York: Viking Press, 1972. New York: Pocket
     Bks., 1972. London: Heinemann, 1972.
     London: Coronet Bks., 1973.

     The novel's "limbo" exists for the wives of
POW's and MIA's. The plot revolves around three
women, each of whom has a husband lost in
Vietnam. One, Mary Kaye, is released from limbo
when she finds out her husband is dead.
Another, Sharon, is driven into the limbo of
madness when she realizes no one will ever be
certain if her husband is alive or not.
Finally, the third character, Sandy, develops a
serious relationship with a professor named

Alan, and must choose between him and her
returning POW husband, Roy. Her choice to
resume her life with Roy leaves Alan in his own
limbo. Throughout the narrative, the American
military looms as villainous as the North
Vietnamese.

16.   Southall, Rita, and Carl Shears. **The Black
      Letters: Love Letters from a Black Soldier in
      Viet Nam**. Washington, D.C.: Nuclassics and
      Science Publishing Co., 1972.

The book is constructed around a series of
letters sent by a black soldier to his
girlfriend. He is stationed at Da Nang near
China Beach. Interspersed among his letters are
scenes of her reactions to his long distance
attention, and his conversations with people on
the base. His letters pledge love, marriage,
and faithfulness. Upon his return, however, he
never calls or goes to see her.

1980–1987

17.   Blair, Cynthia. **Battle Scars**. New York:
      Ballantine Bks., 1983.

The title of this book actually describes
everyone's wounds: the unhealed wounds of a
family which lost its son and brother in
Vietnam, and the wounds of a still readjusting
veteran. Both sets of scars multiply as main
characters Kate and Ben attempt to develop a
lasting relationship, an attempt which forces
them both to refight old battles and open old
wounds in the struggle for a final healing.

18.   Boyd, Candy Dawson. **Charlie Pippen**. New
      York: Macmillan Publishing Co., 1987. New
      York: Puffin Bks., 1988.

The novel is written for children and young
adolescents. The main character, Charlie, is
black. Her father is a scarred Vietnam veteran,
and although the family has remained together,
many of their problems stem from his failures to
deal with the war. Charlie is obsessed with the
desire to understand the Vietnam War, for if she

can, she believes she will then help her father.
She intensively researches the war, sneaks off
on a secretly planned trip to see the Wall, and
becomes the instrument by which her father
begins to come to terms with his painful
memories.

19. Davis, Patti, with Maureen Strange Foster.
     Home Front. New York: Crown Pubs., 1986.
     Boston: G.K. Hall and Co., 1987. New York:
     Ivy Bks., 1987. New York: Ballantine Bks.,
     1987. London: New English Library, 1987.

     This is a nearly autobiographical account
based on Reagan's daughter's life during the
1960's and early 1970's. The main character,
Elizabeth (Beth) Canfield, views these years as
a high school and college student in a flashback
sequence after her father, former governor of
California, has become President. Beginning
with her adolescent years in an Arizona boarding
school, she describes her awakening to sex,
politics, and a quest for personal identity.
Her first love, Greg, becomes a Vietnam vet, and
his changes are woven closely into her own
awakening and rebellion as the protest movement
develops. The growth of her value system pits
her against her parents' radically conservative
views. The birth of her own social
consciousness allows her to perceive the horrors
of the war for both alienated youths at home and
those returning from Vietnam.

20. Degens, T. **Friends**. New York: Viking Press,
     1981.

     The novel is written for young people
although its themes are sophisticated and
somewhat brutal. A young girl on the verge of
adolescence, Nell, is the heroine, and it is
through her life's events during her sixth grade
year that the book's Vietnam connection exists.
Nell's attachment to the war is both personal
and cultural. She absorbs the war daily from
television until it becomes grist for children's
games (e.g., the Tet game she creates). The war
is a backdrop to the novel's events, yet it is
not detached scenery. It and the protestors
subtly impact on Nell throughout. Her only

direct attachment to war comes from an older
friend who is drafted, writes her frequently,
and comes to see her as he waits for orders for
Vietnam.

21.   Dickason, Christie. **The Dragon Riders**.
         London: Century Hutchinson, 1986. London:
         Coronet Bks., 1987. Published as **Indochine**.
         New York: Villard Books, 1987. New York:
         Bantam Bks., 1988.

      The book is an epic novel of Vietnam from the
      1920's to the 1960's. The first part develops
      the key characters: the young Vietnamese boy,
      Luoc, bent on revenge on the French colonials
      for the death of his father, and Ariane, a young
      French governess in Saigon who marries Luoc.
      Together they parent the story's heroine, Nina,
      who is born at the end of the first part of the
      three-part novel. Nina grows up in Dalat,
      living with her wealthy parents through the
      Vietminh victory over the French, the partition
      of her country, and the coming of the Americans.
      Heiress to a large opium enterprise and an
      accomplished guerrilla fighter, Nina's
      subsequent encounters include a great deal of
      romance and danger.

22.   Didion, Joan. **Democracy**. New York: Simon and
         Schuster, 1984. New York: Pocket Bks., 1985.

      The book's plot occurs in 1975. The first
      two-thirds establishes the characters in famous
      extended families--the Christians and the
      Victors--both of whom wield wealth and power,
      the latter family in American politics. The
      Vietnam War serves as a backdrop to sections of
      this part of the novel, but Vietnam becomes a
      focus in the latter third, when the daughter of
      Inez and Harry Victor determines to get a job in
      Vietnam near the time of the fall of Saigon.
      The plot then centers on her "rescue" in April,
      1975, and her mother's subsequent break from
      their past artificial life. The novel closes as
      Inez works with refugees in Kuala Lumpur.

23.   Dodd, Susan. **No Earthly Notion**. New York:
         Viking Press, 1986. New York: Penguin Bks.,
         1987.

This is a novel only peripherally dealing with Vietnam or its effects. Muranda and her brother, Lyman Gene, grow up in Kentucky. After their parents' deaths, he graduates, goes into the Army and is sent to Vietnam. The experience leaves him mute and only vacantly attentive to those about him including his sister who attends his needs. Only his unending voracious appetite drives him, a drive which becomes their only connection and which she tries to ignore until his extreme obesity kills him. Her life goes on from there, slowly renewing itself in spite of another major loss later in the book. It is a novel about loneliness, strength, growth, and despair with Vietnam as a part of the causes and effects.

24. Farrington, Carolyn G. "Blowin' In the Wind: A Story of the Sixties." Ph.D. diss., State University of New York at Albany, 1986.

This is the story of a family and the changes each experiences during the 1960's. The Vietnam War, as well as other social issues and events, impacts on the characters' lives, causing serious crises and important resolutions.

25. Hawkins, Evelyn. **Vietnam Nurse**. New York: Zebra Bks., 1984.

This romance novel is set in Vietnam. The main character, Sybil, is a nurse, and she and her friends find ways to help each other cope with the pain they see. When Sybil meets Brian, a Green Beret constantly being sent on dangerous missions, she falls in love. He is killed on his final mission. Devastated, she nonetheless returns to nursing and tries to cope with this latest tragedy.

26. Hazzard, Mary. **Idle and Disorderly Persons, A Novel**. Seattle: Madrona Pubs., 1981.

Hazzard writes a novel of the homefront during the Vietnam War years, 1969-71. The Wyatts, their marriage, and their friendships are focused on as a kind of case study of what the times did to individuals and their families. As wife Phoebe Wyatt becomes more involved in

protesting the war, she consequently becomes
more independent. Husband Daniel finds he needs
the support of a more helpless, adoring mate,
and he drifts into an affair. Almost every
major relationship in the book dramatically
alters in part due to the deep social and
personal questioning caused by war issues. The
novel's conclusion finds Phoebe continuing to
liberate herself from her past.

27. Heckler, Jonellen. **Safekeeping**. New York:
      Ballantine Bks., 1983. New York: G.P.
      Putnam's Sons, 1983. New York: Fawcett
      Pubs., 1984. London: Futura Publications,
      1984. London: Macdonald and Co., 1984.

      The novel's main character is Judy Greer, a
POW wife who, after five years of waiting
without word from her captured husband, Ron,
finally reaches her limit with her existence in
limbo. Because of her husband's importance to
the military (he is a specialist on China), she
is discouraged from seeking a divorce, an action
which in the eyes of the military might
traumatize him or leave him with no will to
live. Judy finally does take a lover, a Capt.
Joe Campbell, who is actually the army's best
"crisis mediator." Unfortunately and
unintentionally, he does become truly personally
involved with her. Ron returns to his family at
the end of the book, leaving Joe Campbell in
limbo.

28. Mason, Bobbie Ann. **In Country**. New York:
      Harper and Row Pubs., 1985. New York:
      Perennial, 1986. South Yarmouth, Mass.: J.
      Curley, 1986. London: Chatto and Windus,
      1986. London: Flamingo, 1987.

      Eighteen-year-old Sam searches for the
reality of her dead father, a soldier killed in
Vietnam when he was eighteen. The plot unfolds
within a frame; she and her Vietnam veteran
uncle, Emmet, travel to Washington, D.C. to see
the Vietnam Veterans Memorial. On the way she
remembers the reasons that prompted her journey.
The inner tale tells of the reconstruction of a
person, a person Sam feels she must come to know
if she is ever to fulfill her own quest for

identity. Through reading her father's letters
and diaries, talking about him with her mother,
and coming to know other Vietnam veterans in her
life, she tries to complete her quest for his
re-creation and her own. The book ends as she
and Emmet face the overwhelming reality of the
Wall, each beginning to come to terms with the
personal legacies left by the war. Ultimately,
the novel is a gripping account of the longterm
impact of Vietnam on American lives.

29. Moore, Elisabeth Sims. **Bend with the Wind**.
     Port Washington, New York: Ashley Bks., 1980.

     The novel's main character is Marty Fountain,
a surgical nurse, who, because of a failed
romance in Boston, flees to Saigon to nurse. En
route, she is coerced by a Dr. Peter Cain into
serving on his staff in Quang Ngai. Once there,
a series of war adventures begins. Marty finds
herself vaccinating and treating the native
population in their villages, experiencing a
helicopter crash in the jungle, and the capture
of her friends by Vietcong while at a
leprosarium. In the midst of these events, she
struggles with another nurse for the affections
of Peter Cain. Finally rescued by South
Vietnamese, she and Peter return to be married.

30. Moulton, Elizabeth. **Fatal Demonstrations**.
     New York: Harper and Row Pubs., 1980.

     Moulton writes a novel which weaves together
the lives and social backdrops of two
generations of people. The main characters are
the grandmother, Isobel, and her long-dead lover
Curtis, a young man who championed the
Sacco-Vanzetti case and who is described in a
series of flashbacks. David and Robin, the
former an English professor who is writing a
biography of Curtis, and the latter, his
girlfriend and Isobel's granddaughter, are also
central to the plot. The time is the 1970's, a
time when anti-war protest was at its height.
The two ages and personalities are contrasted
and compared as the plot unfolds against the
backdrop of the Vietnam War.

31. Okimoto, Jean Davies. **Jason's Women**. Boston:

Atlantic Monthly Press, 1986. Boston:
Little, Brown, 1986. New York: Dell
Publishing Co., 1988.

This is a novel written for adolescents. The
story centers on a shy 16-year-old, Jason Kovak.
With his older brother gone and his Mom and Dad
recently divorced and acting like singles again,
Jason is alone, which complicates his natural
shyness and reticence. While trying to locate a
new job, he is hired by an eccentric old lady to
be both her campaign manager (she wants to run
for mayor) and her all-around handyman. One of
his tasks is to help Thao, a 16 year old
Vietnamese refugee, to speak English better.
The last half of the book explores the growing
relationship of the two adolescents, each lonely
and alone in a different way. How each grows
and gains confidence from the friendship
completes the book.

32.   Phillips, Jayne Anne. **Machine Dreams**. New
        York: E. P. Dutton/Seymour Lawrence, 1984.
        New York: Pocket Bks., 1985.

Phillips' novel chronicles two generations of
one family in which father and son serve in
World War II and the Vietnam War respectively.
Each section of the first half of the book is
told from the point of view of the mother, Jean,
or the father, Mitch. In the second half of the
book, the growth of their children, Danner and
Billy, proceeds until each is a young adult, and
Billy confronts a critical decision. Either he
must continue college to avoid the war, or allow
himself to be drafted. He is drafted and is
sent to Vietnam. Finally, the notice of his MIA
status arrives, and the novel closes with two
poignant sections describing Danner's reactions
and adjustment to his fate.

33.   Singer, Marilyn. **The First Few Friends**. New
        York: Harper and Row Pubs., 1981.

The main character, a young college student,
returns from a year's study abroad. The year is
1968, and she comes from an idyllic year of
romance to a society filled with demonstrations
over social issues and the Vietnam War. The

book traces her growth. At her return she grows
closer to a group of old girlfriends, playing at
unconventional lifestyles. These are her first
friends back, but numerous male friends
challenge her naive and romantic ideals that the
former group perpetuates. One male friend is
drafted, considers dodging, then serves. He is
wounded and returns to become part of the VVAW.
Another, a black militant, becomes her closest
friend and lover. These last few people,
because they hold ideals that are socially
realistic, become her true "friends."

34. Walsh, Patricia. **Forever Sad the Hearts**. New
       York: Avon Bks., 1982.

       Kate Shea, an American nurse, joins a
government hospital staff in DaNang sponsored by
the Better World Organization. Their mission is
to treat civilian Vietnamese casualties and to
train Vietnamese medical personnel as part of
the "Vietnamization" plan. People abound
throughout the plot: sarcastic Margaret, a
British nurse; Tom and Shelley, a nurse and her
corpsman lover; various doctors; and the
Vietnamese pupils at the hospital. While Kate's
love affair with a Green Beret, Dan, is central,
enough strands weave through the plot creating a
vision of the normal workings of a hospital.
The incidents also reveal the struggle to
survive and assist others in the midst of graft,
corruption, and the personal pain of losing
friends. The ending of the book finds Kate
leaving Vietnam to try to begin her life anew.

35. Wartski, Maureen Crane. **A Boat to Nowhere**.
       Philadelphia: Westminster Press, 1980. New
       York: New American Library, 1981.

       In this children's novel, a Vietnamese boy,
Kien, fleeing the Communist regime in southern
Vietnam, finds a home in a small Vietnamese
fishing village. Two children, Mai and Loc,
Grandfather, and he flee on the boat "Sea
Breeze" after the Communists take over the
village. In the second section, the three find
themselves "boat people," and experience the
hardships and alienation common to these
refugees. Finally, an American freighter picks

them up and they are promised sponsorship in
America.

36. Wartski, Maureen Crane. **A Long Way from Home**.
       Philadelphia: Westminster Press, 1980. New
       York: New American Library, 1982.

       This novel is the sequel to **A Boat To
Nowhere** and tells the story of Mai's, Loc's, and
Kien's new home. Both Mai and Loc adapt
quickly, but Kien runs away to another town
which hosts a thriving Vietnamese community.
There he experiences a different kind of
American-Vietnamese conflict on this soil, one
caused by bigotry and narrow-mindedness toward
immigrants. At the end of the novel, he returns
to his new parents.

37. White, Teri. **Tightrope**. New York: Mysterious
       Press, 1986.

       After a first chapter set in Saigon at its
fall in 1975, the book becomes a "cops and
robbers" detective story. All the main
characters (two policemen and three criminals)
as well as many of the subsidiary ones, are
Vietnam veterans. The three criminals attempt
to retrieve stolen diamonds lost in Saigon,
while the two detectives slowly discover their
scheme. The climax naturally finds the three
criminals subdued and the police solving the
case. Many of the minor characters involved in
the last parts of the book are Vietnamese
immigrants in America. Woven into the plot are
the human asides of romance, family problems,
and friendships among veterans suffering from
the war's effects.

38. Wolitzer, Meg. **Caribou**. New York:
       Greenwillow Bks., 1984. New York: Bantam
       Bks., 1986.

       This is an adolescent novel about 12-year-old
Becca Silverman and her family in 1970. The
novel opens as she, her 19-year-old brother, and
their parents watch the draft lottery on
television. Upon learning that his birthdate is
the first called, her brother Stevie decides to
leave for Canada. His decision alienates his

parents but not Becca, who, in her own way, must
make her own stand both against the war and for
her own independence. The rest of the book's
plot revolves around her completion of an
anti-war mural and her visit to her brother in
Canada. The book ends as she returns home,
hoping that one day her brother may be able to
return also.

39. Wolkoff, Judie. **Where The Elf King Sings**.
     Scarsdale, N.Y.: Bradbury Press, 1980.
     Published as **A Stranger in the Family**. New
     York: Scholastic Book Services, 1980.

     The book appears to be an adolescent novel.
The main character, Marcie, is 12. Her father
is a Vietnam veteran who returned home in 1972
only to find he suffers from nightmares about
his best friend's death in Vietnam, nightmares
which are partly responsible for his alcoholism.
Through Marcie's eyes, the author tells of the
family's near breakup, but the novel concludes
on a hopeful note.

Short Fiction

1960-1969

40. Richie, Mary. "Hunt and Destroy." **New American Review**, no. 6 (1969): 64-68. Also in **The Fact of Fiction: Social Relevance in Short Stories**, edited by Cyril Gulassa, 99-103. San Francisco: Canfield Press, 1972.

 The story concerns a corporal, Jimmy, who while on patrol takes a pet snake from a captured Vietcong prisoner. He manages to keep the poisonous snake through the rest of his tour without it biting him.

41. Robertson, Dorothy, trans. **Fairy Tales From Vietnam**. New York: Dodd, Mead, and Co., 1968.

 This is a translation of eight famous tales of Vietnam. The book of stories is framed by a holiday occasion at the home of the Nguyen family on the night of the annual Children's Festival and Lantern Parade.

1970-1979

42. Bambara, Toni Cade. "The Sea Birds Are Still Alive." In her **The Sea Birds Are Still Alive: Collected Stories**, 71-93. New York: Random House, 1977. New York: Vintage Bks., 1982. London: Women's Press, 1984.

 Several people cross a river on a ferry. Although none speaks to another, Bambara shows us the thoughts and actions of each individual. Central to the story is a young girl who throws bread to the sea birds while hungry refugees look on.

43. Boyle, Kay. "You Don't Have To Be a Member of the Congregation." In **Little Victories, Big Defeats: War as the Ultimate Pollution**, compiled by Georgess McHargue, 11-18. New York: Delacorte Press, 1974. New York: Random House, 1977. New York: Dell Publishing Co., 1978.

A writer sees a potential story about the silent man sitting day after day in the darkened corner of a church. The man is on a hunger strike protesting the war in Vietnam. After waiting in vain for anyone to communicate with the striker, the writer finally notices a young soldier approach the man to tell him he has decided not to go to Vietnam. The writer realizes that a story can now be told.

44. Grau, Shirley. "Homecoming." In her **The Wind Shifting West**, 41-54. New York: Alfred A. Knopf, 1973.

A young girl lives alone with her widowed mother. She receives word that a distant friend, a young man, has been killed in Vietnam. Her mother and her friends use the occasion to relive the girl's father's death in World War II. Finally, the young woman challenges the older adults' glorification of war, admitting her thoughts about the waste and destruction all wars represent.

45. Kaplan, Johanna. "Dragon Lady." **Harper's** 241 (July 1970): 78-83. Also in **Writing Under Fire: Stories of the Vietnam War**, edited by Jerome Klinkowitz and John Somer, 22-34. New York: Dell Publishing Co., 1978.

Ling Sut On is a Chinese descendent who lives in Cholon with her rather undistinguished extended family. Her grandfather, a learned and still well-respected man, and she sustain a special relationship, and because of this, he selects her to attend school. Years later during the Vietnam War, she becomes an educated young woman who is a member of the NLF and a sniper.

46. Kumin, Maxine. "The Missing Person." In **The Best American Short Stories, 1979,** edited by Joyce Carol Oates, 234-242. Boston: Houghton Mifflin Co., 1979. Also in **The Best of Tri-Quarterly**, edited by Jonathan Brent, 152-160. New York: Washington Square Press, 1982.

The major character in this story is a woman

Ellie, who, along with her husband, Alan,
travels to New York City to see her
ex-daughter-in-law in a play. Her son, Jay, is
an MIA in Vietnam. Once in New York, she and
Alan become separated. Unable to locate him,
she reports him missing. In the course of
dealing with this problem, Ellie comes to terms
with Jay's probable death.

47. Lowell, Susan. "David". **The Southern
Review** 7 (January 1971): 254-264.

The story is told from the point of view of a
young girl who is attracted to a young man named
David. Both are high school graduates; she
plans to attend college, while he will join the
Marines. As their relationship grows, aspects
of David's character and hers are revealed. He
is a free spirit, but he is determined not to
alter her future in any way. Even though their
relationship fades, his memory remains strong
for her and she worries for his safety.

48. Oates, Joyce Carol. "Out of Place." In her
The Seduction and Other Stories, 154-164.
Los Angeles: Black Sparrow Press, 1975. New
York: Fawcett Pubs., 1980. New York:
Ballantine Bks., 1984.

A young man returns from Vietnam severely
wounded; he is nearly blind and has lost one
leg. Although he has become well-adjusted
himself, he is made to feel guilty and out of
place by the negative comments of the college
anti-war protestors he encounters.

49. Rascoe, Judith. "Soldier, Soldier." In her
Yours, and Mine: Novella and Stories,
164-179. Boston: Little, Brown and Co.,
1973.

Two people, Nick and Nola, find themselves
outcast from their social groups, he
because he is a Vietnam veteran, she because she
breaks up with her boyfriend who is a leader in
the Resistance Movement. The two are drawn to
each other, and Nola finds herself obsessed with
wondering what Nick's wartime experiences were
like.

50.   Smith, Kathleen.   "Letters from Viet Nam."   In
         The Fallen Angel and Other Stories, edited by
         Mel Cebulash, 115-120.   New York: Scholastic
         Book Services, 1972.

      This is a story about a lonely vet who writes
      a high school girl he never personally knew.
      Through their letters they come to know each
      other.   Wounded, he returns to a hospital where
      she visits him.   He dies as she sings a favorite
      song of his at his request.

51.   Yates, Ethel.   "Seeds of Time."   In **Alabama
         Prize Stories, 1970**, edited by O. B. Emerson,
         262-273.   Huntsville, Ala.: Strode Pubs.,
         1970.

      The story is about three friends who find
      themselves out drinking.   One, Harry, shortly
      after joins the Marines and is sent to Vietnam.
      Severely wounded, he returns to his friends.
      Again, they reflect on each others' pasts and
      futures together, each having lost opportunities
      for a future during the intervening year.

1980-1987

52.   Abrams, Linsey.   "Secrets Men Keep."
         Mademoiselle 91 (August 1985): 144-46,
         279-83.

      The story's main characters include members
      of one family.   One, a father and a husband, is
      a wounded Vietnam veteran. He is seen only
      through the thoughts and conversation of Ellen
      and Jeffrey, his wife and son, and his sister
      Joanne as they all spend their day at the beach.
      Most of the day's events lead to a culminating
      insight for Ellen: each family member has been
      wounded by her husband's Vietnam experiences and
      his permanent paralysis from a Vietcong attack.
      But the story's end, Jeffrey's rescue from
      drowning by two strong men, leaves Ellen and
      Jeffrey more hopeful of a more fulfilling life.

53.   Alberts, Laurie.   "Veterans." In **Love Stories,
         Love Poems: An Anthology**, edited by Joe David
         Bellamy and Roger Weingarten, 56-64.   San
         Diego: Fiction International, 1982.

The woman character in this story examines her current and past attractions to Vietnam veterans. With each, including her current friend, Stephan, she incessantly probes them for details of their war experiences, always trying to see what they have seen. The story concludes as she finds herself alone again.

54. Casper, Susan. "Covenant with a Dragon." In **In the Field of Fire**, edited by Jack Dann, and Jeanne Van Buren Dann, 305-324. New York: Tom Doherty Associates, 1987.

   This is a vet's story about his ESP-like discovery of the existence of his half-Vietnamese child in the American city he now lives in. His discovery and his subsequent claiming of the child are aided by the supernatural threat of the Vietnamese mother whose spirit exists within a token. Her threat will destroy his present existence unless he claims responsibility for their child.

55. Creighton, Jane. "My Home in the Country." In **Unwinding the Vietnam War: From War Into Peace**, edited by Reese Williams, 49-67. Seattle: Real Comet Press, 1987.

   The first half of this story allows us to see the main character, a young girl, growing up in the sixties. Described are her early years, experiences with anti-war protest, and her parents' deaths. The last half of the story finds her haunting constantly the Vietnam Memorial, gaining sustenance from watching its effect upon everyone else. It has become her home in this country.

56. Erdrich, Louise. "A Bridge." Chapter in **Love Medicine**, 130-142. New York: Holt, Rinehart and Winston, 1984. New York: Bantam Bks., 1987.

   The narrator focuses alternately on two characters--the young runaway girl, Alberdine, and Henry, the young Vietnam veteran. By chance they meet in Fargo, North Dakota, and spend a night together. Upon awakening, he explodes into violence, thinking he is in Vietnam, and he

hits her. The story ends with Henry weeping
over her, unable to cross a bridge to normalcy.

57. _____. "The Red Convertible."
    Chapter in her **Love Medicine**, 143-154. New
    York: Holt, Rinehart and Winston, 1984. New
    York: Bantam Bks., 1987.

    This is another chapter, later in **Love
    Medicine**, about Henry and his brother, Lyman.
    The story is told from Lyman's point of view an
    occurs about a year later than "The Bridge."
    Much of the story recounts the psychological
    changes Lyman perceives in his brother after
    Henry's return from Vietnam. The story
    culminates with Henry's suicide by drowning,
    which Lyman caps by submerging their car next t
    him.

58. Fowler, Karen. "The Lake Was Full of Artificia
    Things". **Isaac Asimov's Science Fiction
    Magazine** 9 (1985): 126-35.

    In this science fiction story, the main
    character, Miranda, is a 50-year-old woman, who
    in the year 2000, wishes to rid herself of guil
    associated with the death of her first lover,
    Daniel, in the Vietnam War. Through a
    psychologist's manipulations of her memories,
    she is able to simulate being with him again, a
    simulation whose purpose is to allow her to
    exonerate herself from guilt associated with hi
    going to Vietnam. As she continues to see him,
    the memories become more real until it is clear
    that Daniel is actually present. In the end,
    they both bring finality to their situation.

59. _____. "Letters from Home." In **In
    the Field of Fire**, edited by Jack Dann, and
    Jeanne Van Buren Dann, 70-89. New York: Tom
    Doherty Associates, 1987.

    The story's structure is contained in a
    series of letters that are really diary entries
    Written to an old boyfriend, they are part of a
    insistent quest by a young woman to finally
    understand what the war was like for her old
    boyfriend. Her letters also chronicle "the war
    at home" during the height of the conflict.

60. Geller, Ruth. "Pat's Friend Norm." In her
     Pictures from the Past and Other Stories,
     187-194. Buffalo, N.Y.: Imp Press, 1980.

         Norm and Pat are childhood friends. He is
     drafted, sent to Vietnam, and returns. They
     stay in touch through the years, however, and on
     one visit to Pat, Norm reveals his deteriorating
     physical condition. He is losing hair and
     noticing scaly patches on his skin. The story
     leaves the impression that the war has left him
     a victim of Agent Orange.

61. Harrington, Joyce. "A Letter to Amy." In **The**
     Year's Best Mystery and Suspense Stories,
     1986, edited by Edward D. Hoch, 83-101. New
     York: Walker and Co., 1986.

         Harrington's narrator is a young man who
     constantly writes his daughter Amy who is living
     with his estranged wife. He never receives a
     reply. As he wonders about her silence, he
     reviews the days following his return from
     Vietnam when he was a veteran with problems
     adjusting. He returned to find his mother dead,
     his father remarried and unwelcoming. Although
     he did marry and father Amy, his life continued
     to spiral downward. He was even fired from his
     first job because of his uncontrollable temper.
     The narrator reveals then that, in a fit of
     anger, he has killed both Amy and his wife and
     is now in prison. Under his mattress lie the
     many letters he has written Amy.

62. Kalpakian, Laura. "Veteran's Day." In **Stand**
     One: Winners of the Stand Magazine Short
     Story Competition, edited by Michael
     Blackburn, Jon Silkin, and Lorna Tracy, 9-30.
     London: Victor Gollancz, 1984.

         A Vietnam veteran returns from the war
     harboring the belief that the government is
     poisoning people's minds and making them totally
     controllable. He is arrested just before he can
     deliver a speech about his beliefs on TV on
     Veteran's Day. The story ends as the veteran's
     sister watches television using a gas mask for
     protection against the government.

63. Kumin, Maxine. "These Gifts." In **Why Can't We**

Live Together Like Civilized Human Beings?,
75-84. New York: Viking Press, 1982.

Two mis-matched young people are forced to be
married after they are discovered having
intercourse. The young husband is drafted soon
after, sent to Vietnam, and returns with a case
of "combat fatigue." He is listless and
unmotivated until his wife nearly dies of a bee
sting. The emergency situation enlivens him
into action again, but as a result of this
incident, both realize that their relationship
cannot last.

64. Mason, Bobbie Ann. "Big Bertha Stories." In
       **Soldiers and Civilians: Americans at War and
       at Home**, edited by Tom Jenks, 202-216. New
       York: Bantam Bks., 1986. Also in **Unwinding
       the Vietnam War: From War Into Peace**, edited
       by Reese Williams, 121-133. Seattle: Real
       Comet Press, 1987.

This story's main character is an
ill-adjusted Vietnam veteran who lives with his
wife and child in Kentucky. A major character
is Big Bertha, a machine at the strip mine where
he sometimes works and which he uses as the main
character in his numerous violent stories. In
these stories, which frighten his son, Big
Bertha is immune to all the effects of violence.
The machine seems to embody the Vietnam
experiences of the major character.

65. Phillips, Jayne Anne. "November and December:
       Billy, 1969." In **Soldiers and Civilians:
       Americans at War and at Home**, edited by Tom
       Jenks, 126-154. New York: Bantam Bks., 1986.

This story is actually a chapter from
Phillips' novel **Machine Dreams**. Billy, the main
character, tries to decide whether to continue
with his meaningless college career or to drop
out and be drafted for Vietnam.

66. Prager, Emily. "The Lincoln-Pruitt Anti-Rape
       Device: Memoirs of the Women's Combat Army in
       Vietnam." In **A Visit from the Footbinder and
       Other Stories**, 103-180. New York: Simon and
       Schuster, 1982. New York: Wyndham, 1982.
       London: Chatto-Windus, 1983. London: Hogarth

Press, 1983. New York: Berkley, 1984. New
York: Vintage Bks., 1987.

The story is a satiric look at war.
Lincoln-Pruitt is a female officer who recruits
prostitutes and equips them with her newly
invented weapon, the L.P.A.R.D. The device,
when inserted, can destroy any man who
penetrates the woman. To test the device, she
and her squad are dropped near a Vietcong
village where, instead of using the devices, the
women fall in love with the men. Only
Lincoln-Pruitt carries out the assignment, after
which she gives her anti-rape device to a
Vietcong woman who plans to use it on American
soldiers.

67.   Taylor, Pat Ellis. "A Call from Brotherland."
      In **The Available Press/Pen Short Story
      Collection**, edited by Anne Tyler, 389-393.
      New York: Ballantine Bks., 1985.

The story's main characters, Okie and Lovern,
are Vietnam veterans. While Lovern's adjustment
after returning from the war is satisfactory,
Okie suffers from PTSD and, unable to find any
help, buries his pain under alcohol and drug
use. Even after seemingly adapting to new
lifestyles near Lovern's family, he belies his
normalcy by killing another man. At the story's
conclusion, Okie's sister reveals that she has
psychologically experienced his tragedy, too, in
her dreams.

68.   Thacker, Julia. "A Civil Campaign." In **New
      Directions 44, An International Anthology of
      Poetry and Prose**, edited by J. Laughlin,
      83-88. New York: New Directions Publishing
      Corp., 1982.

The story is about a returning disabled black
vet. Embittered and disillusioned, he and his
wife Leah try to begin life together again.
Much of the story describes their adjustment to
both the sexual and emotional relations in their
lives.

69.   Vaughn, Stephanie. "Kid MacArthur." **New**

Yorker 60 (December 17, 1984): 46-56. Also
in **Prize Stories, 1986: The O. Henry Awards,**
edited by William Abrahams, 226-244. Garden
City, N.Y.: Doubleday and Co., Inc., 1986.

An older sister recounts when she and her
brother came of age in an Army family. Vaughn
describes the father's induction of the brother
into the experience of war and the military as
he grows up; shooting game and shooting contests
pepper his education. Ultimately, the sister
goes to college, while her brother goes to war
in Vietnam. Coming home, he exhibits the
characteristics of many psychologically
disturbed vets. He is now a loner, goal-less,
and overly preoccupied with an old buddy who
lives in a mental institution.

70.   Wilhelm, Kate. "The Village." In **In the Field
of Fire**, edited by Jack Dann, and Jeanne Van
Buren Dann, 158-168. New York: Tom Doherty
Associates, 1987.

The story contains two narrators, Mildred
Carey and Mike Donati. She describes the events
of small town life in America on a typical
morning; simultaneously, he shares the maneuvers
of his patrol in Vietnam. Each one's "normal"
routine continues until the story's end when
readers realize that Mildred's small town is
being attacked by the Mike's soldiers. Wilhelm
gives an ironic and reversed perspective on
being under attack in war.

No Dates

71.   Gigante, Cathy. "When I Was Young." **Samisdat**
n.v., n.d.: 40-42.

A young girl tells of growing up unaware of
the Vietnam War. She lives, as a pre-schooler,
through the deaths of Kennedy, of Oswald, the
election of Nixon, and the death of Bobby
Kennedy. Vietnam is a John Wayne movie,
portrayed only distantly in news pictures. As
she matures, so does the war under Nixon. The
narrator finishes by recapturing the war in
print, marvelling at how she missed it as a

child; now she appreciates it only abstractly.
With this new although abstract awareness,
however, comes the fear that the Vietnam
experience could reoccur.

Poetry

Poems by Women

1960-1969

72. Choun, Linda. "Life in Our Hands." **Quixote**
     1, no. 7 (June 1966): 57.

     The poet wonders how many more generations of
     people will be at war.

73. Gibson, Barbara. "Letter from the Vietnamese
     People." **Quixote** 1, no. 7 (June 1966): 58.

     The letter's speaker is the Vietnamese
     nation, which faults American generals,
     politicians, and media for both using and
     destroying them.

74. Levertov, Denise. "A Marigold from North
     Viet Nam." **Quarterly Review of Literature** 16
     (Fall 1969): 100.

     The marigold, its brilliance, loveliness, and
     resiliency, is compared to Viet Nam.

75. McCabe, Susan. "Vietnam as History." **Quixote**
     1, no. 7 (June 1966): 42.

     The poet sees clearly that Americans have
     been fighting against a people's achievement of
     freedom because we could not recognize in the
     Vietnamese a kinship to our own revolution and
     war for freedom.

76. Piercy, Marge. "The Organizer's Bogeyman." In
     her **Hard Loving**, 65-67. Middletown, Conn.:
     Wesleyan University Press, 1969.

     The poet, in an understated style, describes
     the fruits of the war as products such as
     orphanages and fear.

1970-1979

77. Berk, Barbara Jane. "Daughter's Father."
     Mirror Northwest 3 (1972): 91-92.

     This poem by a daughter describes her
     father's stoic handling of his two sons' deaths,
     supposedly in the Vietnam War.

78. Brown, Crystal. "Liberation." **Samisdat,** 17
     (1978): 33.

     This brief poem graphically portrays the
     waste in Hue after Tet.

79. _____. "Living On an Icon Translating
     Vietnamese Folk Poetry." **Samisdat** 17 (1978):
     32.

     This is a poem describing the inherent beauty
     in the folklore and legends of the Vietnamese,
     made all the more visible by the destruction of
     war.

80. Czapla, Cathy Young. "Twelve Years Later (for
     Geoff Kline)." **Samisdat** 17 (1978): 44.

     A woman wonders what happened to an old
     friend who volunteered for service. She still
     dreams about him.

81. Giggans, Patricia. "Two Poems: One and Two."
     Aphra 3, no. 3 (Summer 1972): 32-33.

     In poem one, the poet speaks to the maimed
     Vietnamese child as if the speaker were guilty
     of bringing its death. In the second poem the
     speaker imagines Vietnam as a tomb and herself
     in it, silent and dead.

82. Griffin, Susan. "Song My." **Up From Under** 1,
     no. 4 (Winter 1971-72): 12. Also in **No More
     Masks! An Anthology of Poems by Women,** edited
     by Florence Howe and Ellen Bass, 309-310.
     Garden City, N.Y.: Anchor Bks., 1973. Also
     in **Women Poets of the World,** edited by Joanna
     Bankier, and Deirdre Lashgau, with Doris
     Earnshaw, 370-71. New York: Macmillan
     Publishing Co., 1983.

This poem presents simultaneous images of an innocent family enjoying a morning contrasted with the mutilated bodies of parents and babies at Song My. These images are linked as the American family reads the newspaper account of the Vietnamese tragedy at Song My.

83. Howard, Vanessa. "Monument in Black." In **Soulscript: Afro-American Poetry,** edited by June Jordan, 3. Garden City, N.Y.: Zenith Bks., 1970.

The poem is about the black person's contribution to American wars, even Vietnam, and the need for recognition of his or her efforts.

84. Jordan, June. "Poem to My Sister, Ethel Ennis, Who Sang 'The Star Spangled Banner' at the Second Inauguration of Richard Milhaus Nixon." In **The Treasury of American Poetry,** edited by Nancy Sullivan, 767-768. Garden City, N.Y.: Doubleday and Co., 1978.

This is an angry poem centering on the two lines of the anthem: "and the rockets' red glare/the bombs bursting in air." These lines suggest to the poet the American bombing of Hanoi, particularly the non-military targets hit under Nixon's orders. Her final question is a kind of plea--when will she (the singer-nation) realize the violent potential for her own destruction in these words, sentiments, and actions?

85. Lakides, Lucy. "Veteran." **Samisdat** 17 (1978): 54.

The poet traces the development of a consciousness of war in one young man, from early games of soldier, from images of heroism offered by media, to the harsh realities thrust upon him by the war experience, through his return. This voyage takes him from hero to anti-hero.

86. Levertov, Denise. "White Phosphorous, White Phosphorous." **Earth's Daughters** 1 (February 1971): 10.

      The poet questions white phosphorus,
comparing it to snow, while its voice speaks of
its indiscriminatory destruction of flesh.

87.   Paley, Grace. "Women in Vietnam." In **No More
     Masks! An Anthology of Poems by Women**, edited
     by Florence Howe and Ellen Bass, 136-37. New
     York: Anchor Bks., 1973.

      This is a poem about the women of Vietnam,
their state, and their part in the war.
Sisterhood and the commonality of all women and
their struggle for freedom mark the poem.

88.   Piercy, Marge. "Curse of the Earth Magician on
     a Metal Land." In **From the Belly of the
     Shark, a New Anthology of Native Americans**,
     edited by Walter Lowenfels, 280-82. New
     York: Vintage Bks., 1973.

      Piercy's poem recounts the helplessness of
protesters against a bureacracy that will not
hear that its destruction of other lands and
people is a destruction of its own people, too.

89.   Rich, Adrienne. "Burning Oneself In." In her
     Diving Into the Wreck, 46. New York: W.W.
     Norton and Co., 1973.

      Rich's poem eloquently describes human
helplessness to stop the destruction of war.

90.   Shay, Norma Joan. "War." **Mirror Northwest** 2
     (Summer 1971): 77.

      The poet remembers daily life with a soldier
whom the war has taken away.

91.   Simon, Rose. "Three Red Ghazals." In **Angel in
     My Oven: A Story Workshop Anthology,** edited
     by John Schultz, 96-97. Chicago: Columbia
     College Press, 1976.

      The speaker's personal experience, developed
with jolting images of isolation, blood, and
war, emphasizes the meaninglessness of all human
relations.

92.   Zamvil, Stella. "Veterans Day." **Samisdat** 17

(1978): 45.

The poet sees a young disabled veteran and begins to wonder which war he fought in. Deciding upon Vietnam, she then wonders how a nation can forget such a conflict when its effects are so externally visible.

1980-1987

93. Bellerson, Fran. "Background." **Minerva: Quarterly Report on Women and the Military.** 4, no. 3 (Fall 1986): 126-133.

    The narrator, through a series of memories, catalogues the events of war, the protests, and the aftereffects on veterans and others.

94. Biedler, Barbara. "Afterthoughts on a Napalm-Drop on Jungle Villages near Haiphong." In **Vietnam and America: A Documented History,** edited by Marvin Gettleman, Jane Franklin, Marilyn Young, and Bruce Franklin, 299-300. New York: Grove Press, 1985.

    The poem graphically describes a peaceful Vietnamese village before and during a napalm attack. The poem was first written when the author was 12 years old.

95. Boris, Norma J. "The Devil." **Minerva: Quarterly Report on Women and the Military** 2, no. 3 (Fall 1984): 136-137.

    A woman nurse recounts the hellish experience of Vietnam and laments that the dream of returning also became a nightmarish reality.

96. Brown, Crystal. "Leaving Vietnam." **Kalliope** 5, no. 2 (1983): 14-17.

    A young mother celebrates a birth of a daughter against the backdrop of a wartorn country.

97. Cannon, Janet. "Vietnamese Girl." **Helicon**

Nine: The Journal of Women's Arts and Letters, no. 14/15 (Summer 1986): 119.

The poet writes of a young Vietnamese girl, now in an American high school, whose memories of the war 10 years later are still fresh.

98.   Coit, Becky.   "A Mother's Plea." In **Reflecting "on the Memories of War"** 1 (1987): 45.

A mother addresses the President and other Americans asking that they help her find out her son's status (he is MIA).

99.   Czapla, Cathy Young.   "Lullaby." In **Vietnam Flashbacks: Pig Iron, No.12,** edited by Jim Villani and Rose Sayre, 79.   Youngstown, Ohio: Pig Iron Press, 1984.

A woman encourages her companion to stay, to rest, to accept that there is no war to fight now even though there may be another in the future.

100.   **Deros.**   Alexandria, Va.: 1981-1987.

Deros is a journal which appears four times a year.   From 1981-87, over 150 women's poems about the Vietnam War and its impact on American lives have been printed in this journal of poetry.   Most deal with themes relating to women's wartime experiences (waiting for lovers and friends, children wondering about lost fathers, and protesting the war at home) although several poems describe nursing in the war.

101.   Farenthold, Lisa.   "Skirmish at the HEB." **Stone Country** 10 (Fall 1982): 74-75.

A woman witnesses the confusion of and then the wounding of a Vietnam War veteran who has problems adjusting to the world once again.

102.   Fields, Cheryl.   "Only Pretend." In **Reflecting "on the Memories of War"** 1 (1987): 4.

In her poem, Fields examines the continuing

myth that war is a game or is heroic, and asks
if humankind should not have learned to teach
its children a different attitude by now.

103.   Hartland, Patricia. "War." In **Reflecting "on
       the Memories of War"** 1 (1987): 5.

       The poem uses terse two word couplets to
describe despair in the aftermath of the war,
but the poem ends on a note of hope and suggests
a way out of personal pain.

104.   Leventhal, Ann. "Snapshot." In **Vietnam
       Flashbacks: Pig Iron No. 12,** edited by Jim
       Villani. and Rose Sayre, 50. Youngstown,
       Oh.: Pig Iron Press, 1984.

       A woman gazes at a picture she took at Da
Nang, remembering herself as a WAC, and
recalling the physical sensations and realities
of living there twenty years ago.

105.   Levertov, Denise. "A Speech: For the Anti-Draft
       Rally." In her **Candles In Babylon,** 92-96.
       New York: New Directions Publishing Corp.,
       1982.

       Levertov strikes out against the ignorance of
young people ready to be drafted for a war many
believe they must fight in for the sake of
abstractions. The poem is a call for peace and
unity among people, not for the support of wars.

106.   Rich, Adrienne. "Dien Bien Phu." In her **The
       Fact of a Doorframe, Poems Selected and New,
       1950-84,** 200-201. New York: W. W. Norton and
       Co., 1984.

       The poem describes the hell that nurses go
through treating the war-wounded and the.
particular shell-shock effects nurses suffer.

107.   _____. "For the Record." In
       **Unwinding the Vietnam War: From War Into
       Peace,** edited by Reese Williams, 375-76.
       Seattle: Real Comet Press, 1987.

       The poet challenges the reader to remember
where he or she was during the war and to take
responsibility for the misery that the war
caused.

108.   _____ . "In the Wake of Home." In
        **Unwinding the Vietnam War: From War Into
        Peace**, edited by Reese Williams, 381-85.
        Seattle: Real Comet Press, 1987.

        The poet poignantly recreates the world of
        the wartorn and homeless children and families.

109.   Storey, Sandra. "Patrol." In **Vietnam
        Flashbacks: Pig Iron No. 12,** edited by Jim
        Villani and Rose Sayre, 17. Youngstown,
        Ohio: Pig Iron Press, 1984.

        A woman imagines herself both walking point
        and following at the rear of a line of men on
        patrol.

Poetry In Collections by Women

1960-1969

110. Connie, Sandra, and Laura Stine, eds. **Green Flag**. San Francisco: City Lights Bks., 1969.

  Compiled as a result of the National Guard's arrests at a noon rally protesting the U. of California's building a fence around People's Park, this collection of poems contains thirteen women's poems. Most center on the protest itself in the park although a few deal with larger issues of the difficulty of attaining peace.

111. DiPrima, Diane, ed. **War Poems**. New York: Poets Press, 1968.

  DiPrima's collection contains poems of her own and ten others. All the others are men. At least two of her own poems here deal with the Vietnam War, one honoring the Buddhist nun who burned herself in 1966 in protest of the war, the other an ironic look at the possible consequences of this war for our nation.

112. Levertov, Denise, ed. **Out of the War Shadow**. New York: War Resisters League, 1967.

  This is an appointment book (peace calendar) published by Levertov and including a number of poems by women. Many deal with imagery of protest; others deal with the tragic human losses in wars.

113. Levertov, Denise. **The Sorrow Dance**. New York: New Directions Publishing Corp., 1967. London: Jonathan Cape, 1968.

  The collection of poems includes a section entitled "Life At War," in which Levertov explores the tragedies of the war. The most well-known titles are "Life At War," "Altars in the Street," and "What Were They Like?," poems which are often anthologized.

1970-1979

114.   Chagnon, Jacqui, and Don Luce, eds. **Of Quiet
       Courage: Poems from Vietnam**. Washington,
       D.C.: Indochina Mobile Education Project,
       1974.

       These poems are by Vietnamese writers,
translated into English. They deal with a
variety of topics: children's views of the war
and love are two among even more traditional
topics.

115.   Cudahy, Sheila. **The Bristle Cone Pine and
       Other Poems**. New York: Harcourt, Brace and
       Jovanovich, 1976. Great Britain: Rampant
       Lions Press, 1976.

       In this collection, all by Cudahy, the first
and last poems seem to deal directly with the
war and war protest. "Plastic," the first,
describes her reaction to a news photo
containing the remains of a war victim. The
last, "Peace March," describes quite sensuously
the progress of a Sunday protest march.

116.   Hollis, Jocelyn. **Vietnam Poems: The War Poems
       of Today**. New York: American Poetry Press,
       1979. Rev. ed., Philadelphia: American
       Poetry Press, 1983.

       Twenty-three poems, all by Hollis, cover
parental perspectives, a soldier's experiences,
and the plight of the returned veterans. The
second edition contains more poetry, and these
vary greatly from the first.

117.   Levertov, Denise. **The Freeing of the Dust**.
       New York: New Directions Publishing Corp.,
       1972.

       The collection includes at least nine poems
of Levertov's which relate to the Vietnam War.
Many, such as "Fragrance of Life, Odor of
Death," or "The Distance," praise the fighting
spirit of the Vietnamese. Others, such as "The
Pilots," or "A Poem At Christmas, 1972, during
the Terror Bombing of North Vietnam," are
clearly anti-American in sentiment.

118. _____. **Relearning the Alphabet**.
     New York: New Directions Publishing Corp.,
     1970. London: Jonathan Cape, 1970.

     The first section of this collection,
     "Elegies," contains several of Levertov's
     well-known poems relating to the Vietnam War:
     "Tenebrae," "Advent 1966," and "A Marigold from
     Vietnam" are among them. These poems in
     particular are often anthologized.

119. _____. **To Stay Alive**. New York:
     New Directions Publishing Corp., 1971.

     This collection contains "Life At War," "At
     the Justice Department, Nov. 15, 1969," and
     "Revolutionary," all of which are commonly
     anthologized. These poems are about Levertov's
     involvement in the anti-Vietnam War protests.
     As Levertov says in the introduction, the poems'
     sentiments extend beyond a protest of this one
     war to the human qualities that make all wars
     inevitable.

120. Luce, Don, John Schafer, and Jacqui Chagnon.
     **We Promise One Another: Poems from an Asian
     War**. Washington, D.C.: The Indochina Mobile
     Education Project, 1971.

     This group of 40 plus poems is written by
     Vietnamese men and women on various topics
     stimulated by the war: peace, family
     situations, attitudes toward women, and growing
     up amidst the war are among some of them.

1980-1987

121. Hollis, Jocelyn. **Collected Vietnam Poems and
     Other Poems**. Philadelphia: American Poetry
     and Literature Press, 1986.

     This collection includes many of her poems
     published in her earlier collections. At least
     six collections are represented; only the first
     two sections contain poetry on the Vietnam War.

122. _____. **Poems of the Vietnam War**.

Philadelphia: American Poetry and Literature
Press, 1980. Rev. ed., 1985.

The earlier collection of poems is written by
Hollis. There are 29 poems on various aspects
of war. The revised edition contains 28 poems
covering a span of topics about the war:
combat, loss, death, and destruction. The
overall theme of the wastefulness of the war
dominates as in all of Hollis' other volumes.

123.   Larsen, Wendy Wilder, and Tran Thi Nga.
       Shallow Graves: Two Women and Vietnam. New
       York: Random House, 1986. New York: Harper
       and Row Pubs., 1987.

These two sections of narrative poetry, one
by an American woman and one by a Vietnamese
woman, capture two stories of life in Vietnam
during the many wars there. Larsen, who knew
co-author Tran Thi Nga during the American war
in Vietnam, writes about being a wife living in
Saigon. Nga's saga reveals almost her entire
personal history, and lends insight into the
curious blend of submission and independence
which characterizes many accounts of Vietnamese
women.

124.   Le, Nancylee. **Duckling in a Thunderstorm**.
       Colorado Springs, Colo.: Rong-Tien Publishing
       Co., 1983.

This collection of prose poetry details Le's
life in Vietnam in the 1960's, and life in
America with her Vietnamese husband after her
return home. As a 19 or 20-year-old, she left
home for Saigon to teach. The book describes her
growing relationship to her husband-to-be,
Thuong, her teaching, her appreciation of the
Vietnamese people, and her political thoughts.
Divided into seven sections, the first five
cover her time in Vietnam and the last two cover
the couple's permanent return and adjustment to
the United States.

125.   Topham, J., ed. **Poems of the Vietnam War**.
       New York: American Poetry Press, 1980.

All 29 poems here seem to be actually

authored by Topham. Subjects cover a spectrum
ranging from parental perspectives on children
in the war, to the soldiers' views on induction,
training, combat, and returning home.

126.   _____. **Vietnam Heroes: A Tribute**.
Claymont, Del.: American Poetry Press, 1982.

At least seven poems in this collection are
by women, most by Jocelyn Hollis. The poems'
tones are uniformly angry and anti-war in
sentiment with American politicians receiving
the blame for the war.

127.   _____. **Vietnam Heroes II: The Tears
of a Generation**. Claymont, Del.: American
Poetry Press, 1982. Rev. ed., 1984.

Seven poems in the original volume are
authored by women, many by Jocelyn Hollis.
Several poems mourn the loss of soldiers in the
war. Some, definitely anti-war, lash out at the
economic motives behind the war.

128.   _____. **Vietnam Heroes III: That We
Have Peace**. Philadelphia: American Poetry
Press, 1983.

Eight poems by women appear in this
collection, again dominated by J. Hollis and
Joan Maiman. Several speakers are clearly
describing the war from a non-combatant point of
view, but a few contain speakers imaginatively
describing combat and the soldier's experience.

129.   _____. **Vietnam Heroes IV: The Long
Ascending Cry**. Philadelphia: American Poetry
and Literature Press, 1985.

The collection contains thirty-three poems.
Only one is by a woman, J. Hollis, and in it,
the speaker is an MIA lamenting the loss of
home, love, and freedom.

Poetry by Women in Other Collections

1960-1969

130. Bly, Robert, and David Ray, eds. **A Poetry Reading Against the Vietnam War**. Madison, Minn.: Sixties Press, 1966.

Two poems by Denise Levertov and Joanna Campbell appear in Bly's collection, both intensely anti-war in tone.

131. Community Council to End the War in Vietnam. **A Poetry Reading for Peace in Vietnam**. Santa Barbara: Unicorn Press, 1967.

At least three women's poems appear in this protest collection. All deal with the horror of war, one specifically about children in the war.

132. Lowenfels, Walter, ed. **Where Is Vietnam? American Poets Respond**. Garden City, N.Y.: Anchor Bks., 1967.

This collection contains ten poems by women writers. Most are protest poems offering images of violence and destruction in war; several are pleas for peace.

133. _____. **The Writing on the Wall: 108 American Poems of Protest**. Garden City, N.Y.: Doubleday and Co., 1969.

This collection of protest poetry includes only Denise Levertov's well-known poem, "What Were They Like?," a poem which focuses on the Vietnamese people whose daily lives are disrupted by the tragedies of war.

1970-1979

134. Barry, Jan, and W.D. Ehrhart, eds. **Demilitarized Zones: Veterans After Vietnam**. Perkasie, Pa.: East River Anthology, 1976.

At least four women's poems appear in this

collection, each describing the realities of
living with a soldier or veteran of Vietnam.

135.   Barry, Jan, Basil Paquet, and Larry Rottman,
       eds. **Winning Hearts and Minds: War Poems by
       Vietnam Veterans**. Brooklyn: 1st Casualty
       Press, 1972. New York: McGraw-Hill Bk. Co.,
       1972.

       Two women's poems appear in this small
collection. Each deals with the woman speaker's
perceptions of combat.

136.   Dater, Lt. Col. Tony, and Lt. Col. Fred Kiley,
       eds. **Listen. The War**. Colorado Springs,
       Colo.: U.S. Air Force Academy Association of
       Graduates, 1973.

       Eighteen women wrote poems which appear in
this volume. Again, many describe the emotions
of a lover or spouse who suffers the loss of a
soldier-lover either psychologically or
physically. One poem's speaker, a child, awaits
the return of an imprisoned father.

137.   Taylor, Clyde, ed. **Vietnam and Black America:
       An Anthology of Protest and Resistance**.
       Garden City, N.Y.: Anchor Bks., 1973.

       Two poems appear in this collection; both are
by black women, Nikki Giovanni and Sonia
Sanchez. Both of their poems are angry at the
senseless loss of black lives in this war.

1980-1987

138.   Barry, Jan, ed. **Peace Is Our Profession: Poems
       and Passages of War Protest**. Montclair,
       N.J.: East River Anthology, 1981.

       This is an extensive collection of protest
poetry, much of it dating back to protest about
the Vietnam War, and much of it written by
women. Over thirty poems are authored by women,
some by Rukeyser and Levertov; many are lesser
known poets. The anthology also contains a few
prose pieces.

139. Ehrhart, W.D., ed. **Carrying the Darkness:**
      American Indochina--The Poetry of the Vietnam
      War. New York: Avon Bks., 1985.

      This collection includes four poems by women
      including Denise Levertov. Each poem presents
      the woman speaker's experiences during this war:
      waiting for a soldier's return, the problems of
      readjustment after the war, and being part of
      the anti-war movement dominate the themes.

140. **Vietnam in Poems**. McLean, Va.: POW-MIA Common
      Cause, [1987].

      At least seven poems by women appear in this
      collection of poetry on the war. Most of these
      poems lament the loss of fathers, lovers, and
      husbands, portray the emotional pain of children
      without fathers, or decry the MIA situation.

1960-1969

141. Garson, Barbara. **MacBird**. New York: Grove
      Press, 1967.

      The play satirizes the politics behind
      Johnson's rise to the Presidency and the
      tensions between the Kennedys and him. In
      structure, plot, and character, the play
      parodies Shakespeare's **Macbeth**, with Johnson
      cast in the ambitious king's role. At Johnson's
      death, Robert Kennedy becomes the leader of the
      country. Garson mocks constantly Johnson's
      domestic and foreign policies, including the
      Vietnam War.

142. Terry, Megan. "Viet Rock". **Tulane Drama
      Review** 11 (Fall 1966): 196-227. Also in **Viet
      Rock**, 19-110. New York: Simon and Schuster,
      1967.

      Dubbed a "folk war movie," "Viet Rock" is
      loosely plotted to show the saga of young men
      born, inducted into the armed services, and
      trained for the Vietnam War. Terry presents
      both men in war and women involved with them in
      an ironic, surrealistic way. The setting shifts
      from America to Vietnam where Terry introduces
      North Vietnamese characters to the cast. The
      play contains two endings; in both, every
      soldier dies.

1970-1979

143. Fornes, Maria Irene. "The Red Burning Light or:
      Mission XQ3." In her **Promenade and Other
      Plays**, 19-60. New York: Winter House, 1971.

      This is a violent satire against the military
      and its involvement in the war. There are hints
      that some of the landscape might suggest
      Vietnam, but Fornes gives no overt mention of
      Vietnam.

144. Gonzalez, Gloria. "The New America." In her

Moving On! Three One-Act Plays, 35-48. New
York: Samuel French, 1971.

A 19-year-old young man flees to Canada with
his girlfriend to avoid being drafted and sent
to Vietnam. The action takes place entirely
within his car; both share their doubts   and
fears of the consequences of their actions as
well as his resolve to continue his journey.

145. Henderson, Nancy. "Honor the Brave." In her
Celebrate America: A Baker's Dozen of Plays,
47-54. New York: Julian Messner, 1978.

In this play for young people, two wounded
vets, Ralph and Ike, visit a friend's gravesite
on Memorial Day a year after the war has ended.
There they meet five women placing flowers on
graves of war dead. In the ensuing dialogue
between the bitter vets and the patriotic women
all eventually come to an understanding that
working for world peace will be the best way to
honor the dead.

1980-1987

146. Mann, Emily. **Still Life**. New York:
Dramatists Play Service, 1982. Also in
**Coming to Terms: American Plays and the
Vietnam War**, 253-325. New York: Theatre
Communications Group, 1985.

The play, told in three movements, is
composed of the monologues of three people who
all appear on stage simultaneously. The three
form a triangle: Mark, a haunted, suffering
Vietnam veteran who is an artist; Nadine, his
older artist lover; and Cheryl, his young and
abused wife.

147. Orr, Mary. **Women Still Weep**. New York:
Dramatists Play Service, 1980.

The play's characters are all females; males
appear only in the portraits of the family's war
dead which hang on one wall in the home. The
setting is 1965, and the plot unfolds around a
daughter who is a Vietnam War protestor. She is
severely hurt at a protest rally and dies. The

family hangs her portrait on the wall along with
the male war heroes.

Literary Criticism

1960-1969

148. Hughes, Catherine. "The Theater Goes to War."
      America 116, no. 20 (May 20, 1967): 759-761.

      Hughes examines the failure of several plays
      about the Vietnam War, including Megan Terry's
      Viet Rock. She criticizes **Viet Rock** for its
      superficial treatment of the issues of America
      in the war, its dialogue of clichés, and its
      stereotypical characters. Another play, **US**, is
      also criticized, and Hughes ends by lamenting
      the quality of plays on Vietnam in general.

1970-1979

149. Bell, Pearl K. "Writing About Vietnam."
      Commentary 66 (October 1978): 74-77.

      Bell writes a review essay in which she
      describes the Vietnam War as the most difficult
      of our American wars to recreate artistically.
      She outlines the problems a novelist faces, then
      analyzes Groom's **Better Times Than These**,
      O'Brien's **Going After Cacciato**, and Herr's
      Dispatches. To Bell, the latter two works
      succeed as fiction and memoir respectively
      because they do not rely on the traditional
      techniques of literature for capturing the
      essence of this war.

150. Kinder, Marsha. "The Power of Adaptation in
      Apocalypse Now." **Film Quarterly** 33, no. 2
      (Winter 1979-80): 12-20.

      The author analyzes Coppola's artistic
      achievements in **Apocalypse Now**, contrasting the
      scenes and elements with its counterpart, **Heart
      of Darkness**. She notes that the deviations from
      Conrad's work were artistically appropriate for
      his film. But, Kinder argues that Coppola's
      main failure in combining **Heart of Darkness** with
      this film lies in his faulty development of the
      character Kurtz.

151.   Maness, Mary. "War Is Glorious: War Is Hell:
         War Is Absurd." **Language Arts** 53 (May 1976)
         560-563.

         Maness analyzes the treatment of war in
         children's literature, limiting the wars to
         W.W.II and the Korean and Vietnamese conflicts.
         The literature she reviews for each war spans
         the three categories in the title, and she
         places Vietnam War literature (**The Man in the
         Box** and **Crossfire**) squarely in the "war is
         absurd" category. Her assessment indicates that
         many authors may have ceased giving children a
         glorious, patriotic view of war. Instead, they
         now reveal its meaninglessness.

152.   Melamed, Lisa. "Between the Lines of Fire:
         Vietnam War Literature for Young Readers."
         The Lion and the Unicorn 3, no. 2 (Winter
         1979-80): 76-85.

         Melamed reviews four novels that concern the
         Vietnam War and are either written for or are
         appropriate for teenagers: Garfield's **The Last
         Bridge,** Graham's **Crossfire: A Vietnam Novel,**
         Haldeman's **War Years,** and Hentoff's **I'm Really
         Dragged But Nothing Gets Me Down.** Melamed find
         that this fiction is so mild that it forsakes
         truth and honesty. She concludes by stating
         that the better reading for young people is the
         war's non-fiction, such as Baez's **Daybreak,**
         Lifton's **Children of Vietnam,** or Kovic's **Born o**
         the Fourth of July.

153.   Messerly, Carol. "The Literature of the Vietnam
         War." **Louisiana Library Association Bulletin**
         35 (Summer 1972): 53-57.

         Messerly notes that the themes of war
         literature in the twentieth century underscore
         the negative qualities of violence. In
         particular, literature of the Vietnam War (e.g.
         The Ugly American, The Prisoner of Quai Dong, o
         Coming Home) introduce themes of moral ambiguit
         about the war, the lack of clarity between
         friend or foe, and disgust with military
         organization. Also discussed is war poetry.
         Messerly mentions the works of two women in
         particular, Mary McCarthy and Denise Levertov.

154.   Pochoda, Elizabeth.   "Vietnam, We've All Been
          There."   **The Nation** 226 (March 25 1978):
          344-346.

          This extensive review essay analyzes two
       Vietnam books by men, O'Brien's **Going After
       Cacciato** and Herr's **Dispatches**. While bothered
       by O'Brien's reliance on the literary techniques
       of Heller and Hemingway, Pachoda finds the novel
       valuable, insightful, and powerful in its
       distinctiveness. She finds **Dispatches** an
       excellent book which, unlike many novels,
       captures the war's paradoxes.

155.   Robinson, Jo Ann.   "Novels and Vietnam."   **Peace
          and Change** 4 (Fall 1976): 12-18.

          Robinson describes several themes
       characterizing the fiction of Vietnam: (1) the
       multiple character types; (2) the flaws of
       American actions in Vietnam; (3) racism; and (4)
       disenchantment, both in the war and afterwards.
       She describes over 20 novels; only one is
       co-authored by a woman.

156.   Vallely, Jean.   "Michael Cimino's Battle to Make
          a Great Movie."   **Esquire** 91 (January 2-16,
          1979): 88-93.

          Vallely's piece opens with her own personal
       story about her brother's wounding in Vietnam.
       Haunted by this, she looked in vain for answers
       in fiction and film, and feels that only
       Cimino's film **The Deer Hunter** comes close to
       expressing the realities of the war for her.
       Much of the article chronicles Cimino's problems
       and successes in making the film.

157.   Welsh, Elizabeth.   "What Did You Write About in
          the War, Daddy?" **Wilson Library Bulletin** 46,
          no. 10 (June, 1972): 912-17.

          Welch writes what she terms "an anti-war
       evaluation of books on Vietnam for Young
       People." Essentially, the article is an
       annotated bibliography of non-fiction works for
       young people. Barbara Dane's **The Vietnam
       Songbook** is the only work by a woman that Welch
       discusses.

158. Winner, Carole Ann. "A Study of American
         Dramatic Productions Dealing with the War in
         Vietnam." Ph.D. diss., University of Denver,
         1975.

      Winner analyzes over ten plays written about
      the Vietnam War, including Megan Terry's **Viet
      Rock** and Barbara Garson's **MacBird**, noting that
      both the authors were anti-war protestors.
      Winner suggests that most playwrights weave
      simplistic black and white attitudes about the
      war into the fabric of their plays, thus
      creating superficial works. The exceptions,
      which she spends more time discussing, are
      Berrigan's **The Trial of the Catonsville Nine**,
      McNally's **Botticelli**, and Rabe's two plays,
      Pavlo Hummel and **Sticks and Bones**.

1980-1987

159. Bellhouse, Mary L., and Lawrence Litchfield.
         "Vietnam and Loss of Innocence: An Analysis
         of the Political Implications of the Popular
         Literature of the Vietnam War." **Journal of
         Popular Culture** 16, no. 3 (Winter 1982):
         157-174.

      The authors argue that the Vietnam experience
      should have altered a kind of blindly innocent
      national mythology which still bars Americans
      from clearly seeing and learning from past
      political and military mistakes. Even though
      numerous pieces of literature centering on
      certain core themes of the war do blast away at
      the mythology, the authors see little hope for
      lasting impact from these works' messages.

160. Benoit, Ellen. "Storyteller." **Forbes** 135
         (June 17, 1985): 194.

      This is a brief overview of the inception of
      Time-Life's multi-volume series, **The Vietnam
      Experience**. Benoit describes author-publisher
      Robert George's ups and downs while trying to
      get the series published.

161. Chambers, Andrea. "Bobbie Ann Mason's In

Country Evokes the Soul of Kentucky and the
Sadness of Vietnam." **People Weekly** 24
(October 28, 1985): 127-129.

The article is not so much a description of
In Country as it is of its author herself, her
solitary past, her roots in rural Kentucky, and
her values and aims as a writer. According to
Chambers, Mason's main literary conflicts center
on staying at home versus leaving home. Mason,
however, describes how **In Country**'s themes grew
beyond this idea after her visit to the Vietnam
War Memorial.

162. Creek, Mardena Bridges. "Myth, Wound,
      Accomodation: American Literary Responses to
      the War in Vietnam". Ph.D. diss., Ball State
      University, 1982.

      Creek's thesis is that the fiction and
non-fiction about the Vietnam War attempt to
refute the American myths which idealize
American perceptions and values. She analyzes
works of Vietnam literature (including Gloria
Emerson's **Winners and Losers**), probing how each
reveals a darker side of the war experience.
Finally, she reviews the most recent body of
literature which tries to assimilate the war
into the American consciousness.

163. Dong, Stella. "The Cinderella Story of **The
      Alleys of Eden**". **Publishers Weekly** 221, no.
      1 (January, 1982): 25-26.

      The brief story chronicles the problems
Robert Olen Butler had while trying to publish
his **Alleys of Eden**. After 20 rejections,
Horizon Press finally published it, and its
reviews read favorably. The article offers good
insights into the difficulties of publishing
Vietnam literature earlier in this decade.

164. Emerson, Gloria. "How Films Lie About Vietnam."
      National Catholic Reporter 17, no. 4
      (November 14, 1980): 7.

      Emerson decries the revisionist perspective
on America and its version of the Vietnam War
which characterizes the films on popular

television currently. Excepting **Friendly Fire**
and **Coming Home,** Emerson finds most showings
(including **The Deer Hunter** and **A Rumor of War**)
to be less than truthful about the war. She
spends a great deal of time describing Peg
Mullen's negative reaction to **Friendly Fire**.

165.   Hasan, Zia. "American Films of the 1970's:
       Through Fantasy (**Star Wars,** 1977), Resolves
       an Era's Concerns About the Threat of Media
       (**Network,** 1976), the Sexual Revolution (**Annie
       Hall,** 1977), and the Vietnam War (**Coming
       Home,** 1978)." Ph.D. diss., Oklahoma State
       University, 1980.

       Hasan contends that many popular films in the
       1970's attempted to deal with the social
       realities of the period. For example, **Coming
       Home** confronts the impact of the Vietnam War on
       people at home or returning home. However,
       Hasan also thinks that because of the film
       medium's capacity to create preferred frames of
       reference, the counterpart to such realistic
       films, the fantasy film, re-emerges as an
       important tool for both escaping and reaffirming
       mythical American values and powers.

166.   Heilbronn, Lisa M. "Coming Home a Hero: The
       Changing Image of the Vietnam Vet on Prime
       Time Television." **Journal of Popular Film
       and Television** 13, no. 1 (Spring 1985):
       25-30.

       Heilbron suggests that television's image of
       the Vietnam veteran is a new treatment, and she
       explores what this change means. Isolating
       "Magnum, P.I." (1980) as the first intensive
       treatment of a vet and his past experiences in
       Vietnam, she then describes other subsequent
       shows in which both the veteran and his
       experiences are integral. Heilbron traces the
       reasons for the shift toward a positive image of
       the veteran, citing the roles the characters
       play and the cinematic tradition in which they
       fit as possible causes.

167.   Heiss, Andrea Brandenburg. "On Foreign Grounds
       Portraits of Americans in Vietnam." Ph.D.
       diss., University of Iowa, 1983.

The portraits studied are ten important works
of fiction and non-fiction written about
Americans in Vietnam from 1961-1975. After a
discussion of the books in a chronological
sequence, Heiss outlines several important
themes, including the use of American
technology, common perceptions of the
Vietnamese, and the conflicts involved in living
in a foreign environment.

168.   Holdstein, Deborah H.   "Vietnam War
         Veteran-Poets: The Ideology of Horror." **USA
         Today** 112, no. 1240 (September 1983): 59-61.

Holdstein's first few paragraphs set the
Vietnam war-poet apart from those of the past.
This poet alone has confronted the war and
experienced it without help from an undisputed
governmental perspective; ultimately, the
Vietnam poet tries to make sense of the war in a
vacuum. Holdstein discusses the poetry of
Rottman, Paquet, and Casey among others, making
particular reference to **Winning Hearts and
Minds**.

169.   Hurrell, Barbara.   "American Self-Image in David
         Rabe's Vietnam Trilogy." **Journal of American
         Culture** 4, no. 2 (Summer 1981): 95-107.

This essay examines Rabe's own biographical
roots and how they may have influenced his
writing. Hurrell's main point seems to be that
Rabe's plays are of cultural importance. As a
trilogy, the plays destroy the image of America
as an ultimate superpower. On another level,
the plays work out the existential theme of the
gulf between self and other.

170.   Jeffords, Susan.   "Friendly Civilians: Images of
         Women and the Feminization of the Audience in
         Vietnam Films." **Wide Angle** 7, no. 4 (1985):
         13-22.

Jeffords discusses aspects of two main images
of women (as passive and as remote from war) as
they appear in three Vietnam war films:
Apocalypse Now, Coming Home, and **First Blood.**
She also describes how each film feminizes

(here, meaning "makes passive") its characters
and ultimately the audiences as well.

171. _____. "The New Vietnam Films: Is the
      Movie Over?" **The Journal of Popular Film and
      Television** 13, no. 4 (Winter 1986): 186-194.

      Jeffords suggests that Vietnam films like
      Rambo or **Missing in Action I** serve several
      popular functions: (1) each attempts to
      symbolically bring an end to the Vietnam War;
      (2) each portrays a faultless image of the
      American soldier; and (3) each leaves open the
      possibility for a new, yet similar American
      intervention by suggesting that the Vietnam War
      is now concluded. Jeffords argues that the
      films portray the negative elements which lost
      the war as "feminine" (weak, inactive), while
      typically masculine values (comradeship, valor)
      define the heroic characters of each film. To
      her, understanding this dynamic is an important
      step in achieving a reconceptualization of the
      war's end.

172. Johnson, Diane. "The Loss of Patriotic Faith."
      In her **Terrorists and Novelists,** 179-192.
      New York: Alfred A. Knopf, Inc., 1982.

      In this short essay, Johnson recounts the
      major facts of the Mullen family case. The
      essay then moves into a criticism of C.D.B.
      Bryan's negative reaction to the intensity of
      the single-mindedness of the Peg Mullen's quest
      for justice. Johnson sharply criticizes Bryan's
      research effort into the entire incident.

173. Karaguerzian, Maureen. "Interview with Robert
      Stone." **Tri-Quarterly,** no. 53 (Winter 1982)
      248-258.

      In this interview Stone talks about the
      process of composing his novel, **Dog Soldiers**.
      Mixed throughout are many rich insights about
      how writers develop their works.

174. _____. "Irony in Robert Stone's
      Dog Soldiers." **Critique: Studies in Modern
      Fiction** 24, no. 2 (Winter 1983): 65-73.

      The author argues that once Stone's plot is

taken as a parallel to America's involvement in
Vietnam, the kind of irony working in the novel
becomes apparent as do the symbolic meanings of
characters and events. The ironies intensify as
the purposeful allusions to Hemingway's war
fiction increase. These allusions offer a
vision of war which ultimately leads to the
world Stone's main characters inhabit.

175. Kearns, Katherine Sue. "Some Versions of
       Violence in Three Contemporary American
       Novels: John Irving's **The World According to
       Garp,** Tim O'Brien's **Going After Cacciato,** and
       Alice Walker's **The Color Purple.**" Ph.D.
       diss., The University of North Carolina at
       Chapel Hill, 1982.

       Kearns argues, with reference to O'Brien's
       book, that there can be no "reasoned, honorable
       action" in the violent landscapes of war. Yet,
       the main character, she contends, is part of a
       struggle to overcome violence and its damaging
       effects. Most of her analysis of this Vietnam
       novel occurs within Chapter 3 of the
       dissertation where she discusses how the violent
       atmosphere of Vietnam leads to a final loss of
       innocence, a loss of connection, and a complete
       isolation for the characters.

176. Kinney, Judy Lee. "The Mythical Method:
       Fictionalizing the Vietnam War." **Wide Angle**
       7, no. 4 (1985): 35-40.

       Kinney examines three Vietnam War films,
       Apocalypse Now, Who'll Stop the Rain, and **The
       Deer Hunter,** which all mythologize the war.
       Kinney argues that these mythic methods allow
       audiences to confront the war indirectly without
       acknowledging the difficult political realities
       involved in the American experience in Vietnam.

177. Leibowitz, Fran. "Recycling American Ideology:
       The Second Coming of Michael Vronsky."
       Telos, no. 47 (Spring 1981): 204-208.

       Leibowitz sees Cimino's film, **The Deer
       Hunter,** as a film which promotes the ideals out
       of which military ventures stem. The vision of
       the Vietnam War here, to her, is one in which

war functions as a kind of birthing-place for
real men. Leibowitz traces the main character's
rebirth into manhood, and the failure of the
other two to attain this birth into the proper
hierarchies of life. She concludes that the
film promotes some dangerous myths in an era in
which the nation must re-evaluate itself.

178. Malone, Anne. "Once Having Marched: American
      Narratives of the Vietnam War." Ph.D. diss.,
      Indiana University, 1983.

      Malone's study uses autobiographical writings
      of men in Vietnam to explore what she considers
      the main focus of Vietnam narratives: the
      relationship between an individual's personal
      goals and the public vision, values, and
      directions. She argues further that in a war in
      which the individual was often left alone to
      interpret the meaning of the war, the narrative
      form itself served to clarify the meaningfulness
      of one's experience.

179. Marquis, Harriett Hill. "'Cries of Communion':
      The Poetry of Denise Levertov." Ph.D. diss.,
      Drew University, 1984.

      Although a dissertation about the entire body
      of works written by Levertov, the study does
      look closely at her poetry published about the
      Vietnam War. Marquis argues that a noticeable
      change in direction in her poetry at the time of
      the war was not just a reaction to the war, but
      part of her poetic development toward a more
      complete vision of communion.

180. Puhr, Kathleen. "Four Fictional Faces of the
      Vietnam War." **Modern Fiction Studies** 30, no.
      1 (Spring 1984): 99-117.

      Puhr describes four types of fiction about
      Vietnam using five major works. The four
      classifications discussed are documentary
      fiction, black humor, propagandist, and
      realistic portrayals.

181. _____. "Novelistic Responses to the
      Vietnam War." Ph.D. diss., St. Louis
      University, 1982.

Puhr discusses thirty-eight novels within a chronological, historical account of the war. The final chapter describes four literary approaches or styles that these novels usually demonstrate, and Puhr analyzes several novels as examples of each style.

182. Richman, Liliane G. "Themes and Ideology in the Vietnam Films 1975-1983." Ph.D. diss., The University of Texas at Dallas, 1984.

Richman considers over 20 films on the Vietnam experience produced from 1975 to 1983. She theorizes that the impact of the war on American society can be better understood by carefully examining the contents of films about the Vietnam experience. In her study, she discusses how this body of films provides clues to American attitudes toward the veterans, the war itself, and national and political issues.

183. Sayre, Nora. "At War in the Movies". **The Progressive** 44 (February 1980): 51-54.

Sayre analyzes the quality of American films on war, noting that some films, **The Bridge on the River Kwai, Paths of Glory,** and several about Korea, begin to depict war as less than glorious. The four Vietnam films reviewed follow this move toward portraying realism rather than glorifying the war (**Coming Home, The Deer Hunter, Hair,** and **Apocalypse Now**).

184. Slocock, Caroline. "Winning Hearts and Minds: The First Casualty Press." **Journal of American Studies** 16 (April 1982): 107-117.

First Casualty Press, the independent publishers of anti-war literature like **Winning Hearts and Minds** and **Free Fire Zone,** is the subject of Slocock's essay. She examines the political uses for which the editors used the publications. The saga of approaches to and rejections by publishers is reviewed and discussed, too, as are the ways the books were structured, written, and marketed in order for the anti-war message to reach the widest public.

185. Smith, Lorrie. "A Sense-Making Perspective in

Recent Poetry by Vietnam Veterans." **American Poetry Review** 15 (November-December 1986): 13-18.

Smith's analysis of Vietnam war poetry delineates three stages in the poetic response to the war: (1) poems of immediate experience during and after the war; (2) the 1970's poems which, through form and structure, seek to bring order to the experience of the war; and (3) poems of the 1980's which bring retrospective visions to the war experience. She gives extensive treatment to Ehrhart's recent poems.

186.   Springer, Claudia. "Vietnam: A Television History and the Equivocal Nature of Objectivity." **Wide Angle** 7, no. 4 (1985): 53-60.

Springer focuses her criticism on the nature of documentaries portraying the Vietnam War. Here, she analyzes the 13-part "Vietnam: A Television History." Springer argues that the series aimed for an objective presentation of the war, but failed because it used inappropriate strategies for achieving objectivity. The result is a series with no point of view about the war, with little in-depth treatment of the issues and events in the war, and virtually no comment on American involvement.

187.   Stewart, Margaret E. "Death and Growth: Vietnam War Novels, Cultural Attitudes, and Literary Traditions." Ph.D. diss., University of Wisconsin, Madison, 1981.

Stewart identifies several American attitudes about war common in the novels of Vietnam. For each of four major attitudes, she compares one positive and one critical novel. Her study also places these eight Vietnam books in the context of past war novels.

188.   Sturken, Marita. "The Camera As Witness: Documentaries and the Vietnam War." **Film Library Quarterly** 13, no. 4 (1980): 15-20.

Sturken discusses the documentary films about

Vietnam, avoiding the narrative films that many
others analyze. She analyzes the importance of
the camera's presence in **Frontline, The War At
Home, War Shadows, Vietnam: An American Journey,**
and **Outtakes**.

189.   Suther, Judith D.   "French Novelists and the
       American Phase of the War in Indochina."
       **Selecta: The Journal of the Pacific Northwest
       Council on Foreign Languages** 4 (1983): 1-9.

Suther analyzes the writing of three French
novelists whose fiction covers the theme of the
American involvement in Vietnam. What links
these very different pieces, she finds, is the
anti-American attitude of the French society
reflected in the stances taken in the novels, a
stance of knowing and ironic detachment.

190.   Wolf, Susan.   "Women and Vietnam: Remembering in
       the 1980's."   In **Unwinding the Vietnam War:
       From War Into Peace,** edited by Reese
       Williams, 243-260.   Seattle: Real Comet
       Press, 1987.

Wolf points out that women who served in
Vietnam were and remain invisible. She
discusses Van Devanter's **Home Before Morning,**
Mason's and Phillips' fiction, and the
perspectives described in **Shallow Graves** as
examples which illustrate woman's perceived role
as outsider to the war experience even though
many experienced war's painful realities.

1980-1987

191. Anisfield, Nancy, ed. **Vietnam Anthology:
     American War Literature**. Bowling Green,
     Ohio: Bowling Green State University Popular
     Press, 1987.

     This anthology is composed of nothing but
     Vietnam fiction. Anisfield includes excerpts
     from novels, short stories, drama, and poetry.
     Along with her preface, she writes an
     introductory essay and shorter introductions to
     each section. Since the anthology is designed
     for use in literature, history, or political
     science classes, she completes each section with
     discussion questions for reflection.

192. Topham, J., ed. **Vietnam Literature Anthology: A
     Balanced Perspective**. New York: American
     Poetry and Literature Press, 1984. Rev. ed.
     Philadelphia: American Poetry and Literature
     Press, 1985.

     Both the original and the revised editions
     present three male authors' poetry on Vietnam
     and a chapter from a novel by another male
     author. There are fewer poems in the revised
     edition by R. L. Barth. Topham's role seems to
     be limited to producing the written introductory
     material.

Biography

1970-1979

193.   Clark, Marjorie. **Captive on the Ho Chi Minh
       Trail**. Chicago: Moody Press, 1974.

       Clark writes of two young men's experiences
as prisoners of both the Lao Communists and the
North Vietnamese. Canadian Lloyd Oppel and his
friend Sam Mattix served as missionaries in
Laos. Captured in Laos, they were turned over
to the NVA and deposited at the Hanoi Hilton.
The book reads like a firsthand account of their
struggles to survive captivity, of their hopes,
despairs, and the routines of prison life. The
narrative ends as they are released after five
months in prison.

194.   Franks, Lucinda. **Waiting Out a War: The Exile
       of Private John Picciano**. New York: Coward,
       McCann, and Geoghegan, 1974.

       Franks met and talked with many American
deserters who lived in Sweden. Selecting
Picciano as representative of hundreds of these
men, she reconstructs his life as an example of
the deserter's experience. Picciano's early
life through high school left him prepared for
college but unable to go, so registration for
the draft was inevitable. After basic training,
he deserted, moved to Canada, then to Sweden.
Details of the life of the deserter in Sweden,
and that country's attitudes toward the deserter
community complete the work, adding to an
understanding of this group's experiences.

195.   Hefley, James, and Marti Hefley. **No Time for
       Tombstones: Life and Death in the Vietnamese
       Jungle**. Wheaton, Ill.: Tyndale House
       Publications, 1974.

       The book recounts the murders of the
Christian Missionary Alliance workers during
Tet, 1968. Three people, Hank Blood, Betty

Olson, and Mike Berge were also captured by
enemy forces at the same time. Forced to march
toward an unknown destination, Blood and Olson
die and are buried in the jungle. Mike Berge's
account of prison life until his release
completes the remainder of the Hefley's book.

1980-1987

196.   Chambers, Andrea. "Ex-Marine Bill Broyles Jr.
        Befriends His Enemy In Vietnam." **People
        Weekly** 26, no. 9 (September 1, 1986): 69-70,
        72.

        This article is the story of William Broyles'
        return to Vietnam in 1984 on his quest to answer
        emotional questions that had haunted him for the
        14 years since the war. Broyles returned to
        better understand the Vietnamese people he
        fought against. The article also gives quite a
        bit of Broyles' personal background.

197.   Dong, Stella. "PW Interviews Army Nurse L. Van
        Devanter." **Publishers Weekly** 223 (March 25,
        1983): 58-59.

        Dong's brief article is a summary of an
        interview with Lynda Van Devanter. The story
        explores her nursing career in Vietnam and her
        decision to write (with Chris Morgan) **Home
        Before Morning**.

198.   Goodwin, Jan. "War Torn: The Story of Two
        Women." **Ladies Home Journal** 102, no. 3
        (March 1985): 80-88, 165.

        As a journalist, Goodwin managed to get
        inside Cambodia to Dong Rek Platform, a refugee
        camp of almost 4,000 Vietnamese. She tells the
        story of Thu, a 35 year old Vietnamese refugee
        with an American husband who had lost contact
        with her children, been in prison after the fall
        of Saigon, and had managed to hang on to life at
        Dong Rek. The article portrays the immensely
        depressing refugee problem and is brightened
        only by Goodwin's news of Cambodia's intentions
        to process refugees like Thu for immigration to
        the United States.

199.   Keenan, Barbara M. **Every Effort: A True Story**. New York: St. Martin's Press, 1980. Rev. ed., 1986.

Keenan writes this book about her first husband, listed as MIA in Vietnam. She narrates her long, hopeful wait for his return, a return promised at many points, but without results. The book is a haunting attempt to expurgate grief and an attempt to bring to consciousness what kind of limbo MIA wives live through.

200.   Levertov, Denise. "Courage of a Poet." **In These Times** 4, no. 17 (March 26 – April 1, 1980): 24.

The short piece is a tribute to Muriel Rukeyser and includes two brief memories of Levertov's and Rukeyser's trip to Hanoi in 1972.

201.   Mahowald, Nancy. "I Never Saw Donnie Cry." **Reflecting "on the Memories of War"** 1 (1987): 18-20.

A sister reviews her brother's life, from his innocent childhood to his deterioration from Agent Orange-caused cancer after his return from Vietnam.

202.   May, Antoinette. **Witness to War: A Biography of Marguerite Higgins**. New York: Beaufort Bks., 1983. New York: Penguin Bks., 1985.

May writes a rather thorough description of the journalist's life from Higgins' childhood until her death of an illness contracted while assigned in Vietnam. The biography reveals Higgins' failures as well as her triumphs professionally and personally, and offers a realistic view of this aggressive woman who excelled as a foreign war correspondent in a man's world. From chapter 23 on, May covers Higgins' final months in Vietnam during the 1963 Buddhist uprisings. The book ends by tracing her slow death.

203.   McKeown, Bonni. **Peaceful Patriot: The Story of Tom Bennett**. Charleston, W. Va.: Mountain State Press, 1980.

McKeown was a college friend of Tom Bennett
a West Virginia conscientious objector who
became a medic in Vietnam. After he was killed
there, McKeown created this portrait of him
using interviews with his family and friends as
well as military resources to compile her book.

204. Moore, Joy Hofacher. **Ted Studebaker: A Man Who
Loved Peace**. Scottsdale, Pa.: Herald Press,
1987.

The book, written for young children, is the
story of the childhood, youth, and adult
military service of Ted Studebaker. A lifetime
member of the Church of the Brethren, Studebaker
finished college, applied for conscientious
objector status, then served two years in
Vietnam with the Vietnam Christian Service. He
was killed in Vietnam, and the book is written
in his memory as an illustration of a peace
loving man's impact on others in the midst of
war.

205. Spelts, Doreen. "She Was a Nurse." **Reflecting
"on the Memories of War"** 1 (1987): 42-43.

The life and death of one of the eight women
to die in Vietnam, Carol Drazba, fascinates
author Doreen Spelts. While a nurse stationed
at the 51st Field Hospital, Tan Sun Nhut, Drazba
was killed in a helicopter crash on her way for
in-country leave.

206. Wilkins, Lillian Claire. "Wayne Morse: An
Exploratory Biography." Ph.D. diss.,
University of Oregon, 1982.

The author writes of Wayne Morse's political
career, including his nearly lone opposition to
the Vietnam War, an opposition which identified
him with the peace movement. Wilkins uses a
psychoanalytical approach to describe Morse's
individual stances on various political issues.

207. Wilson, Joan Hoff. "Peace is A Woman's Job ...
Jeannette Rankin and American Foreign Policy:
Her Lifework As a Pacifist." **Montana** 30, no.
2 (April 1980): 38-53.

This article continues Wilson's writing about
Jeannette Rankin's work as a pacifist, focusing
on her attempts until her death in 1973 to sway
American foreign policy away from aggression.
In this piece, Wilson traces Rankin's efforts on
behalf of pacifism from the 1920's until her
death during the Vietnam War. Wilson's analysis
suggests that Rankin was not a Communist, but
instead believed that all countries needed to
see themselves as interdependent. She traces
Rankin's push for world disarmament, her
domestic reform measures, and her second term in
Congress. Labeling her protest of America's
involvement in the Vietnam War as her final
protest, Wilson examines Rankin's role both as
an anti-war protestor and symbol of the peace
movement.

Autobiography

1960-1969

208. Bevel, Diane Nash. "Journey to North Vietnam."
     Freedomways 7 (Spring 1967): 118-128.

     Bevel is a black woman who was active in the
     anti-war movement. She accompanied a group to
     Hanoi in 1966. Her visit included tours of
     bombed areas in Hanoi, talks with North
     Vietnamese citizens, visits to their hospitals,
     and interviews with government officials who
     further indoctrinated the group about U.S. war
     crimes.

209. Eby, Omar, and June Saunder. **House in Hue**.
     Scottsdale, Pa.: Herald Press, 1968.

     This is June Saunder's story of her
     experiences during the 1968 Tet Offensive.
     Seven Americans with the Vietnam Christian
     Service, she among them, were stranded in Hue
     for eight days, and she narrates the events of
     those days of waiting for rescue.

210. Husselblad, Marva, with Dorothy Brandon.
     **Lucky-Lucky: A Nurse's Story of a Provincial
     Hospital in Vietnam**. New York: M. Evans and
     Co., 1966. Philadelphia: J.B. Lippincott
     Co., 1966.

     The book is an account of Husselblad's three
     years (1962-65) in Vietnam as a nurse. She was
     stationed at the Chen-Y-Vien Hospital in Natrang
     and supervised the daily routine there. Stories
     of her daily routines at the hospital, the
     people who impacted on her life, and the daily
     tragedies comprise the book. Two important
     threads run through her narrative: observation
     of Vietnamese customs, and the growing American
     military role before and after Diem's
     assassination.

211. Manion, Gina O'Brien. **Mama Went to War**.
     Shepherdsville, Ky.: Victor Publishing Co.,
     1966.

Pat and Gina Manion, residents of Indiana,
decided to visit their son, Lt. Daniel Manion,
in Vietnam. In this little book, Gina Manion
describes the decision, plans, and trip to the
Far East. Upon arriving in Saigon, they found
themselves unable to see their son immediately,
so Gina Manion describes in great detail the
life of the city in the midst of war. The book
provides an interesting point of view on the
growing hostilities.

212. Schuyler, Phillippa Duke. **Good Men Die.** New
       York: Twin Circle, 1969.

Schuyler was a black woman correspondent in
Vietnam. A composer also, she spent time in
Vietnam entertaining troops and learning the
ways of the Vietnamese people. She writes here
of her experiences before she became a casualty
of the war herself. Schuyler particularly
abhors the "no win" policies dominating American
operations in Vietnam.

213. Smith, Mrs. Gordon [Laura Irene]. **Victory in
       Viet Nam.** Grand Rapids, Mich.: Zondervan
       Publishing Hse., 1966.

Smith and her husband, former missionaries in
South Viet Nam, returned there in 1956 to
central Viet Nam to continue their missionary
work. They located dozens of tribes which had
received little or no missionary contact, and
began visiting villages. Several tribes they
worked with, the Katu, the Cua, the Hrey, for
example, are described as are the events of
their lives until 1964. Not only are church
projects and personal anecdotes shared, but
glimpses of the war between the French and the
Viet Minh and of the increasing American
involvement pervade each section.

214. Sontag, Susan. **Trip to Hanoi.** New York:
       Farrar, Straus and Giroux, 1968. London:
       Panther Bks., 1968.

Sontag was invited to visit Hanoi. During
her visit, she first imagines the Vietnamese as
childlike and innocent people, particularly as
compared to herself, her own values, and

sensibilities. Slowly discovering that her imagination of these people and the realities did not mix, Sontag allows herself to appreciate finally the real Vietnamese by putting aside her own cultural lenses and accepting the actual cultural differences that exist. The book gives a revealing, sensitive picture of life in the North.

1970-1979

215. Bennett, Marilyn. **Help! What Do I Do Now? The Adventures of a Young Missionary Nurse in Vietnam.** Nashville, Tenn.: Southern Publishing Association, 1976.

Bennett was the director for a school of nursing in Saigon during the war. The school, funded by the Adventists, was her home for two years. She tells of her feeling of mission to serve in Vietnam even though she was very afraid, and of her arrival at the hospital. Most of the book details her experiences in the hospital, caring for Vietnamese (including Vietcong), the war's encroachment upon the city, the men she associates with, and the Vietnamese friends she makes.

216. Elkins, Marilyn Roberson, ed. **The Heart of a Man.** New York: W. W. Norton and Co., 1973.

Elkins' husband Frank was a pilot who was listed as missing in action in 1966. She received his diary among his personal effects which became the gist of this book. The excerpts extend from May, 1966, to October, 1966, when he was lost. The entries tell of flights, missions, friends lost, and reveal as well the deeply held fears and emotions of a fighter pilot.

217. Emerson, Gloria. "An American Woman's Vietnam Diary." **Vogue** 159 (January 1, 1972): 74-76, 117.

The piece is a series of excerpts from

Emerson's diary, vignettes of the war-ravaged
people, both American and Vietnamese. The
entries run from June to October of 1971.

218. Geyer, Georgie Anne. **Buying the Night Flight:
      The Autobiography of A Woman Foreign
      Correspondent**. New York: Delacorte Press,
      1975. New York: Seymour Lawrence, 1983.

      The book is about the career of journalist
Georgie Geyer. Only several pages are about her
time in Vietnam.

219. Herrgesall, Margaret, comp. **Dear Margaret,
      Today I Died: Letters from Vietnam by Lt.
      Col. Oscar Herrgesall**. San Antonio, Tex.:
      Naylor Co., 1974.

      Margaret Herrgesall compiled letters from her
husband beginning when he arrived in Long Binh
in February, 1972, and ending with his final
note in July of that year. The letters give a
sense of some of the routine of a Colonel's day
in Vietnam.

220. Krich, Claudia. "Vietnam Journal: Witness to
      the War's End." **Ms.** 5, no. 1 (July 1976):
      108-116.

      Krich was co-director of the AFSC Relief
Project in Quang Ngai, South Vietnam. After
April 30, 1975, her husband and she stayed until
July to witness the transitions. The article is
composed of excerpts from her diary of those
months. The excerpts begin on April 17 after
she fled Quang Ngai for Saigon, so she and her
friends witness Thieu's resignation, the advance
of the PRG, and they hear the evacuation of the
Americans. Extremely interesting is her account
of daily life as it proceeds methodically in
spite of the chaos around them. Krich's piece
is a nice inside view of the paradoxes of war.
Many conversations recorded after April 30 bring
out thoughts, fears, and the range of emotions
of the Vietnamese people.

221. Miller, Carolyn Paine. **Captured!** Chappaqua,
      N.Y.: Christian Herald Bks., 1977.

Miller, her husband, and children were one of
several families of missionaries living at
Banmethuot in March, 1975. As the PRG forces
advanced through the countryside, the Millers
and several others were taken prisoner and held
by Communist forces for several months. She
describes the various camps and conditions they
survived. Of particular interest is Miller's
portrayal of the enemy whom she presents as
intelligent and often kind.

222. Rutledge, Howard, and Phyllis Rutledge. **In the
Presence of Mine Enemies**. Old Tappan, N.J.:
Fleming H. Revell Co., 1973. Boston: G.K.
Hall and Co., 1974. New York: Pyramid Bks.,
1975.

This is Captain Howard Rutledge's story of
his imprisonment for eight years in North
Vietnam. Shot down in November, 1968, he was
captured by villagers, then shipped to Hanoi to
"Heartbreak Hotel," the "Zoo," and various parts
of the "Hanoi Hilton." His narrative is infused
with coming to grips with his mortality and his
faith. The last one-fourth of the book is by
Phyllis Rutledge who describes what the eight
years of waiting was like for her. Her daily
fears, her problems with her children and his
return into their lives, compose her part of the
narrative.

223. Smith, Laura Irene Ivory [Mrs. Gordon]. **Ten
Dangerous Years**. Chicago: Moody Press, 1975.

This is Laura Smith's story of her husband's
and her missionary work in Vietnam from the
mid-1960's to the mid-1970's. Smith elaborates
from her personal perspective on the events
during that decade in Vietnam.

224. Trembly, Diane L. **Petticoat Medic in Vietnam**.
New York: Vantage Press, 1976.

Trembly was a doctor in Vietnam from 1970-72
employed by U.S. AID. Beginning with her
departure from the United States, she describes
the high points of her 18 months' service in
Vietnam.

225. Williams, Marion. **My Tour in Vietnam: A
      Burlesque Shocker**. New York: Vantage Press,
      1970.

          Marion Williams, a black women, came to
      Vietnam in 1967 as both a journalist and
      volunteer nurse. The book, while a vehicle for
      retelling her experiences, serves also as a
      platform for espousing her political beliefs
      about the American involvement in Vietnam.
      Squarely anti-communist, she believes in the
      American role as a "world policeman."
      Nevertheless, she perceives the negative aspects
      of America's presence in Vietnam. The book
      reads like a catalogue of wrongdoings by both
      Vietnamese and Americans, wrongs which Williams
      sees as roadblocks to American victory in
      Vietnam. Williams also discusses cultural
      aspects of South Vietnam including the place of
      women and the role of black Americans in the
      war.

1980-1987

226. Alpert, Jane. **Growing Up Underground**. New
      York: William Morrow and Co., 1981.

          Alpert's book, written in three parts,
      describes her life in the 1950's and 1960's.
      Beginning with her earliest memories, she
      recreates her "passages" toward her anti-war
      protests, her feminism, her fugitive status, and
      finally, toward a personal renewal.

227. Boardman, Elizabeth Jelinek. **The Phoenix Trip:
      Notes on a Quaker Mission to Haiphong**.
      Burnsville, N.C.: Celo Press, 1985.

          Boardman was the only woman crew member on
      the Phoenix Trip, a relief voyage to North
      Vietnam. Against the backdrop of other Quaker
      Action Group war protest activities, she tells
      of her growing personal involvement in
      protesting the war. She shares the process of
      making the decision to take the trip, her
      feelings about the publicity it brought her
      family and her, and the details of the Phoenix's
      voyage to Haiphong and Hanoi with its boatload

of medicines and other items. Once she returned
home, she received many letters, both supportive
and threatening, and she shares some of these at
the end of the book.

228. Borton, Lady. **Sensing the Enemy: An American
      Woman Among the Boat People of Vietnam**. New
      York: Dial Press, 1984.

Borton, a feminist with a Quaker background,
writes of her work among Vietnamese refugees
during two stays in Southeast Asia. Borton's
writing aims to give the American public a
portrait of the Vietnamese people who, even now,
Americans still fail to see as people holding a
legitimate perspective of their own on the war.

229. Browne, Corinne. **Casualty: A Memoir of Love
      and War**. New York: W.W. Norton and Co.,
      1981. New York: Stein and Day, 1987.

In **Casualty**, Browne writes about the
Vietnam Veterans Chapel, a memorial built many
years ago in New Mexico by Victor Westphall in
honor of his son David who died in Vietnam in
1968. Meant to be a monument dedicated to all
fallen soldiers in Vietnam, the chapel drew a
large number of visitors, including Corinne
Browne, throughout the 1970's. Browne found
herself possessed by the structure's mysterious
symbolism, one which drew her back continually.
On her subsequent visits, she learns about
David's life and interviews his mother,
receiving a woman's perspective on war and the
death of one's children. This book is a look at
women's responses to war in the early years of
Vietnam as well as a description of one early
attempt to force national recognition of Vietnam
veterans.

230. Deegan-Young, Terre. "Donut Dollies."
      Reflecting "on the Memories of War" 1 (1987):
      33-34.

Deegan-Young reflects on her 1971 experience
as a Donut Dollie. Rather than retell of all
her visits, she gives a capsule summary of her
work, then describes the pain and the emotional
drain of having to be available to cheer others
up while having nowhere to release her own pain.

231.   Innis, Wendy. "Mango Showers." In **Viet Nam
       Flashbacks: Pig Iron 12**, edited by Jim
       Villani, and Rose Sayre, 21-25. Youngstown,
       Ohio: Pig Iron Press, 1984.

       As a twenty-seven year old woman, Innis was
       volunteer worker in Laos in 1966, where she
       didn't really expect the Vietnam War to
       influence her life. Most of the selection
       derives from her diary from February 6-23, 1966
       She also discusses and comments on the American
       role in Laos, describing in particular the
       various factions at war and the CIA's heavy rol
       there during this period.

232.   Musgrove, Patches [Helen]. **Vietnam: Front Row,
       Center**. 2 vols. Santa Ana, Calif.: Patches
       Publishers, 1986.

       In these 1400 pages, Patches Musgrove detail
       her life in Vietnam from 1966-72. While the
       subtitle bills her as a war correspondent for
       those years, the memoirs actually show that she
       was a fashion designer and business manager in
       the Far East. After these ventures failed in
       Vietnam, she became a press correspondent.
       Beginning her war coverage with the Big Red One
       she eventually reported the war with many other
       units; her collection of their patches earned
       her her name. Her many visits include stays
       with MASH units, Naval fleets, the Green Berets
       Korean allies, the Seabees, Marines, and the
       Coast Guard. The book is notable for its
       re-creation of real people through lengthy
       dialogues and descriptions of every event that
       Musgrove encountered both Vietnamese and
       American. Of interest, too, is Musgrove's
       description of the Tet Offensive, her personal
       fight with corruption there, and excerpts from
       her articles sent home to the **Jacksonville
       Journal** in Florida.

233.   Nasmyth, Virginia, and Spike Nasmyth. **Hanoi,
       Release John Nasmyth: A Family Love Story**.
       Santa Paulo, Cal.: V. Parr Publishing, 1984.

       Jointly authored by POW "Spike" Nasmyth and
       his sister, Virginia, the story unfolds through
       their alternating narratives. One concerns the

situation at home after Spike Nasmyth's MIA
status was announced, and Virginia Nasmyth shows
the slowly disintegrating relationships within
the family largely due to the excess stress
caused by Spike's MIA status. The second
narrative thread is Spike's, and he reveals his
experiences both as a captive in Vietnam and as
a returned and readjusting POW.

234. Noel, Chris, with Bill Treadwell. **Matter of
      Survival: The "War" Jane Never Saw.** Boston:
      Branden Publishing Co., 1987.

      Noel was the Armed Forces Radio and
Television's counterpart of Hanoi Hannah. She
describes her visits to camps and her
entertainment shows in Vietnam. The aftermath
of being in Vietnam left her suffering from PTSD
symptoms like many others, so the last part of
the book explores her continuing personal
struggle to adjust. In spite of the war's
legacy, she clings to her pro-American beliefs.

235. Roth, Patricia. **The Juror and the General**.
      New York: William Morrow and Co., 1986.

      Roth, an elementary art teacher, was on the
jury for the Westmoreland v. CBS, et al. trial.
She gives an often humorous insider's view of
the process, revealing the daily ups and downs.
Roth's account of the trial's progress is also
the story of one woman's development from
ignorance of the issues about the war to a
better, more informed understanding.

236. Stockdale, Jim, and Sybil Stockdale. **In Love
      and War: The Story of a Family's Ordeal and
      Sacrifice During the Vietnam Years**. New
      York: Harper and Row Pubs., 1984. New York:
      Bantam Bks., 1984.

      The authors, by retelling their experiences
in alternating chapters, recapture Jim
Stockdale's combat and prison experience and
Sybil Stockdale's personal "war on the
homefront." The first one-third of the book is
spent describing childhood, young adulthood,
marriage, early career, and family decisions.
Most of the narrative deals with his capture and

imprisonment as well as Sybil's own attempts to
confront the tragedy. Particularly interesting
are both his survival tactics in prison and her
as an outspoken POW wife constantly lobbying on
behalf of the POW-MIA's. His release and
information about their readjustment after 1973
complete this very detailed account.

237.   Van Devanter, Lynda, with Christopher Morgan.
       **Home Before Morning: The Story of an Army
       Nurse in Vietnam.** New York: Beaufort Bks.
       Pubs., 1983. New York: Warner Bks., 1984.

       Van Devanter has written a definitive version
of the American nurse in the Vietnam War.
Although the book describes her Vietnam
experience, it also is a record of the journey
of a woman's consciousness. Beginning with her
childhood and describing her nursing training,
Van Devanter develops a portrait of herself as a
patriotic, Kennedy-era believer in America's
rightness. Her Army training and her stationing
in Vietnam are all graphically described as are
the people and relationships in her life. From
combat zone through the return home, the impact
of the war is shared by this woman who became
haunted by the war and who went from a political
innocence to an experienced, hurt, and sometimes
cynical veteran.

1960-1969

238.   Lynd, Alice, ed. **We Won't Go: Personal
       Accounts of War Objectors**. Boston: Beacon
       Press, 1966.

      Lynd organized this collection of twenty-four
stories told by men and women war protestors.
Their stories share the events of and reasons
behind their rebellion against the draft and
service in the Vietnam War. Two women, sharing
one narrative, speak from the perspective of the
imprisoned protestors' spouses.

239.   Sheehan, Susan. "A Vietnamese Woman."
       McCall's 94, no. 6 (March 1967): 48, 50, 52,
       143.

      Sheehan's article is a portrait of a South
Vietnamese peasant woman, Nguyen The Lan, who
finds herself in the midst of war. Sheehan lays
out Lan's early life, the life she shares with
her husband and children at present, and her
cultural, economic and physical surroundings in
the first pages. Then Sheehan centers on the
impact of the war for Lan and her family. Of
greatest impact was the rule of Diem, harsh for
Lan since the family were Cao Daists. This
piece offers a rare glimpse of the war through a
peasant's eyes and this view reveals the
existence of a people with few political
connections or ideas about the war and who only
hope to live through it and survive.

240.   _____. **Ten Vietnamese**. New York:
       Alfred A. Knopf, 1967. London: Jonathan
       Cape, 1967.

      This is a very early oral history of sorts.
Susan Sheehan interviewed and wrote of the lives
of ten Vietnamese. These perspectives on a
growing war come from a wide-ranging group of
"ordinary" people: a peasant, a refugee,
soldiers, a prisoner, other adults, and a young
orphan. The group includes both North and South

Vietnamese. Sheehan introduces each person's
current condition followed by a past personal
history. Their views on the war, politics, and
the American involvement expand the entries, bu
Sheehan also interweaves historical and
political events among all the narratives.

1970-1979

241.   Wyatt, Barbara Powers, and Capt. Frederick
       Wyatt, eds. **We Came Home.** Toluca Lake,
       Calif.: P.O.W. Publications, 1977.

       The Wyatts' book consists of hundreds of
personal experience stories told by American
POW's after they were released in 1973 and 1974
Each alphabetical entry shows a photograph and
narration of the veteran's experiences in
prison. The end of the book lists the 648
returning POW's and all the MIA soldiers.
Civilian POW's and MIA's are also listed.

1980-1987

242.   Blake, Jeanne. "No Houses, No Gardens." In
       **Unwinding the Vietnam War: From War Into
       Peace,** edited by Reese Williams, 178-208.
       Seattle: Real Comet Press, 1987.

       This article-length series of eight
interviews shares the experiences of Meo
refugees moving from Laos to the United States.
Many of these people assisted the U.S. during
the Vietnam War and the invasion of Laos.
Presented here are excerpts from eight
conversations; all describe leaving home and
coming to the U.S., the past life versus the
new. Clearly, these peoples' experiences share
common themes: homelessness, material losses,
and personal loss. Some conversations also
touch on women's rights.

243.   Brandon, Heather, ed. **Casualties: Death in
       Vietnam, Anguish and Survival in America.**
       New York: St. Martin's Press, 1984.

       Brandon's format is interesting; she

interviews clusters of friends and family of
dead Vietnam war heroes. Most entries
concentrate on the theme of "aftershock" for the
people left behind--wives, lovers, friends,
children, parents. In a sense, the title
alludes to "casualties" at home after the death
of a soldier in the war.

244. Byrd, Barthy. **Home Front: Women and Vietnam**.
      Berkeley, Calif.: Shameless Hussy Press,
      1986.

      This is an oral history of nine women most of
woman remained in the U.S. during the Vietnam
War, but in some way had their lives changed
because of the war. The women are reporters,
teachers, wives and friends of soldiers who were
KIA or MIA; and the women are both American and
Vietnamese.

245. Freedman, Dan, and Jacquelin Rhoads, eds.
      Nurses in Vietnam: The Forgotten Veterans.
      Austin, Tex.: Texas Monthly Press, 1987.

      Freedman and Rhoads interviewed nine nurses
about their experiences in Vietnam. Their
insights include many of the now well-known
characteristics of combat-related positions that
women served in. The editors' well-written
introduction focuses on the nurses' roles in
this war.

246. Marshall, Kathryn. **In the Combat Zone: An Oral
      History of American Women in Vietnam**.
      Boston: Little, Brown and Co., 1987.

      Twenty women's voices bring together their
diverse experiences in and reactions to the
Vietnam War. The women represented come from
many backgrounds; some are nurses, civilians, or
volunteers for relief work. Each woman
discusses why she went to Vietnam, her memorable
experiences there, and her feelings upon her
return home. Past and current biographical
material is available for each woman's entry.

247. Palmer, Laura. **Shrapnel in the Heart: Letters**

and **Remembrances from the Vietnam Veterans
Memorial**. New York: Random House, 1987. New
York: Vintage Bks., 1988.

Palmer investigated the collection of letters
and poems left at the Vietnam Memorial by
individuals. She traces the mementos found next
to 29 men's names. The book is composed of the
letter or poem and the stories behind each as
told to Palmer by the soldier's friends, wives,
lovers, or families who left the keepsakes.

History

1954-1959

248. Farley, Miriam. "Vietnam Kaleidoscope." **Far Eastern Survey** 24 (May 1955): 77-78.

   Farley describes the political infighting among various military, religious, and political groups in South Vietnam in 1955. Specifically, she reports the upheavals and resolutions in April and early May, 1955.

249. Hammer, Ellen. **The Struggle For Indochina**. Stanford: Stanford University Press, 1954.

   Hammer's extensive study, while published in 1954, the year of the French defeat, actually deals with the French control of Vietnam, the loss of that control in World War II, and the tensions between French, Vietnamese, and Chinese after World War II when France reoccupied the country. The last half of the book concerns the French war with the Vietnamese, and her final chapter outlines the future problems Americans may have in Vietnam.

250. _____. "Viet Nam, 1956." **Journal of International Affairs** 10, no. 1 (May 1956): 28-48.

   This extensive article reveals the roots of Viet Nam's current political status. Hammer begins with the rule of Gia Long in 1802, and traces the rise and fall of French Colonialism and its effects on the Vietnamese people. She spends much time discussing the political moves underlying the Geneva Conference and the transformation of the North by the Viet Minh into a solidly Communist territory. In fact, Hammer spends the last half of the article debunking the myth that the Viet Minh gave unwitting allegiance to the Communists as well as the myth that if South Viet Nam postpones the national elections, they will remove the threat of the Viet Minh Communists.

251.   Klein, Wells C., and Marjorie Weiner.
          "Vietnam." Part V, Chapters 17-21, in
          Governments and Politics of Southeast Asia,
          edited by G.M. Kahin, 315-411.   Ithaca, N.Y.
          Cornell University Press, 1959.

          In this first edition of Kahin's book, Wells
          and Weiner cover the history of Vietnam from the
          French governance until the Geneva Conference in
          1954.   In Chapters 18-20, they discuss South
          Vietnam's economy, social, and political
          structure as well as specific problems the South
          Vietnamese currently must solve.   The final
          chapter covers these same topics about North
          Vietnam.   The contrasting information between
          the North and South is of particular interest.

1960-1969

252.   Hammer, Ellen. **Vietnam: Yesterday and Today.**
          New York: Holt, Rinehart and Winston, 1966.

          Hammer geographically sketches Vietnam,
          moving then to a discussion of the people and
          their characteristics.   After a brief history of
          Vietnam, the remainder of the book analyzes the
          impact of international conflicts on the
          struggle to reunify Vietnam.   The two Vietnams
          are pictured as victims of the superpower
          conflicts.   In one section, Hammer discusses the
          role of women, primarily those of North Vietnam.

253.   Higgins, Marguerite. **Our Vietnam Nightmare.**
          New York: Harper and Row, 1965.

          This is an account of the American effort in
          Vietnam which indicts America's involvement
          based on a "profound ignorance" about Vietnamese
          realities.   Higgins' conversational style makes
          the history easy to read even though her
          rhetoric rings with strongly anti-American
          involvement sentiment.

254.   Jumper, Roy, and Marjorie Weiner Normand.
          "Vietnam." Part V, Chapters 17-23, in
          Governments and Politics of Southeast Asia,
          2nd ed. Edited by G.M. Kahin, 375-524.
          Ithaca, N. Y.: Cornell University Press,
          1964.

In this second edition, Normand and Jumper
offer an updated description of the social,
economic, and political situation in both North
and South Vietnam. The historical survey covers
much of the same detail as in the previous
edition. While the organization of the
remaining chapters is similar to the first book,
information on the politics, economy, and
problems of each country is considerably
changed. The section on North Vietnam
encompasses three chapters and offers a more
detailed view of the Communist controlled north.

255. Strong, Anna Louise. **Some Background on the
       United States in Vietnam and Laos**. New York:
       Far East Reporter Pubs., 1965.

Strong attended an international solidarity
conference in Hanoi on world-wide U.S.
imperialism, and this pamphlet is part of her
conference report. The actual focus of the
conference, however, was the war in Vietnam.
Participants passed resolutions demanding U.S.
withdrawal from Vietnam. Published, too, is a
summary of South Vietnamese views of the U.S.
involvement in the war including the manifesto
of the NLF.

1970-1979

256. Adams, Nina. "The Last Line of Defense." Vol.
       5 of **The Pentagon Papers: Critical Essays**,
       edited by Noam Chomsky and Howard Zinn.
       Senator Gavel Edition, 143-155. Boston:
       Beacon Press, 1972.

Adams argues that the Pentagon study cannot
be seen as a history of the war in Vietnam or of
Vietnam itself because of its numerous flaws.
The study's conclusion concerning the major
question, "What went wrong in Vietnam?" is that
the means to win the war ought to have been
different. This conclusion, to Adams, is a
direct result of the flaws. She outlines what
the study actually reveals about administrative
lies, the economic motives for American
involvement, the narrow political assumptions of
leaders, and the failure on the part of its
authors to understand American history. In

failing to pose important questions and examine
them objectively, the report recreates a
dangerous fantasy world unrelated to current and
alternative understandings of the war.

257. _____. "The Meaning of Pacification:
Thanh Hoa Under French Rule, 1885-1908."
Ph.D. diss., Yale University, 1978.

Adams examines one major province under the
rule of the French colonials in order to
illustrate the widely variant French and
Vietnamese perspectives on politics, society,
and history. She carefully traces the reasons
for and the forms of resistance used by the
Vietnamese against the French in this province,
then catalogues the disruptive results of the
French conquest to the native resistance. In
essence, French conquest set the stage by the
early 20th century for a future use of force by
the Vietnamese to earn their freedom.

258. Hammer, Ellen. "Perspective on Vietnam."
Problems of Communism 25 (January-February
1976): 81-84.

Hammer's piece is an extended review essay on
four books on the Vietnam War. She prefaces the
review with a brief history of the war and the
partition of Vietnam in 1954. The four books
she applauds as careful and scholarly
reconstructions of the period of Vietnamese
history and politics from the early 1950's to
the early 1960's.

259. Lamb, Helen. **Vietnam's Will to Live:
Resistance to Foreign Aggression from Early
Times through the Nineteenth Century**. New
York: Monthly Review Press, 1972.

In the introduction to this book, Lamb
provides the book's link to the Vietnam War.
Noting that in the midst of our war, no one has
bothered to pay any attention to the Vietnamese
history of resistance, Lamb suggests that the
very key to understanding Vietnam's success in
defeating two world powers may lie in the
historical roots of their existing nationalism.
She attempts to shed some light on the nature of

the Vietnamese who waged the war in the 1960's and 1970's. Finally, she covers the Vietnamese resistance to both the Chinese and the French through the early 1900's, concluding the book with two chapters assessing the lessons of resistance learned by the Vietnamese and which they apply continually.

260. Marshall, Rachelle. **A Brief Account of Vietnam's Struggle for Independence: America's Longest War**. Philadephia: Women's International League for Peace and Freedom, 1975.

This 34-page history of struggle in Vietnam speaks to high school readers, outlining the chronology of the Vietnam War from 1954 to 1975. Marshall relates the background leading up to the American involvement and concludes with several pages of discussion on the nature of politics, corruption, anti-war sentiment, as well as speculation about why the United States stayed in Vietnam.

261. Young, Marilyn B. "Revisionists Revised: The Case of Vietnam." **Newsletter of the Society for the History of American Foreign Relations** 10, no. 2 (June 1979): 1-10.

Young argues that American historians and writers are rewriting the history of the Vietnam War and whitewashing the American purposes, role, and experiences in the war. Finding this a tragic block to true analysis and progress as a nation, she calls for an admission of our true aims, and acknowledgment of our own wrong in intruding in Vietnam. This confrontation with national self is the nation's only way to deal with this past war realistically according to Young's ideas.

1980-1987

262. Hammer, Ellen. **A Death in November: America in Vietnam, 1963**. New York: E.P. Dutton, 1987.

Hammer examines the Diem coup, both

describing and analyzing the historical events
that led to it. Chronologically, the book
outlines the year 1963 beginning with the Ap Bac
confrontation until a few days after the
November coup. Within this chronology though,
Hammer creates a panoramic view of the Vietnam
War from the 1940's until 1963. The chapters
are full of details of the lives, thoughts, and
decisions of key Vietnamese and Americans (Diem,
Ho, Lodge, Nolting, for example), and she vaults
from the past to present, from Diem to Ho, South
to North, Vietnamese to American, while weaving
themes together. Clearly, Hammer's history is
sympathetic to Diem's rule and his desire to rid
himself of the Americans. He comes across as a
leader often outwitted by the American
government.

263.   Mabie, Margot C. J. **Vietnam, There and Here**.
         New York: Holt, Rinehart and Winston, 1985.
         New York: H. Holt and Co., 1985.

         This is a children's or adolescent's history
of Vietnam and a very complete and clearly
written account of many aspects of the war.
Beginning with a history of the wars in
Indochina, Mabie moves to the French occupation
in the 20th century, pausing in her chronology
to compare the two key nationalist figures, Ho
Chi Minh and Ngo Dinh Diem. She traces the
steps toward American involvement and escalation
under three Presidents, then explores several
American reactions; hawks, doves, and the
anti-war protestors are among them. Mabie
concludes the book with the communist
encroachment from 1973 to 1975 in South Vietnam.

264.   Werner, Jayne. "A Short History of the War in
         Vietnam." **Monthly Review** 37, no. 2 (January
         1985): 14-21.

         Werner argues in this article that American
involvement in the war extends from the point
when the first American was killed there--in
1946. In fact, she says, by 1954, 80-90% of the
French war effort in Vietnam was being paid for
by U.S. dollars. Most of the article is spent
proving false these three basic beliefs about
American involvement: (1) that the war was a

rebellion against an independent South; (2) that
it was a war between North and South; (3) that
the North was responsible for war escalation.
Werner gives very straightforward retellings of
the progress of the war grouped around these
three myths.

265.   Young, Marilyn B.   "Old Wine in New Bottles:
         'Reinterpreting' the Vietnam War." **Southeast
       Asia Chronicle**, no. 93 (April 1984): 9-25.

       Young hits hard at the "revisionist"
interpretations of American involvement in the
Vietnam War. She focuses on Fox Butterfield's
essays and his scholarship, criticizing his
slanted reinterpretation of America's part in
the war. Young notes important anti-war
scholars that were left out of his
interpretations, and is critical of his claims
that academic America has suffered from an
unconsciousness about the war.

266.   _____. "The U.S. Invasion of
       Vietnam." **Monthly Review** 38 (October 1986):
       49-55.

       In this review essay, Young analyzes
extensively George Kahin's book, **Intervention.
How America Became Involved in Vietnam**. On all
points, she finds Kahin's book a valuable
contribution to the many analyses of America's
involvement in the war. Specifically, she finds
particularly interesting Kahin's descriptions of
political debates and decisions made during the
Johnson administration, as well as the nature of
the bribery used to induce South Korea and the
Philippines to send troops.

Politics

The American Government

1954-1959

267. Durdin, Peggy. "Saigon in the Shadow of Doom."
New York Times Magazine, section 6 (November
21, 1954): 7, 40, 42, 44, 46.

Characterizing Saigon both during and after
the French defeat as a city which "fiddles while
the fire approaches," Durdin contrasts the
serious political and military threat of the
Communist North with the continued apathy,
corruption, and carefree climate of the South
Vietnamese capital. Durdin then analyzes the
reasons for the city's isolation and false
security. Her fear is that Saigon, one of the
last European dominated cities, will not
transform itself into a Vietnamese city strong
enough to withstand the Communists. Its
blindness and corruption, only masked by its
surface beauties, create a tragic situation.

268. _____. "There is No Truce in Vietnam."
Reporter 11, no. 12 (December 30, 1954):
23-27.

Durdin wrote this piece just after the
temporary separation between North and South
following the rout of the French at Dienbienphu.
Calling American policy "short-sighted," she
questions American motives and warns that this
"cold" war will be potentially dangerous to
Americans and Vietnamese alike. Most of the
article compares and contrasts the North and
South--economically, politically, and
militarily, and it ends with the warning that
America will not be able to save a country
unless the country itself participates in the
process.

269. _____. "Vietnam Awaits Independence
and/or Annihilation." **Reporter** 10 (April 27,
1954): 21-23.

Durdin describes the plight of the

non-Communist Vietnamese nationalists on the eve
of the French defeat and withdrawal from
Vietnam. She reports that many fear that a
Communist ruled state would be as oppressive as
colonial rule had been. The solution to many is
an organized, strong, energetic government which
would hold out against the Vietminh. Durdin
analyzes why the Bao Dai (and Buu Loc)
government failed to meet the needs of
non-Communist Vietnam, and she judges that the
Cao Dai, Dai Viet, and Hoa Hao are not strong
and united enough to emerge as an effective
opposition. She concludes the article by
suggesting that perhaps Ngo Dien Diem would be
able to consolidate non-Communist Vietnamese
elements.

270.   Farley, Miriam. **United States Relations With
       Southeast Asia with Special Reference to
       Indochina, 1950-55.** New York: Institute of
       Pacific Relations, 1955.

       Farley's report was expanded and revised
during the first nine months of 1955. She
attempts to examine the successes and failures
of American policies in Southeast Asia during
the early 50's, and she specifically traces
American goals, actions, and alliances in the
region, emphasizing all that led to the 1954
Geneva conference and to the division of
Vietnam. Included, too, is a brief summary of
the Bandung Conference.

271.   Hammer, Ellen. "The Struggle for Indochina
       Continues: Geneva to Bandung." **The Pacific
       Spectator.** Supplement to vol. 9 (Summer
       1955): 1-40. Published as **The Struggle for
       Indochina Continues: Geneva to Bandung.**
       Stanford: Stanford University Press, 1955.

       Hammer's long article begins by clearly
pointing out the false assumptions America held
about the Vietnam situation at the time of the
French defeat in 1954. Analyzed is the United
States' role at the Geneva conference and the
results of the conference itself in which the
disharmony among western nations' views of
Vietnam clearly appeared. Hammer describes
extensively the problems confronted by the Viet

Minh after the Geneva settlement, and follows
with a parallel analysis of the problems
confronting competing political units in the
South. The article concludes with a warning
about the immense power behind the Vietnamese
search for their own independence.

1960-1969

272. Bromley, Dorothy. **Washington and Vietnam: An
      Examination of the Moral and Political
      Issues**. Dobbs Ferry, N.Y.: Oceana Pubns.,
      1966.

      The purpose of Bromley's short book is to
      clarify events of the war for average Americans
      who are being increasingly confused by the
      complex issues the war generated. Bromley gives
      the historical and political background for the
      American involvement in the war, covering the
      Geneva agreements, the U.S. support of Diem, and
      the slow escalation of the war. The book
      clearly opposes American involvement in
      Vietnam.

273. Fitzgerald, Frances. "The Struggle and the War:
      The Maze of Vietnamese Politics." **The
      Atlantic** 220 (August 1967): 72-88.

      Fitzgerald attempts to force American readers
      to see the Vietnamese struggle through the lens
      of their politics and psychology, not through
      American perspectives. She asserts that to find
      solutions for the Vietnam War, Americans must
      understand the issues involved as a Vietnamese
      would. Fitzgerald outlines the political and
      social goals of this Confucian-based society,
      the importance of the village, the meaning of
      revolution in that culture, the messages
      implicit in the varying languages of the South,
      and the probable realities of the future for
      North and South Vietnam.

274. Higgins, Marguerite. "Ugly Americans of
      Vietnam." **America** 111 (October 3, 1964):
      376-382.

      In a very ironic tone, Higgins writes an "I

told you so" article in which she berates
American political leaders for operating
gullibly in Vietnam. One false assumption she
accuses leaders of is that the South Vietnamese
were ready for an American-style democracy, and
another is that Diem was an anti-democratic
leader who could do no right, and, if removed,
would leave the country better off. She expose
the Communist core of the Buddhists led by Quan
Tri as another example of American misjudgments
about the realities of Vietnam. Finally,
Higgins meticulously traces other American
mistakes as time inched toward November and
Diem's assassination.

275.   Jeffries, Jean.   "Why Vietnam is Kennedy's War.
       National Review 20 (April 23, 1968): 396-397
       411.

       Jeffries analyzes the Schlesinger, Sorenson
and Galbraith opinions explaining that the
current Vietnam War is Johnson's and that the
Vietnam War under Kennedy was a totally
different war, motivated by differing agendas
for both countries. Jeffries takes each
component of these assertions and, using John
Kennedy's own remarks, demonstrates that the
current war is Kennedy's also.

276.   Kuebler, Jeanne.   "Task in South Viet Nam."
       Editorial Research Reports 1 (April 17,
       1963): 287-304.

       The article reports on the risks the U.S.
will take if it becomes more involved in a war
in South Viet Nam. Kuebler details factors
which cause unease: (1) the American senators'
lack of confidence in Saigon after surveying th
political situation in the country and finding
it regressing; (2) the unease of the American
military over the internal politics of the Sout
Vietnamese military; (3) the mixed results of
the hamlet programs; (4) the drawbacks American
advisors experience in training the indigenous
population; (5) non-Communist opposition to
Diem; and (5) American opposition to an
impending war. In essence, the article points
out many reasons which make a widening of
American involvement unwise.

277.   Lamb, Helen.   "The Negotiations That Are
            Possible."   **Minority of One** 8 (January 1966):
            16-17.

        This brief article sets a context for Lamb's
        assertions that negotiations could only occur
        with Hanoi or the NLF if the war escalation
        ceased and withdrawal of American troops and aid
        occurred.

278.   _____.   "The Paris Exiles."   **The Nation**
            197, no. 4 (August 10, 1963): 65-68.

        Lamb interviews exiles from Vietnam about
        their perceptions of the "undeclared" war there
        and of Diem's rule.   She interviews people who
        are opposed to Diem and Communism and those who
        are Communists and neutralists.   All the exiles
        were critical of the American military conduct
        and of American economic aid to a faltering, now
        dependent, South Vietnam.

279.   _____.   "President Johnson's Peace
            Offensive."   **Minority of One** 8 (December
            1965): 11-12.

        Lamb discusses the United States statements
        of desire for a negotiated peace settlement
        complete with the actions to the contrary.   She
        probes the causes for such duplicity.

280.   _____.   **The Tragedy of Vietnam: Where Do
            We Go From Here?**   New York: Basic Pamphlets,
            1964.

        In an attack on America's role in Vietnam,
        Lamb retells the beginnings of the Vietnam civil
        war, carefully describing the conflict in the
        South as a "grass roots" one not instigated by
        the North.   Her arguments cover the feelings of
        pro-neutralism felt by even many of the South
        Vietnamese themselves, and the reluctance of
        America to allow a reunification.   The pamphlet
        ends with a call for a new Vietnam policy.

281.   _____.   "Vietnam: The Long Stalemate is
            Ending."   **National Guardian** 16 (September 26,
            1964): 7.

        Lamb describes the gradual escalation by the

U.S. in 1964, mentioning that the war threatens
now to swallow both Laos and Cambodia. She sees
the current crisis now centering on President
Khanh's inept use of power which prompted
further Buddhist uprisings, and argues that the
American government must decide whether to
declare war or to enter negotiations.

282.   Lenart, Edith.   "End Game in Paris." **Far
        Eastern Economic Review** 65 (August 1969):
        370-372.

        The article describes and updates the
        progress, or lack thereof, of the Paris peace
        talks from December to August. Lenart gives
        much attention to President Nixon's Eight-Point
        Peace Plan.

283.   _____. "Stubbornly Last Summer." **Far
        Eastern Economic Review** 63, no. 1 (December
        29, 1968): 18-20.

        This is a chronological and political
        analysis of the preparation for the Paris talks
        from May to December. Lenart details carefully
        the international politics behind the scenes.

284.   McCarthy, Mary. **Hanoi**. New York: Harcourt
        Brace and World, 1968.

        A counterpart to **Vietnam**, this book reveals
        McCarthy's insights into the realities of life
        in North Vietnam. Much of the book concerns
        her self-discoveries engendered by this visit to
        the North.

285.   _____. **Vietnam**. New York: Harcourt
        Brace and World, 1967.

        McCarthy contrasts Saigon, an almost totally
        Westernized city, to the Vietnamese countryside
        at war. Interspersed are her liberal views on
        the politics behind the war.

286.   _____. "Vietnam: Solutions." **New
        York Review of Books** 9 (November 9, 1967):
        3-6.

        McCarthy focuses on several works of Vietnam

war critics, and finds that, while many offer
concise and apt criticisms of American war
policies, each one's suggestions for ending the
war are poorly thought out. She discusses the
problems inherent in critics' solutions, then
puts forth her own idea of how Americans might
end the war.

287. Mears, Helen, and J. Alexander. "The Big Risks
       of Little Wars." **The Progressive** 26 (October
       1962): 23-27.

       The authors fear that American involvement in
Vietnam could trigger nuclear conflict. They
foresee certain risks as an outcome of American
involvement: (1) escalation of the ground war;
(2) U.S. bombing attacks on North Vietnam; and
(3) the possible involvement of China. Factors
increasing the probability of these outcomes are
the weakness of the Diem government's support in
the countryside, the support of the guerillas by
the South Vietnamese peasants, and the warnings
by China and the U.S.S.R. to the U.S. if it
remains at war in Vietnam. Finally, they
predict that the undeclared war could become
more expansive than the Korean War.

288. Starner, Frances. "LBJ's Doctrine for Asia."
       Far Eastern Economic Review 53 (September 29,
       1966): 635-637.

       Starner discusses the vagueness of Johnson's
policies for the American presence in Asia. To
her, such vagueness is due to the
administration's ambivalence towards China and
its burdensome commitments to Vietnam. The
vagueness encompasses contradictory statements
about America's future involvement in Asia.

289. Trilling, Diana, and Mary McCarthy. "On
       Withdrawing from Vietnam: An Exchange." **New
       York Review of Books** 10, no. 1 (January 18,
       1968): 5-10.

       Trilling's position opens this debate. She
argues that, while she is an opponent to the
war, an American withdrawal will open the door
to a subsequent bloodbath in South Vietnam.
McCarthy responds by noting that we cannot

predict a bloody outcome, and, in any case,
South Vietnamese working for U.S. interests must
have been aware of the risks in the first place.
Thus, while the ethics of withdrawal are an
issue, they should not be the deciding factor in
the United States' decision to leave. Both
women's arguments admit there are no easy
avenues out of Vietnam and that American
withdrawal is a complex issue at best.

290.   Woodward, Beverly. "Nuremberg Law and U. S.
        Courts." **Dissent** 16 (March-April 1969):
        128-136.

        Woodward reviews the assertions of David
Mitchell, Capt. Levy, and the Ft. Hood Three
concerning the application of the Nuremberg
Charter to their personal situations. In each
instance, these cases came before American
courtrooms. Although in all three situations
the men lost, several Supreme Court opinions
suggest deeper national issues present in these
cases, specifically the question of whether
Americans were involved in an illegal war.
Woodward analyzes carefully the issues of law
involved.

1970-1979

291.   Bell, Coral. **The Diplomacy of Detente: The
        Kissinger Era**. New York: St. Martin's Press,
        1977.

        Bell analyzes the concept "detente" as an
American political strategy used by Henry
Kissinger (1969-77) in relationship to China and
the Soviet Union. One chapter is spent
analyzing "detente" as an important part of the
American withdrawal from Vietnam.

292.   Brodine, Virginia, and Mark Selden. **Open
        Secret: The Kissinger-Nixon Doctrine in Asia**.
        New York: Harper and Row Pubs., 1972.

        Of the three essays included in the volume,
only the first is co-authored by the book's two
editors. They review Kissinger's bases for his
foreign policy and the concepts associated with

the central aim of international stability. An
extensive analysis of Nixon's stand on
Asian/U.S. relations follows the Kissinger
section. Finally, the two sections are brought
together as Selden and Brodine explore the
results of Kissinger's plans for achieving both
Nixon's and his own goals through the Vietnam
War.

293.   Fitzgerald, Frances. "Annals of War: Johnson's
            Dilemma." **New Yorker** 48 (July 22, 1972):
            53-68.

        This fourth part of a five part series on the
Vietnam War explains thoroughly the response of
President Johnson to the NLF build-up in the
South from 1965-68.

294.   _____. "Can the War End?" **New
            York Review of Books** 20 (February 22, 1973):
            13-14.

        Fitzgerald argues that the war, as fought by
the American politicians, may never end. She
views America's signing of the Paris Accords as
an open-ended method of staying involved in
Vietnamese matters. That was an act that
promises peace, but does not demand closure;
thus the way remains for an unending American
involvement. Fitzgerald views Thieu's and
Nixon's actions as detrimental to any political
healing. She concludes by suggesting what
Nixon's next steps must be.

295.   _____. "The End is the
            Beginning." **The New Republic** 172, no. 18
            (May 3, 1975): 7-8.

        Fitzgerald queries the numerous repetitions
of history as the 25 year American involvement
in Vietnam comes to a close. Characterizing
American policy as one of "rigid
repetitiveness," Fitzgerald maintains that none
of the four Presidents serving during the war
ever pursued it for real foreign policy issues.
Fitzgerald asserts heatedly that all reasons
given for sustaining the war can be reduced to
one: a few powerful men refused to accept any
solution but winning and refused to see that

their power and credibility with the American
public had dissolved over the years of war.

296. _____. "The Offensive-I: The View
      from Vietnam." **New York Review of Books** 18
      (May 18, 1972): 6-13.

      Fitzgerald describes the lack of American
surprise at a recent offensive launched by North
Vietnamese military, and she criticizes American
intelligence failures. Cutting through the
American and South Vietnamese rhetoric,
Fitzgerald reassesses the meaning behind the
offensive concluding that: (1) the ARVN are
still poorly prepared to handle the military war
without American aid; (2) the North Vietnamese
did not attack from desperation as Americans
claim, but from strength; (3) the attack was not
a final attempt at a total victory which was
flouted, but merely one victory along the way to
a final one. Fitzgerald believes this leaves
Nixon with no face-saving measures; he must
either risk an all-out war or withdraw.

297. _____. "Vietnam: The Future."
      New York Review of Books 14 (March 26, 1970):
      4-10.

      Fitzgerald criticizes heavily Nixon's
"Vietnamization" plan, saying that it really
means a continued support of anti-Communist
governments, but with fewer American troops
involved. Essentially, it is a similar strategy
as that attempted after 1954. Fitzgerald shows
that not only will "Vietnamization" not win the
war, but it actually retards any true gains.
She elucidates again her point that Vietnamese
thinking differs drastically from American,
which is and has been the crux of this American
fiasco. The only solution she sees for ending
the war is the return of political matters to
Vietnamese hands.

298. Frederick, Cynthia. "The Vietnamization of
      Saigon Politics." **Bulletin of Concerned
      Asian Scholars** 3 (Winter-Spring 1971): 5-14.

      Frederick returned to Saigon in 1971 for six

days before she was expelled. The article warns
that the anti-American feelings of the
Vietnamese people are slowly surfacing and
becoming visible in acts of mob demonstrations
and violence. After citing several recent
examples, Frederick then describes the
activities of various dissenting elements
especially in the urban areas. She projects
then where this Vietnamese peace movement might
lead.

299. Giles, Barbara M. "My Lai and the Law: An
      Analysis of How International Law Relates to
      the My Lai Incident and Its Cover-Up." Ph.D.
      diss., University of Tennessee, 1978.

      Giles' study analyzes the international laws
of war as they pertain to the My Lai massacre
and the legal controls relating to the incident.
Her analysis finds that the processes of
implementing and enforcing the laws of war are
at best faulty because of the reliance on the
military establishment for the governance of
those processes.

300. Giles, Lydia. "Washington's Psywar." **Far
      Eastern Economic Review** 77, no. 36 (September
      2, 1972): 20.

      Giles reveals that as America bombed North
Vietnam, the pilots also dropped propaganda
leaflets, toys, and games. The result has been
a stepped up counter-propaganda campaign and
more efforts by the North to communicate well
its political decisions and details to its own
public.

301. Gray, Francine (du Plessix). "Kissinger: The
      Swinging Sphinx." **Ramparts** 11 (December
      1972): 33, 34, 58-62.

      Gray deals with two recent books on
Kissinger's life, but the article is far more
than a review of these books. She gives some
background to Kissinger's life while assessing
him at present as a case of powerful "grey
eminence" who has woven a spell over women and
the American public. Danielle Hunebelle's
personal memoir of Kissinger is first described

as an example of Gray's point, then she
discusses Landau's **Kissinger: The Uses of Power**,
a serious analysis of the man behind the facade.
This book describes a Kissinger Gray believes
does exist.

302.   Kearns, Doris. **Lyndon Johnson and the
        American Dream**. New York: Harper and Row,
        Pubs., 1976.

   Kearns determined to analyze Lyndon Johnson's
life through the stages of his career.
Throughout, she balances images of the man in
private and in public, both in the arena of
politics and after his retirement in the late
1960's. Part of her thesis involves an analysis
of his decisions from the viewpoint of a man who
was shaped by a different America than the
country of the 1960's.

303.   _____. "Lyndon Johnson's Political
        Personality." **Political Science Quarterly** 91
        (Fall 1976): 385-410.

   The focus of Kearns' article is to review
not only Johnson's political personality, but to
analyze the interplay between persons and
institutions in America using Johnson's life as
a model. Thus, she sheds new light on the
recent American political system. Kearns
describes the forces shaping Johnson's
personality from his childhood on and
demonstrates how he applied those attributes to
the advancement of his political career. In the
final 10 pages, she analyzes his decisions about
the Vietnam involvement in terms of his
personality and leadership style, and draws
conclusions about the implications of his
political career for the American Presidency.

304.   Krause, Pat, ed. **Anatomy of An Undeclared
        War: Congressional Conference on the Pentagon
        Papers**. New York: International
        Universities Press, 1972.

   The book is the edited transcript of
proceedings of the conference on the Pentagon
Papers sponsored by 19 Congressmen in 1971 for
the purpose of raising public consciousness

about the war. The participants' anti-war
sentiment remains clear from the transcripts
which are grouped around themes like
"culpability and responsibility" and "the war is
grinding on."

305.   Lamb, Helen. **Studies on India and Vietnam**.
       New York: Monthly Review Press, 1976.

       This is a collection of her essays and
reviews previously published and brought
together in two sections, the first on India and
the second on Vietnam. The Vietnam essays
include: "The Paris Exiles," "Three Letters to
the New York Times," "The Tragedy of Vietnam,"
"Vietnam: The Long Stalemate is Ending,"
"President Johnson's Peace Offensive," and "The
Negotiations That Are Possible," along with four
book reviews of writings on Vietnam.

306.   McCarthy, Mary. **Medina**. New York: Harcourt
       Brace Jovanovich, 1972.

       McCarthy covers the trial of Ernest Medina,
Calley's company commander in Vietnam. After
summarizing the trial, McCarthy questions the
acquittal, pointing out flaws in the process of
prosecuting Medina and questionning the results
for the nation of both Calley's and Medina's
prosecution.

307.   _____. **The Seventeenth Degree**. New
       York: Harcourt Brace Jovanovich, 1974.

       The book is a compilation of four other
pieces on Vietnam: **Vietnam, Hanoi, Medina,** and
Sons of the Morning, an extended discussion of
Halberstam's **The Best and the Brightest**.

308.   Porter, Ethel. "Vietnam and the Collapse of the
       American Democratic Faith: The Meeting of
       Ethics and Ideology in History, 1963-1969."
       Ph.D. diss., Yale University, 1978.

       Porter tries to determine the process by
which moral and political ideas become the
principles upon which one acts in national
affairs. Her analysis covers only the Johnson
war years, a time of excessive war escalation,

and she uses the metaphors and symbols of
governments and the opposing protest groups'
rhetoric to uncover the process of forming
principles.

309.   Starner, Frances.   "Pacification in South
         Vietnam: Any Umbrellas?" **Far Eastern
         Economic Review** 69, no. 28 (July 9, 1970):
         19-20, 69-71.

       The article proclaims that pacification
efforts do not work in the Delta area.   As an
example, Starner uses Kien Hoa province as a
case study.   The hamlets are like armed camps,
secured and constantly under watch, bridges are
guarded, and hamlets show war scars.   Although
government statistics point to a widening
security and less enemy action, the local peopl
perceive the situation as highly dangerous.

310.   Welch, Susan.   "Groups and Foreign Policy
         Decisions: The Case of Indochina, 1950-56."
         Ph.D. diss., University of Illinois,
         Urbana-Champaign, 1970.

       Welch uses the period of 1950 through the
late 1950's as a decision-making case to which
she applies various theories of organizational
behavior.   Closely examined are the American
government's deliberations about aiding the
French government until 1954 and the Diem
government afterward.   Welch argues that a
simplistic view of the situation such as
"Communist vs. anti-Communist" structured
decision-making styles during this period, not
only of the American government but of the press
and the American public as well.

311.   Welch, Susan, and Walter Oliver.   "Interest
         Groups, Ideology and the Costs of
         Participation." **Rocky Mountain Social
         Science Journal** 12 (April 1975): 81-98.

       The authors pose a thesis about the United
States' political processes: that multiple
interest group involvement in decisions will be
high if costs are low and outcomes positive, and
vice versa. They use the U.S. decisions about

Indochina involvement in the 1950's as their
case in point.

1980-1987

312. Dailey, Ann Ricks. "The Development of
      Adolescents' Political Attitudes." Ph.D.
      diss., The Johns Hopkins University, 1981.

      This research looks at developmental changes
      in the formation of adolescent political
      attitudes from high school, college, the
      military, through first jobs. One of the four
      political attitudes analyzed was attitude toward
      the Vietnam War. (These data were collected in
      1966-1974.) For this one attitude, the
      researchers found that years of schooling
      affected anti-Vietnam War attitudes. Attending
      college and having high occupational goals
      during high school related to opposition to the
      war, also.

313. Dixler, Elsa. "Back to the 1960's": Conference
      at Hofstra University on the LBJ Presidency."
      The Nation 242 (April 26, 1986): 573-574.

      Dixler attended the Hofstra University
      conference covering LBJ's Presidency. One
      session, "The Vietnam War in Perspective"
      included Tom Hayden, Daniel Ellsberg, Walt
      Rostow, and other prominent figures from the
      1960's. Dixler's observations are that the "war
      criminals" and the "S.D.S.'ers" all look alike
      now twenty years later. She seems nostalgic for
      the old days, but realizes, like everyone at the
      conference, that it is time to live in the
      present and leave former selves and times
      behind.

314. Donnelly, Dorothy Jeanne Carlson. "American
      Policy in Vietnam, 1949-1965: A Perceptual
      Analysis of the Domino Theory and Enemy Based
      on the Pentagon Papers." Ph.D. diss., The
      University of Pittsburgh, 1980.

      Using all three editions of **The Pentagon
      Papers,** Donnelly describes the growing
      involvement of Americans in Vietnam from roughly

1945 to 1965. In particular, she traces the
notion "domino theory" through documentation
during those years, revealing its presence as a
powerful idea in some form or other in the
thinking of most political figures dealing with
the war. In essence, Donnelly suggests that
this idea obscured the nature of the real
importance (or lack of it) of the Vietnam War.

315.   Fitzgerald, Frances. "How Does America Avoid
        Future Vietnams?" In **Vietnam Reconsidered:**
        Lessons from a War, edited by Harrison
        Salisbury, 300-305. New York: Harper and
        Row, Pubs., 1984.

        Fitzgerald's thesis is that there is nothing
easier to avoid than future Vietnams since we
went out of our way from 1954-64 to create the
Vietnam War in the first place. Then, in a ver
ironically written article, she reviews a list
of people and describes lessons for the future.

316.   Judson, Janis. "The Hidden Agenda:
        NonDecision-making on the U. S. Supreme
        Court." Ph.D. diss., The University of
        Maryland, 1986.

        Judson discusses the concept of
nondecision-making on the part of the Supreme
Court and the judicial purposes that dissents t
nondecision-making serve. As an example, she
reviews Justice Douglas' dissents relating to
the Vietnam War which were instrumental in
encouraging consideration of the
constitutionality of the war.

317.   Schlagheck, Donna Marie. "Contextual and
        Conceptual Content Analysis in the Study of
        Foreign Policy Decision-Making." Ph.D.
        diss., The University of Minnesota, 1985.

        This research completes a case study of Henr
Kissinger's definitions of the events he faced
in Vietnam negotiations. A content analysis of
Kissinger's verbal productions (written and
oral) reveals the conceptual bases for both his
understanding and his decision-making about the
Vietnam War and the peace negotiations.

Vietnamese Government

1954-1959

318. Hammer, Ellen. "Progress Report on Southern
       Viet Nam." **Pacific Affairs** 30 (September
       1957): 221-235.

       Hammer reports that the Diem government in
       South Viet Nam has control of the country, the
       loyalty of the southern Vietnamese, has
       eliminated all political dissention, achieved
       economic successes, and held off successfully
       the Communist threat. Her article analyzes the
       steps Diem took to secure political stability;
       she applauds his emasculation of the Binh Xuyen,
       Cao Dai, and Hoa Hao sects, his deposing of Bao
       Dai, and his agrarian reforms as necessary acts
       for achieving support for his government.
       Hammer predicts future problems with the
       reliance of the economy on American aid and
       help, but remains confident about the future of
       economic independence in the South and of
       dominance over the Communist North.

1960-1969

319. Adams, Nina. "Man in the Middle." **New York
       Review of Books** 13 (September 11, 1969):
       42-44.

       This is a review essay, but as much about Ho
       Chi Minh as it is about Jean Lacouture's book **Ho
       Chi Minh** and Philippe Devillers' and his **The End
       of A War**. Adams begins by describing the
       particular blend of nationalism and communism
       which influenced Ho, and follows this with a
       lengthy description of Lacouture's senstive and
       complete character analysis in the first book.
       She finds the co-authored book, **The End of a
       War**, well-documented.

320. Close, Alexandra. "The Voters of Vietnam."
       Far Eastern Economic Review 57 (September
       10-16, 1967): 505-506.

       Close analyzes the victory of the Thieu-Ky

ticket which is based on one-third of the total
poll. Nearly two-thirds of the electorate
refused to register support for the pair. Close
points out the recriminations among candidates
as well as the U.S. part in influencing these
elections.

321.   Deepe, Beverly. "Fall of the House of Ngo."
        Newsweek 62, no. 20 (November 11, 1963):
        27-31.

        Deepe describes the coup from its set-up to
the last several hours of the Ngo brothers'
lives. She also sketches biographies of the
major coup leaders--Major General Duong Van
Minh, Major General Tran Van Don and Brigadier
General Ton That Dinh. The tone of the article
is sharply anti-Diem and hopeful for the new
regime.

322.   _____. "War in the Pagodas: Who is the
        Enemy?" **Newsweek** 62 (September 2, 1963):
        35-38.

        Deepe reports on the Diem crackdown on the
Buddhist uprisings in the summer of 1962. She
reveals Ngo Dinh Nhu's use of his Special Forces
units to act against the Buddhists. Also
discussed is the world's horrified reaction to
Diem's actions and the subsequent Vietnamese
student protest. Deepe concludes by noting the
growing unrest with the American presence in
Vietnam.

323.   Fitzgerald, Frances. "The Long Fear:
        Fresh Eyes on Viet Nam." **Vogue** 149 (January
        1, 1967): 110-11, 139.

        Fitzgerald writes about the Delta region in
South Vietnam and its curious aloofness from
both the controls and influences of the
Americans, the Saigon government, and the Viet
Cong. She focuses on An Giang, a province
dominated by the Hoa Hao, and An Xuyen,
dominated by Viet Cong. Fitzgerald's
description of the people, the American
advisors, and the life in the countryside
underscores the gap between the realities in

Vietnam and the anticipated outcomes of the
Americans.

324. _____. "The Tragedy of Saigon."
     Atlantic Monthly 218, no. 6 (December 1966):
     59-67.

     Fitzgerald describes a Saigon urban quarter
turned slum, labeling it an example of the "new
face of Vietnam." As the war continues and more
people leave their rural communities, many end
up in Saigon where, poor, disease-ridden, and
hopeless, they become politically ripe for Viet
Cong purposes. The article graphically details
the bureaucratic ineptness which contributes to
Saigon's political and economic disorganization,
a condition which contributes more than the war
to South Vietnam's internal trouble. To
Fitzgerald, the American presence greatly
enhances these conditions.

325. Gannett, Betty. "The NLF Offensive in Vietnam."
     Political Affairs 47 (March 1968): 1-9.

     Gannett describes the growing American
skepticism about the President's and the
American military's statements of impending
victory after the 1968 Tet Offensive. She
quotes from speeches by Robert Kennedy, Mike
Mansfield, Drew Pearson, and many others
concerning a profound doubt about an American
victory. She ends by calling for a re-education
of Americans on the Vietnam War aimed at
ultimately dismantling American war efforts in
Vietnam.

326. Hammer, Ellen. "South Viet Nam: The Limits of
     Political Action." **Pacific Affairs** 35
     (Spring 1962): 24-36.

     Hammer notes that after years of apparent
peace and progress, the situation in South Viet
Nam has become dangerous. The article attempts
to analyze the underlying elements which may
have contributed to the new chaos defining the
South. Hammer blames the Viet Cong, who
remained a strong force in the South after 1954,
and drew off many dynamic leaders to their side,
consequently leaving the new Diem government

with poor administrators. Saigon intellectuals
too, remained aloof to the Diem government. In
essence, while the South's government remained
fragmented and its policies unfocused, the Viet
Cong elements became increasingly united around
common goals. In spite of her analysis, Hammer
concludes her article with the hope that the new
government can succeed in remaining democratic.

327.   Hayes, Marcia. "Plague Goes to War." **Far
       Eastern Economic Review** 59 (March 7, 1968):
       418-420.

       Hayes states that bubonic plague cases
increased after the Tet Offensive which in
itself reinforced conditions for the
communication of the plague. The W.H.O. blamed
the epidemic on the war; human displacement and
loss of vegetation also contributed. Fears
include its reaching epidemic proportions and
the spreading of the disease to other countries

328.   Higgins, Marguerite. "Saigon Summary."
       America 110, no. 1 (January 4, 1964): 18-21.

       Higgins points out that there were more
suicides by fire, and more protests after the
Diem coup and under the new military junta than
under Diem and Nhu. She argues that Americans
should question the assumption that the previous
self-immolations and protests were proof of
state-wide, intensive persecutions of Buddhists
by Catholic Diem. Follow-up visits by Higgins
did not bear out evidence that Diem persecuted
the population on religious grounds. In fact,
the religious uprisings were politically
motivated, she contends, yet, the image of
religious persecution by international press
paved the way for Diem's downfall. The article
pokes holes in the rationale for supporting
anti-Diemist attitudes after the coup d'etat.

329.   Hope, Marjorie. "Guns, Butter--Or Chinh Nghia?
       War/Peace Report 6 (August/September 1966):
       14-16.

       Hope argues that the Vietnamese and
Confuscian concept of political right, "chinh
nghia," is a powerful force motivating the

Vietnamese to stand behind a leadership which serves the cause of independence and democracy for the people. Hope describes historical and successful leaders as well as those who were not in order to illustrate the importance of this concept. She insists that the Buddhists now exhibit this leadership capability, but that the U.S. will continue to support an ineffective and unsupported regime.

330. Kelly, Gail. "Origins and Aims of the Viet Cong." **New Politics** 5 (Winter 1966): 5-16.

Kelly focuses on the dearth of reliable information about the NLF, but, by piecing together what facts are available, tries to determine its origins, its organization principles, and its future plans for South Vietnam. Origins begin with the Vietminh, and Kelly deduces that the group's present composition consists of Vietminh cadre, NVA, and South Vietnamese. She meticulously describes NLF operations and programs. Kelly does not see a promising future for South Vietnamese should the NLF sponsored fighters win, but nor does she believe that the South's current regime serves the South any better. In fact, from her perspective, only the Buddhist movement may offer true hope.

331. Luce, Clare Boothe. "Lady Is For Burning: The Seven Deadly Sins of Madame Nhu." **National Review** 15 (November 5, 1963): 395-99.

In a pro-Madame Nhu article written after her 1963 visit to America, Luce enumerates the unfounded reasons for the American dislike for Madame Nhu: nepotism, bigotry, her underhanded political maneuverings, her tyrannical use of power, and her support in the persecution of the Buddhists are among the offenses cited. For each of these points, Luce offers at length a defense of the First Lady of Vietnam's actions, thoughts, and behaviors.

332. Paley, Grace. "Report From the DRV." **Win Magazine** 5, no. 16 (September 15, 1969): 5-9.

Paley and others took a three week trip to

Hanoi in order to escort three American POW's
home. Her visit separates into several phases:
she describes first how Hanoi looks, then the
villages and the bombing destruction around the
countryside. Paley concludes with descriptions
of the returning pilots' captivity and their
attitudes toward the war. Their views, she
finds, clearly define them as warmongers.

333.   Strong, Anna Louise. **Cash and Violence in
       Laos and Vietnam.** New York: Mainstream
       Pubs., 1962.

       Strong argues that American "neo-colonialism
in Southeast Asia was established on the twin
principles of cash and violence. That is, there
is no formal ownership of a country, but
instead, political deals made with native ruler
allowed the acquisition of some property,
including bases for establishment of military
support. Thus, both profit and power were
attained. Strong argues that, in particular,
the U.S. operated in Laos under these
principles, thus dividing the country and
continuing to subject it to American will.
South Vietnam was targeted in such a way too.

334.   _____. "Exclusive: An Interview
       with Ho Chi Minh." **National Guardian** 13, no
       32 (May 22, 1961): 7.

       Strong recalls meeting Ho Chi Minh in Hanoi;
she was the first U.S. citizen to come to his
country during these years. Her talk with him
reveals the progress made in the North and
relations with both South Vietnam and Laos.
Strong ends the piece with praises for Ho Chi
Minh's quality of leadership.

1970-1979

335.   Emerson, Gloria. "The Consequences for South
       Vietnam: Each Day is A Separate Ordeal."
       Saturday Review 55, no. 47 (December 1972):
       52-57.

       Emerson describes the effects of the war in

the South as a daily hell for the Vietnamese.
She relies on portraits of poverty-stricken
Vietnamese, bands of children, and scarred
veterans, troops, and hamlets to drive home her
point that war has done little but destroy the
future of the South Vietnamese people. She
believes they will never recover.

336. Fitzgerald, Frances. "Annals of War: A Cave on
      the Karl Marx Mountain." **New Yorker** 48 (July
      15, 1972): 33-49.

      The third article in this series describes
      the guerrillas and the NLF organization.
      Concentrating on Ho Chi Minh's leadership,
      Fitzgerald analyzes why the Marxist doctrines
      became the major influential idea in Vietnamese
      nationalism.

337. _____. "Annals of War: Fire In
      the Lake." **New Yorker** 48 (July 1, 1972):
      36-52.

      This series of articles during July of 1972
      is based on Fitzgerald's book, **Fire In the Lake**.
      The first of five articles covers the general
      background of the major cultures playing out the
      war.

338. _____. "Annals of War: Sovereign
      of Discord." **New Yorker** 48 (July 8, 1972):
      34-54.

      This second part of a five-part series of
      articles concentrates on the reign of Ngo Dinh
      Diem.

339. _____. "Vietnam: Behind the Lines
      of the 'Cease-Fire' War." **The Atlantic** 233
      (April 1974): 4-18.

      In this first of a three part article,
      Fitzgerald, seeking to understand more about the
      Vietnamese who resist the U.S. and the South
      Vietnamese government, moves behind the lines to
      interview these leaders of the NLF. Her
      discoveries include the elaborateness of
      invisible boundaries between GVN and PRG-held
      territory, and tales of the numerous GVN

cease-fire violations. Fitzgerald frequently
notes the characteristics and attitudes of the
cadres.

340.   _____. "Vietnam: The Cadres and
        the Villagers." **The Atlantic** 233 (May 1974)
        4-16.

        In this second of a three-part article,
Fitzgerald continues describing her visit with a
PRG commanding officer in Chuong Thien Province,
a liberated area.   Then she reveals her
findings from her travels about the true
political sympathies of the people in many of
the GVN-controlled villages. Not surprisingly,
most had been less ill-treated by liberation
cadre and favored those soldiers over the Saigon
regime's soldiers.

341.   _____. "Vietnam: Reconciliation."
        The Atlantic 233 (June 1974): 14-27.

        This article concludes Fitzgerald's
description of the "enemy." Throughout her
visits to Cu Chi, the areas around Da Nang, and
many other villages, she finds stories revealing
the strong resistance by pro-Liberation Front
villagers to the French, GVN, and American war
efforts. Seeking to find and describe the keys
to this inner strength and durability, she
retells their many horrors, pains, and
anguishes, finally uncovering, for her, the
source of the people's energy--that sense of
history which gives perspective on current
events. Analyzed subsequently are the aims for
reconciliation of South and North Vietnam as
members of the PRG view them.

342.   Hodgkin, Liz. "People's War Comes to the Towns:
        Tet 1968." **Marxism Today** 22, no. 5 (May
        1978): 147-153.

        Hodgkin briefly outlines the Communist
advances and attacks on areas of South Vietnam
during Tet, 1968. Analyzed, too, is the reason
for the ARVN's and American forces' surprise,
but she spends most of the article assessing the
meaning of Tet for the entire war effort.
Hodgkin draws most of her analysis from the

Vietnamese use of their own traditional military and political strategies, concluding that the use of attacks on large towns furthered the war of liberation.

343.   Niehaus, Marjorie. "Vietnam 1978: The Elusive
        Peace." **Asian Survey** 19, no. 1 (January
        1979): 85-94.

        Niehaus analyzes why, since the end of the American involvement in the Vietnam War in 1973-75, the country has failed to reconcile and reconstruct both northern and southern halves. Focusing on the poor economic situation first, Niehaus sees the wars with Kampuchea and China, the exodus of many skilled and productive Vietnamese, the natural disasters of the late 1970's, and the confiscation of private business, as several causes of the current economic plight. Complicating the nation's plans are its uneasy relations with almost every country except the Soviet Union. The current ideological reasons for a continued U.S.-Vietnam division are explored, too.

344.   Nutt, Anita L. **On the Question of Communist
        Reprisals in Vietnam**. Santa Monica, Calif.:
        Rand Corp., 1970.

        Nutt defends Nixon's point of view that if American troops left South Vietnam and as a consequence, the country fell to the Communists, a virtual bloodbath of reprisals would occur. Peace defenders claim there were few reprisal measures in the 1950's, but Nutt argues that the deaths during the agrarian reforms in the North were actually camouflaged reprisals against citizens who had cooperated with the French.

345.   Pond, Elizabeth. "South Vietnam: the
        Tran-Ngoc-Chau Affair." **The Atlantic** 227
        (May 1971): 19-29.

        Pond takes issue with the American attitude toward President Thieu's arrest of Tran Ngoc Chau. She claims that Chau's arrest stems from the fact that the anti-Communist opposed Thieu. Pond delves into Chau's political history, pointing to his avowed nationalism and

anti-Communism. This makes the incident and th
American support of it more reprehensible to
her.

1980-1987

346.   Gough, Kathleen. "Is Vietnam Socialist?"
       Contemporary Marxism 12/13 (Spring 1986):
       3-13.

       Gough believes that Vietnam, while moving
       toward industrialization, is also moving closer
       to a true socialism. She analyzes various
       aspects of the society and politics; the
       dominant Communist Party and the Women's Union
       are two of these.

International Extensions of the War

1954-1959

347. McVey, Ruth. **The Calcutta Conference and the South East Asian Uprisings**. Ithaca, N.Y.: Southeast Asia Program, Department of Far Eastern Studies, Cornell University, 1958.

In these reports, McVey covers the decisons and background information of the 1940's conference in Calcutta which dealt with the unrest of all of Southeast Asia, including Vietnam.

348. Morley, Lorna. "Menaced Laos." **Editorial Research Reports** 2 (September 23, 1959): 717-734.

Morley investigates the Laotian government's report that rebel groups in its country are being directly supported by North Viet Nam. Sufficiently alarmed, the U.N.'s Security Council investigated the claims. She includes a brief history of the Pathet Lao and its relationship to Communist North Viet Nam. Most of the article, however, retells the history of the Viet Nam War under the French and the repercussions of this eight year conflict for Laos.

1960-1969

349. Bell, Coral. "Security in Asia: Reappraisals after Vietnam." **International Journal** 24 (Winter 1968): 1-12.

Bell speculates about the implications of an end to the war in Vietnam for Americans, Vietnamese, and surrounding Southeast Asian countries. Describing the status of the war as "fighting while negotiating," Bell outlines future American dilemmas prompted by ending the war, and calls this war a case study in how not to handle a people's war.

350. Kuebler, Jeanne. "Thailand: New Red Target."

Editorial Research Reports 2 (September 15, 1965): 665-682.

Kuebler's article describes the growing threat of Communist terrorism in Thailand from neighboring Laos, North Viet Nam, and China. She describes security problems, the kind of threats from the other Communist dominated countries, and the nature of Thailand's military cooperation with the U.S.

351.   Perazic, Elizabeth. "Little Laos Next Door to Red China." **National Geographic** 117, no. 1 (January 1960): 46-69.

Written by a woman on location in Laos with her husband, the article features Laos from geographic, economic, philosophical-religious, cultural and political perspectives. Told through a personal account of arrival and adjustment in the country, each of the above aspects of Lao life is described using personal incidents as well as the lives and conditions of people Perazic met there.

352.   Pilkington, Betty. "Vietnam: The U.N. Peeks In." **The Nation** 197, no. 14 (November 2, 1963): 273-275.

This short article blasts the U.N. "fact-finding" mission to South Vietnam in the wake of the Buddhist unrest in 1963. Pilkington accuses the Diem government of stacking the delegation's membership and the U.N. of sharing expenses with Diem's government for the visit amidst other irregularities. She also spells out the U.S.'s position -- that it is to American advantage to pursue the visitation tactic, thus pushing the issue out of the debating arena as quickly as possible.

353.   Starner, Frances. "The White Horses: Korean Troops in Vietnam." **Far Eastern Economic Review** 57 (September 21, 1967): 567-572.

Starner visited Phu Yen province at Tuy Hoa and reports on the two regiments of the White Horse Division, the South Korean Division with responsibility for offensive operations there.

Both American and ARVN regiments offer support,
too. The sometimes ruthless Korean methods
contrast with their sponsorship of many welfare
projects. However, their methods are judged
effective since the area seems to be under
control. The article shifts away from this
topic in the last half and discusses the
generally shakey political situation in the
province.

354.   Strong, Anna (Louise). "Peking's View of the
          Tonkin Gulf's Incidents." **National Guardian**
          16 (September 26, 1964): 3.

Strong describes both Peking's and Hanoi's
reactions to the second Tonkin Gulf incident
which prompted air attacks by Americans on North
Vietnam. Both nations saw clear victories in
world opinion for North Vietnam and in the
boosted morale of the North.

355.   Urrows, Elizabeth. "Recurring Problems in
          Laos." **Current History** 57, no. 340 (December
          1969): 361-363, 367.

Urrow's article fills in the political
history of Laos from 1955, describing the
expansion efforts of the Pathet Lao who are
supported by the North Vietnamese. She also
describes the build-up of the American
involvement in Laos, describing its purpose in
terms of the "domino theory" espoused by Dulles
in the 1950's. This theoretical basis continues
through successive administrations in spite of
the increasing opposition in the American
Congress.

356.   Weill-Tuckerman, Anne. "Vietnam at the U.N."
          The Nation 202 (February 14, 1966): 169.

The writer discusses the failure of the
American attempt to gain U.N. support for its
Vietnam policies. Because of the increased
bombing, the U.N. fails to believe that
America's actions are aimed at achieving peace.
The real tragedy to Weill-Tuckerman is that
American leaders obviously believe their own
slogans. It seems painfully obvious to her that

negotiations on American terms would be
impossible to achieve.

1970-1979

357. Adams, Nina. "Patrons, Clients, and
      Revolutionaries: The Lao Search for
      Independence, 1945-1954." In **Laos: War and
      Revolution**, edited by Nina Adams and Alfred
      McCoy, 100-120. New York: Harper and Row,
      1970.

      Adams meticulously recounts the Laotian
      political moves in the 1940's for, not only
      survival, but attempted greater independence as
      a country. Her analysis describes the country's
      moves for more independence in spite of a long
      steady dependence on French colonials, internal
      struggling amongst the ruling elite, and
      distrust of neighboring governments.

358. Blakkan, Renee. "Women Meet Indochinese in
      Canada." **Guardian** 23, no. 29 (April 17,
      1971): 5.

      Blakkan gives her own version of the women's
      anti-war conference on April 7-9 in Toronto,
      Canada. One theme of the conference dealt with
      the war as a feminist issue. Not only is the
      health of women victims endangered by the war,
      but females also serve in military roles. The
      story discusses briefly the internal splits
      within the women's groups against the war.

359. Coburn, Judith. "Cambodia: War at the End of
      the Tunnel." **Ramparts** 12 (July 1973): 40-44.

      Coburn writes of post-Vietnam War Cambodia
      which, in 1973, found itself in the throes of a
      war similar to Vietnam's. Coburn retraces the
      American efforts there from 1970-73, calling
      Cambodia America's "bottomless pit," and showing
      just how, politically and militarily, the U.S.
      efforts and aims failed in that country.

360. Colbert, Evelyn. **Southeast Asia in
      International Politics, 1941-1956**. Ithaca,
      N.Y.: Cornell University Press, 1977.

Indonesia and Indochina in international affairs, focusing primarily on the post-World War II years to the mid-1970's. In her introduction, Colbert traces briefly the rise and fall of colonialism in the region, leaving the rest of the book to deal with the post-WWII struggles for independence among those countries. A whole section deals with the Geneva settlement and the resulting "two Vietnams." A final section suggests future options for Vietnam.

361. Cousins, Judith, and Alfred McCoy. "Doing It Up In Laos: Congressional Testimony on United States Aid to Laos in the 1950's." In **Laos: War and Revolution,** edited by Nina Adams and Alfred McCoy, 340-56. New York: Harper and Row, Pubs., 1970.

The authors' article is stridently negative about the American establishment and funding of a modern army in Laos whose purpose was to "stem the tide of encroaching Communism." They argue passionately that American efforts, vastly complicated by a misunderstanding of the country's culture, created a highly corrupt army. Much of the article's substance derives from testimony at the House Commission on Government Operations concerning economic and military aid to Laos. This testimony revealed corruption among Americans involved in aid programs also.

362. Frederick, Cynthia. "Cambodia: Operation Total Victory." **Bulletin of Concerned Asian Scholars** 2, no. 47 (April-July 1970): 3-19.

Frederick's article explores U.S. motives for the Nixon administration's invasion of Cambodia after Sihanouk was ousted by Lon Nol in 1970. Most of her article retraces Sihanouk's earlier consolidation of power through political decisions that slowly alienated various segments of his power base until the 1970 coup. Frederick also analyzes the close relationship between the Khmer Rouge and Sihanouk, and concludes with the warning that Americans could face another long war in Cambodia.

363.   Hammer, Ellen. "Indochina: Communist But
            Nonaligned." **Problems of Communism** 25
            (May-June 1976): 1-17.

        Hammer notes that in 1976, for the first time
    in over 20 years, the Laotian, Cambodian, and
    Vietnamese governments hold an ideology in
    common. Hammer pieces together the details of
    the uneasy coexistence of the three governments,
    including documentation of military conflicts
    among them and of political meetings. The
    article's focus then moves to the issues of
    political alliance with both China and the
    Soviet Union which the three Indochinese nations
    face, relations with the rest of Indochina, and
    the formation of ASEAN. Hammer senses that the
    three nations prefer a non-aligned status in
    international politics.

364.   Janover, Madeleine. "Vietnam." **Off Our Backs**
            5, no. 3 (March 1975): 4.

        This is an article about the Women of Vietnam
    Conference held in Montreal, Canada in February,
    1975. The conference proposed to reveal more
    about the effects of the war on Vietnamese
    women, to offer support to them, and to talk
    about third world women's struggles in the U.S.
    Topics such as women's roles, liberation, women
    prisoners, and political futures dominated and
    promoted cross-cultural learning and
    understanding.

365.   Leighton, Marian Kirsch. "The Kremlin and the
            Vietnam Conflict." Ph.D. diss., Columbia
            University, 1979.

        This is a complete examination of the place
    of Southeast Asia, Vietnam included, in the
    national interests of the Soviet Union from 1917
    on. Leighton details Vietnam's rise in
    importance, including the assistance and support
    given to Ho Chi Minh.

366.   _____. "Perspectives on the
            Vietnam-Cambodia Border Conflict." **Asian
            Survey** 18 (May 1978): 448-457.

        The article covers the recent border

conflicts between Vietnam and Cambodia, particularly in areas where Cambodians and Vietnamese live on "the wrong side" of the border. The border clashes usually instigated by the highly nationalist Cambodians seem aimed at slowing Hanoi's consolidation of rule with South Vietnam, a move the Cambodians fear would lead to future Vietnamese expansion into their own territories. Leighton also discusses evidence that the Chinese and Soviets involved themselves in the increasing conflicts.

367. _____. "Vietnam and the Sino-Soviet Rivalry." **Asian Affairs** 6, no.1 (September-October 1978): 1-31.

Leighton traces the focal points of the Chinese and Soviet rivalries in Vietnam. Most obvious are the Vietnam-Cambodia conflicts and the problem of the "overseas Chinese" in Vietnam. She describes each superpower's aid and history of support to Vietnam along with the benefits and dangers Vietnam reaps from exploiting the rivalry.

368. Niehaus, Marjorie. **A Chronology of Selected Statements by Administrative Officials on the Subject of Postwar Reconstruction Aid to Indochina: April 7, 1965 - April 4, 1973.** Washington, D.C.: Library of Congress, Congressional Research Service, 1973.

Niehaus' record of statements offers comments on postwar reconstruction aid to Indochina by officials in both the Johnson and Nixon administrations. This reference tool of 19 pages contains directly quoted statements.

369. Sullivan, Marianna. "DeGualle's Policy Toward the Conflict in Vietnam, 1963-1969." Ph.D. diss., University of Virginia, 1971.

The study examines DeGaulle's attitudes toward the Vietnam War during the U.S. involvement from 1954 through the mid-1960's. Sullivan describes DeGaulle's stances on the American presence in Vietnam, his understanding of Vietnamese internal politics, and the link

between these attitudes and DeGaulle's own
international goals for France.

370.   _____. "France's and The
        Vietnamese Peace Settlement." **Political
        Science Quarterly** 89 (June 1974): 305-324.

   Sullivan states that France's post-Peace
Accords policies in Vietnam can only be
understood in light of events affecting policy
from 1968-73. Noting France's thawed attitudes
toward the U.S. after the peace negotiations
began, Sullivan discusses the reasons for that
reversal. She elaborates on France's diplomatic
role in furthering the peace talks as well as
that country's intended future relationship with
post-war Vietnam.

371.   _____. **France's Vietnam Policy:
        A Study in French-American Relationships**.
        Westport, Conn.: Greenwood Press, 1978.

   This book analyzes France's positions on
American involvement in Vietnam from 1963-73
when France was governed by DeGaulle. The first
section discusses the roots of France's
attitudes in terms of DeGaulle's international
aims and his concern over American world
dominance. Subsequent sections describe the
historical reasons for anti-American sentiment
concerning Vietnam while the last part explores
the reasons for DeGaulle's increasingly harsh
criticism in the 1960's of America's Vietnam
policies.

372.   Summers, Laura. "Cambodia: Model of Nixon
        Doctrine." **Current History** 65, no. 338
        (December 1973): 252-256.

   Summers' article analyzes the political
situation in Cambodia and describes the failure
of the Nixon Doctrine as it applied to relations
with Cambodia. Summers concludes that the war
in Cambodia continued only because of American
policy, that the country's fate was not a model
of good foreign policy but a sacrifice to it.

1980-1987

373. Becker, Elizabeth. **When the War Was Over: The
      Voices of Cambodia's Revolution and Its
      People**. New York: Simon and Schuster, 1986.
      New York: Touchstone Bks., 1987.

      Becker is an American journalist who was in
      wartime Phnom Penh, so she describes the rule by
      the Khmer Rouge in Cambodia. Her book is also a
      socio-cultural and historical analysis
      describing how and why this reign of terror
      existed. Drawn partly from records, from
      interviews, and her own experiences in Cambodia
      as a **Washington Post** reporter, Becker begins the
      book with a look at the country's historical
      development from the mid-1800's on, weaving into
      this the roots and rise of key power figures in
      the Khmer Rouge. Subsequent chapters are spent
      on the Khmer running of the country after the
      1970's victory. She also covers extensively the
      country's conflicts with Vietnam, and the
      effects of American participation in both
      countries.

374. Gough, Kathleen. "Roots of the Pol Pot Regime
      in Kampuchea." **Contemporary Marxism** 12/13
      (Spring 1986): 14-48.

      Gough's lengthy analysis explores the
      influences which shaped the Pol Pot government.
      In addition to Maoist influences, she describes
      the influence of Hitler and Stalin. However,
      more similar to Pol Pot's efforts is the Asiatic
      Mode of Production, a medieval form of society
      characterizing Kampuchea of the ninth through
      the fifteenth centuries. Gough concludes with a
      summary of lessons to be learned from the Pol
      Pot experience.

War Commentary

1960-1969

375. Bentley, Helen. "Our Aging Merchantmen and
          Viet Nam." **Navy Magazine** 9 (April 1966):
          16-21.

          Bentley reveals that most of the cargo ships
      transferring supplies to the Viet Nam War are of
      World War II vintage. Her article calls for
      replacement of this seapower, which at this
      time, had not been planned. She points out the
      potential and near consequences of dependence on
      such an old fleet of ships.

376. _____. "The U.S.-Built Ports of South
          Viet Nam: End of the Life-Line for Allied
          Forces." **Navy Magazine** 10 (May 1967): 35-37,
          40.

          Bentley describes the building of seaports
      and airports in South Viet Nam and the reasons
      for this. She describes ports at Cam Ranh Bay
      and Sattahip along with those at Vung Ro, Qui
      Nhon, and Newport.

377. Canova, Pamela, and James Hessman. "The Casualty
          Reports: Some Startling Statistics." **Armed
          Forces Journal** 106 (August 2, 1969): 16-18.

          This report notes that American war
      casualties in Vietnam are up by 30% during
      Nixon's first six months in office. Citing this
      as a political dilemma, the authors outline the
      concrete steps Nixon has taken to address this
      issue.

378. Carper, Jean. **Bitter Greetings: The Scandal
          of the Military Draft**. New York: Grossman,
          1967.

          Carper lashes out at the corruption
      characterizing the Selective Service's Draft
      system during the Vietnam War. She digs up

every ghost to support her thesis that
corruption governs a draft that the nation does
not need: (1) President Johnson's authorization
of a study of it, with the subsequent hiding of
the results; (2) the myth of a manpower
shortage; (3) the biased constitution of members
of the draft boards; (4) the bias in draft
deferment policies which cause selection of
minorities and lower socio-economic classes.
All of these factors underlie the need for draft
abolishment. Carper puts forth a case for its
aboliton as well as for measures of reform if,
at all necessary, the draft must remain.

379.   Chapelle, Dickey. "Helicopter War in South
         Vietnam." **National Geographic** 122, no. 5
         (November 1962): 722-754.

         Chapelle covers the "helicopter war,"
describing assaults by South Vietnamese and
American advisors on a Viet Cong stronghold, and
on Ap My Thanh, Vinh Quoi, and Vinh Loi. Much
of the article stresses the important role the
helicopter does and will play in the war: its
use in evacuating wounded, delivering supplies,
and airlifting soldiers. As is usual in
Chapelle's writing, detailed portraits of the
soldiers who lead the air and ground fighting
pepper the report.

380.   Chapelle, Dickey. "Water War in Vietnam."
         National Geographic 129, no. 2 (February
         1966): 272-296.

         Chapelle travelled with and wrote about the
River Assault Groups of the Vietnamese Navy and
their patrols on the Mekong River. Chapelle,
who went with the Vietnamese and American
advisor on the patrol and on a landing force
expedition, describes these two missions. Now
armed as many correspondents were in Vietnam,
she describes the contest at Vinh Long with the
Vietcong and her forces' subsequent rescue by
the patrol boats. Two themes dominate the
article: the mounting Vietcong attacks on the
Americans and her questionning of the need for
war as a solution for political divisions.

381.   Chapelle, Dickey. "With the Paratroopers."

Reader's Digest 80 (February 1962): 292-298.

This short piece describes Chapelle's night trip into battle action with paratroopers in South Vietnam. They weather a Viet Cong ambush, one of the many that Chapelle covers during this time period in the war. She uses the experience to restate her belief in America's cause against Communist aggression.

382. Deepe, Beverly. "Vietnam: New Metal Birds." **Newsweek** 60 (October 29, 1962): 37-38.

This story includes direct reporting by Deepe on American ground forces versus the active role of the American air forces. Examples of American involvement come from soldiers stationed around A Chau in South Vietnam.

383. Fitzgerald, Frances. "Vietnam: The People." **Vogue** 149 (May 1967): 174, 260-63.

Fitzgerald traces the maneuvers of two American Marine batallions, using the successful operation (no contact made) to drive home her point that the American military has created an abstract Vietnam made of time, coordinates on a map, numbers of bodies, and myths. Their Vietnam is one which has no point of contact with the realities of the Vietnamese people. Fitzgerald argues that even the language of the military heightens the abstractness of the war for the Americans involved.

384. Gellhorn, Martha. **A New Kind of War**. New York: Manchester Guardian, 1966.

The "new kind of war" refers to the American effort to help the South Vietnamese "win the hearts and minds" of the people. She spent her visit to Vietnam observing people; she reports on the abysmal conditions of the hospitals, the orphanages, and the homeless in Saigon. Gellhorn concludes by sharply bringing home the dichotomy between the rhetoric and the real war.

385. Herrera, Barbara. **Medics in Action**. Mountain View, Calif.: Pacific Press Publishing Association, 1968.

The book is a kind of composite biography of
the "medic's experience" in Vietnam. Along with
John Steel's photography, her captions describe
many aspects of the medic's life such as combat,
hospital work, and off-the-job life.

386.   Mayer, Jean.   "Starvation As a Weapon:
       Herbicides in Vietnam." **Scientist and
       Citizen** 9, no. 7 (August-September 1967):
       115-121.

Mayer writes about the effectiveness of
starvation as a weapon of war. Taking the
American military's effort to annihilate food
crops (the source of the Viet Cong's sustenance)
in order to deplete the enemy's offensive as a
case in point, Mayer examines the effects of
starvation on people both in past conflicts and
in this one. She concludes that civilians may
be the hardest hit group by this war tactic,
thus increasing the number of refugees and
resulting ultimately in a failure to halt the
Viet Cong force.

387.   Pohle, Victoria. **Vietcong in Saigon: Tactics
       and Objectives During the Tet Offensive.**
       Santa Monica, Calif.: Rand Corp., 1968.

The author based her study on over 400
interviews conducted in Saigon and Gia Dinh
Province soon after the 1968 Tet Offensive. She
describes the myriad political and military
tactics used by the Vietcong during the
Offensive, and the civilian populace's reaction
to those tactics. Finally, Pohle generalizes
about future implications. For example, she
concludes that residents of Saigon will remain
passive in future conflicts and that future
peace negotiations might persuade many
Vietnamese to reconsider their accommodations of
the Vietcong.

388.   Pohle, Victoria, and Constantine Menges. **Time
       and Limited Success as Enemies of the
       Vietcong.** Santa Monica, Cal.: Rand Corp.,
       1967.

Pohle and Menges argue that there is little

need to fear that a protracted war will hurt
American-GVN military strength, but, in fact,
the war's longevity hurts the Vietcong. They
argue that as Vietcong local demands increase,
the peasants will become increasingly
disenchanted with them. As time passes,
breakdowns within their own ranks will occur.

1970-1979

389.   Coburn, Judy (Judith). "Nightmare on Rte. 9:
            The Target Was Us." **Off Our Backs** 1, no. 22
            (May 27, 1971): 8-9.

        Coburn describes a trip she took as a
reporter with American and South Vietnamese
troops on Rte. 9 toward Laos. A sudden air
attack on their groups leaves her speechlessly
assisting Larry Burrows with casualties.
Striking is her comparison to reports by
Americans of their attacks; now she knows the
unseen reality left behind on the ground.

390.   Emerson, Gloria. "Arms and the Woman."
            Harper's 246 (April 1973): 34-45.

        Emerson writes a scathing diatribe about Army
officers. Using her two years in Vietnam from
1970-72, she characterizes the officers she met
as simple-minded, pretentious, and stupid men.
On the other hand, GI's were often smarter and
more sensitive to the truths of the war and the
Army than officers gave them credit for. Much
of the article is a series of vignettes which
illustrate the heroism of the GI's and the
indifference and callousness of the officers.
Interspersed, too, are various comparisons of
her experience as a woman with her male
counterparts.

391.   _____. "A Gift From ARVN." **Esquire**
            84 (November 1975): 104, 105, 152-157.

        Emerson writes of the homeless and unloved
ARVN army hoping that their worth to Americans
was to let us know that we cannot indulge in
illusions in the future like "Vietnamization."

Most of the article describes the battles they fought and their living conditions.

392. Hessman, James, and Margaret Berkowitz.
      "Vietnam Casualty Report: The Downward
      Trend." **Armed Forces Journal** 107 (February
      14, 1970): 19-21.

      The article asserts that Nixon is now
reducing U.S. combat casualties in the Vietnam
War. Numerous statistics supporting the
downward trend appear in charts, but the authors
do delineate causes of concern for the U.S.,
following that with an outline of Hanoi's
dilemmas. They ultimately conclude that the
Americans and South Vietnamese will be
victorious.

393. Knoll, Erwin, and Judith McFadden, eds. **War
      Crimes and the American Conscience**. New
      York: Holt, Rinehart and Winston, 1970.

      The editors attempt to record the trials in
America and to examine the nature of war crimes
perpetrated by America during the Vietnam War.
The book includes a section on Vietnam, focusing
on the My Lai massacre.

394. Mobley, Peggy. **Analysis of Vietnamization,
      GVN Control, Decline, and Recovery, December
      1971 to June 1972**. Ann Arbor, Mich.: Bendix
      Aerospace Systems Division, 1972.

      Mobley's study was designed to help determine
what factors characterize those provinces which
lost people from GVN control to enemy control
after the Spring Offensive in 1972. She
determines what factors characterize provinces
that regain GVN control of people quickly vs.
those which do not after an offensive action.
In the former case, provinces lost to enemy
control generally experience frequent attack.
Many boast few or very poor GVN sponsored
social, economic, and developmental programs.
Those provinces with strong social programs tend
to be reclaimed more quickly also after
offensive actions.

395. Shapley, Deborah. "Herbicides: AAAS Study Finds

Dioxin in Vietnamese Fish." **Science** 180
(April 20, 1973): 285-286.

The article is a report on the research of
two Harvard scientists. They completed their
study using fish bought from open markets in
Vietnam in 1970. The fish came from areas
heavily sprayed during the U.S. defoliation
campaigns, and their findings showed that the
fish contained significant quantities of dioxin,
known to cause significant birth defects.
According to Shapley, the scientists' study
provides solid evidence that dioxin did enter
the Vietnamese diet. Two repercussions may
occur: (1) the Center for Responsive Law asked
the Environmental Protection Agency to suspend
uses of several dioxin related herbicides; and
(2) the Air Force plans to sell surplus Agent
Orange to other countries would be now delayed.

396. _____. "Herbicides: Academy Finds
Damage in Vietnam After a Fight of Its Own."
Science 183 (March 22, 1974): 1177-1180.

Shapley details the "troubled process" that
produced the National Academy of Science's
report on the use of herbicides in the Vietnam
War. She maintains that the internal squabbling
amongst members of the herbicide committee and
the report's review panel colored the written
results. Amongst its statements, the report
reveals that South Vietnam's mangrove forests
suffered extensive, long-term damage, inland
forests were severely damaged, and there was
crop destruction. While not finding conclusive
evidence of links between herbicide use and
human health issues, the report suggests that a
strong relationship exists. Finally, the report
found that herbicide warfare has a significant
negative effect on Vietnamese opinions of the
American presence.

397. _____. "Herbicides: DOD Study of
Viet Use Damns with Faint Praise." **Science**
177 (September 1, 1972): 776-779.

Shapley reports that the Department of
Defense's study on the effectiveness of
herbicides during the Vietnam War found only

limited usefulness for such warfare. Her
analysis of the report, which tried to point out
as much usefulness as possible, shows that the
document contained weak arguments for herbicide
use. One implication is that the report will
not support the Nixon Administration's continued
interpretation of the Geneva Protocol, an
interpretation which exempts herbicides from its
bans.

398.   _____. "Rainmaking: Rumored Used
         Over Laos Alarms Arms Experts, Scientists."
         Science 176 (June 16, 1972): 1216-20.

Shapley follows up on references in **The
Pentagon Papers** that the U.S. military used
climate modification as part of its escalation
of the war effort. Specifically described are
experiments with rain-making over Laos and parts
of the Ho Chi Minh Trail. She also relates the
civilian meteorologists' reactions to this
possibility. This group worries about the
global long-term effects of this tampering.

399.   _____. "Technology in Vietnam: Fire
         Storm Project Fizzled Out." **Science** 177
         (July 21, 1972): 239-41.

In this report, Shapley describes three
failed attempts from 1965-67, authorized by the
DOD, to light "fire storms" in the heart of
South Vietnam's most valuable timber country.
The military purpose was to clear the jungle
canopy and expose Viet Cong bases, but all
attempts failed. The revelation of this
attempted use of incendiary technology caused
criticism of the military's environmental
warfare.

400.   Shields, Patricia. "The Determinants of Service
         in the Armed Forces During the Vietnam Era."
         Ph.D. diss., The Ohio State University, 1977.

Shields' study focuses on the recruitment
process during the Vietnam Conflict (1966-73).
She describes the enlistment figures as compared
to draft statistics and profiles the people who
served during this time. Among the discoveries
from the study are: (1) black high school

graduates risked greater chances of induction
although high school graduates as a group were
burdened most heavily; (2) black fathers tended
to enlist more than other groups; (3) the
pressure of possibly being drafted is a strong
predictor of service, especially during 1966-68.
In essence, the study indicates that people of
different races did respond differently to the
likelihood of service.

401. Starner, Frances. "Negotiating with B-52's."
      Far Eastern Economic Review 78 (December 30,
      1972): 10-12.

      Starner probes the reasons why the
Nixon-Kissinger team would fail to sign the Nine
Points, and instead unleash B-52's on Hanoi
during December after the talks. Focusing on
President Thieu's objections as a part of the
reason, she cites at least five points of
negotiations that Saigon officials disagreed
with, and suggests Kissinger's ineptness at
negotiating during this phase forced Nixon to
make changes. These changes in turn caused
Hanoi to stall at signing the agreement,
leading, of course, to the B-52 raiding
incident. Starner labels this bombing raid a
major political mistake in the negotiating
process.

1980-1987

402. Hoiberg, Anne. "Military Effectiveness of Navy
      Men During and After Vietnam." **Armed Forces
      and Society** 6, 2 (Winter 1980): 232-245.

      Hoiberg undertook a study to determine how
Navy personnel responded to the pressures of the
Vietnam War during and after the war. Beginning
with a brief history of the Navy's role in
Vietnam, she then outlines the questions,
methods of research, and population statistics
for the study. Among the results were: (1) men
in Navy service in 1966 performed effectively
and often remained in the service while
continuing to be highly adaptable; (2) men who
experienced hostile action in Vietnam and were
hospitalized suffered more injuries; (3) Vietnam

veterans not experiencing hostile action had
highest stress-related disorders and
hospitalization instances.

403.   Shields, Patricia. "The Burden of the Draft:
        The Vietnam Years." **Journal of Political an**
        Military Sociology 9 (Fall, 1981): 215-228.

        Shields' study investigates the draft
likelihood for both whites and blacks during th
Vietnam War. The results of the study show tha
two variables which accounted for differences i
draftability between the two races: education
deferments and health. White men were more
likely than blacks to receive deferments becaus
of educational pursuits. The data suggests tha
white men were able to use marginal health
limitations to gain 1-Y status more than blacks
Numerous comparisons further result from the
study. Shields recommends that to make the
draft more equitable in the future, student
deferments, among other factors, should be
disallowed.

404.   _____. "Enlistment During the
        Vietnam Era and The 'Representation' Issue o
        the All-Volunteer Force." **Armed Forces and**
        Society 7 (Fall 1980): 133-151.

        The author studied enlistment patterns durin
the Vietnam War. Separating the data by races,
she discovered that about 19% of blacks and
whites had enlisted. She establishes
differences in reasons for the enlistments for
each race.

1960-1969

405.   Shaffer, Helen. "Treatment of War Prisoners."
       Editorial Research Reports 2 (July 12, 1967):
       499-516.

       Focusing on the Viet Cong's execution of an
       American prisoner of war, Gustav Hertz, the
       article then describes the atrocities committed
       on prisoners by both the Viet Cong and South
       Vietnamese forces. Fears that prisoners'
       treatments in North Viet Nam may be no better
       permeate the account, and Shaffer describes
       examples of mistreatment including reprisal
       killings, the public exhibition of American
       prisoners in the North, and threats to try
       captured pilots as war criminals. Much of the
       article is a short history of the changing
       treatment of prisoners of war as modern warfare
       emerged in the twentieth century.

1970-1979

406.   Barton, Jane. "Vietnamese Women--POW's in South
       Vietnam." **Off Our Backs** 3, no. 7 (April
       1973): 1, 67.

       The article covers the stories of Vietnamese
       women who were arrested and held by the Thieu
       government in South Vietnam. Barton, who was
       with the American Friends Service Committee,
       confirms the conditions of the women prisoners
       at Quang Ngai which she visited. Held on
       suspicion of being Viet Cong or for other
       political reasons, most women showed signs of
       being brutally tortured although American
       advisors were present near the prison compounds.

407.   Bink, N., trans. "Letter from a Vietnamese
       Sister." **Up From Under** 1, no. 3
       (January/February 1971): 45-46.

       This piece is a translation of a letter
       written by Mme. Nguyen Thi Binh, a delegate of
       the PRG of South Vietnam to the Paris Peace

Conference. She addresses American women,
denounces American aggression, and calls for
everyone to work for a speedy end to the war.

408. Buckley, Priscilla. "Prisoners of War: They
      Also Serve." **National Review** 22 (July 28,
      1970): 786-787, 801.

      Buckley reports on the concerns of wives of
MIA and POW husbands. Three wives visited her
and all four discussed the attempts by peace
delegations, by Perot, and by political
negotiation, to account for the MIA's and
prisoners. An overwhelming theme was the wives
suspicions and disdain of North Vietnam and of
American anti-war protestors in contrast to
their belief in the constant efforts of the
American government to deal with the POW issue.

409. Christopher, Luella Sue. **Prisoners of War in
      Indochina, 1971-72: Legal Issues, Policies
      and Initiatives of Major Parties to the
      Conflict, and Efforts to Secure Release**.
      Washington, D.C.: Library of Congress,
      Congressional Research Service, 1972.

      Written in three parts, this report includes
an introductory summary and appendices. Part I
describes the major differences in the way the
North Vietnamese and the Americans and South
Vietnamese applied the Geneva Convention
stipulations to POW-MIA's. Christopher
denounces the North Vietnamese interpretations
of the war and the relations of the Geneva
Convention to it and cites instances where North
Vietnam broke many articles. Sections II and
III detail U.S. and South Vietnamese attempts to
get prisoners released.

410. Colebrook, Joan. "Prisoners-of-War."
      Commentary 57, no. 1 (January 1974): 30-37.

      This is an account of Colebrook's interviews
with American POW's from both the Korean and
Vietnam Wars. Her belief is that the treatment
of POW's by the North Vietnamese was reminiscent
of the kinds of torture meted out during the
Stalin era in Russia. She points out that many

American North Vietnamese sympathizers are not able to see this relationship.

411.   David, Heather. "Ill-Treated POW's Ignored at Home." **Navy: The Magazine of Seapower** 13, no. 6 (June 1970): 22-28.

David charges that the plight of American POW/MIA's has not reached America's conscience yet, and that the issue remains invisible. David discusses why, under the Nixon Administration, the POW-MIA families are allowed to express their sentiments publicly. Finally, other strategies for publicity that various concerned groups use complete her piece.

412.   _____. **Operation Rescue**. New York: Pinnacle Bks., 1971.

David, a journalist and Pentagon correspondent, covers the ins and outs of the Son Tay raids. The first two chapters describe the raid itself, and succeeding chapters recount the planning of the raid and reactions to the failure to find American prisoners at the site. She devotes the last chapter to the POW wives' responses to the Song Tay raid.

413.   Davidon, A. "Mme. Thanh, a Political Prisoner." **Win Magazine** 9, no. 29 (October 4, 1973): 8-9.

Davidon's story tells of the war resistance and consequent imprisonments of a woman South Vietnamese lawyer, Mme. Ngo Ba Thanh. Mme. Thanh's peace efforts are described, her many imprisonments as a result of her protests, and her latest escapade. She is an example of the suspected violations by President Thieu who had denied holding any political prisoners during this phase of the war.

414.   Morgan, Cindy. "U.S. Vietnam POW's ... Where Did They Go From There?" **Countermeasures** 2 (May 1976): 42-46.

Morgan elected to follow up on the whereabouts and jobs of selected Vietnam POW's three years after their releases from North

Vietnam. After a general summary on jobs,
locations, and feelings of veteran POW's, she
singles out half a dozen to spotlight. Noting
that most men are not in career work which
involves developing survival or evasion
techniques for soldiers in combat, she does find
two ex-POW's working on these contacts. Each
elaborates on the training needs for high risk
candidates for potential prisoners of war.

415. Standerwick, Caroline. "Missing in Action: How
         Agony of Vietnam Lingers." **U.S. News and
         World Report** 77 (December 30, 1974): 30-31.

      Standerwick is the wife of MIA Colonel Robert
Standerwick, a pilot shot down over Laos in
February, 1971. Her article recounts her
frustrating quest to find information on her
husband and her growing disillusion with the
American government's efforts.

1980-1987

416. Beck, Melinda, with Mary Lord and Ron LaBreque.
         "Exploiting the MIA Families?" **Newsweek** 101
         (April 11, 1983): 34.

      Beck discusses the renewed interest in the
Reagan administration and on the part of the
public in accounting for the over 2400 still
missing Americans in Vietnam. The story centers
on the suspicion that tales of sightings of
Americans are false and most likely self-serving
for the teller. The families of POW-MIA's are
guardedly watching the resurgence of interest.

417. Coburn, Judith. "Last Patrol." **Mother Jones**
         12, no. 2 (February-March 1987): 36-45.

      Coburn, a former war correspondent,
accompanied six members of the Vietnam Veterans
of America to Hanoi and Ho Chi Minh City as part
of that group's continued effort to assist the
reinstatement of communications between America
and Vietnam. The visit triggers memories of
combat years, complicating somewhat the main
mission of the group which is to visit a
crash-site of an American plane and to obtain

information on MIA's. As the visit progresses, each person grapples with a private search for atonement.

418.   Martin, Ann. "Families of Vietnam War POW's and MIA's: The Ordeal Continues." **USA Today** 112, no. 2468 (May 1984): 32-37.

Stating that the manner in which the U.S. government continues to manipulate the families of POW-MIA's has rarely been considered, Martin encourages examination of this problem. Most of her article presents a detailed historical account of POW-MIA wife activism during the Johnson and Nixon administrations. The account continues with a history of the League of Families of American Prisoners and Missing in Southeast Asia and that group's political encounters with the Ford, Carter and Reagan administrations.

419.   Robotham, Rosemarie. "Still Missing." **Life** 9, no. 7 (July 1986): 39-42.

Robotham raises this issue: although many more men were unaccounted for in both World War II and Korea, we did not search for them persistently, so why do the Vietnam MIA's haunt the national conscience still? After speculating on possible answers, she develops two portraits of family members of MIA soldiers who, upon receiving remains of their relatives, found that their identities could not actually be proven. The article concludes as she notes the political complications which may continue to hamper obtaining an adequate accounting of the missing.

1960-1969

420.   Bernadette, Sister Marie. "Sisters Escalate
          Service in Vietnam." **Hospital Progress** 48,
          no. 6 (June 1967): 28-30.

          The story describes the Medical Mission
       Sisters' hospital in Qui Nhon, South Vietnam.
       Stampeded by refugees, various sisters describe
       the inability of the hospital to efficiently
       care for them. Much of the article, however,
       uses vignettes of the sisters' work to support
       the praise for their efforts.

421.   Dean, Ruth. "Navy and Marine Corps Wives Do
          More Than Stand and Wait." **Navy: The
          Magazine of Seapower** 11 (November 1968):
          20-23.

          The article relates the various activities of
       Navy wives whose husbands are serving during the
       Vietnam War. Described is "Wifeline", a support
       program for Navy wives with husbands away.

422.   Dickens, Martha L. "Very Few Dull Moments in My
          Unforgettable Two Years As AID Nurse in
          Vietnam." **Weather Vane** 37, no. 4 (August
          1968): 3-4, 32-34.

          Dickens was a civilian "nurse advisor" with a
       U.S. AID medical team stationed in Da Nang in
       1966 to 1968. Much of her description centers
       on the characteristics of Vietnamese hospitals,
       Vietnamese nursing, and the AID nurses' roles.

423.   Drake, Katherine. "Our Flying Nightingales in
          Vietnam." **Reader's Digest** 91 (December
          1967): 73-79.

          Drake writes about the Air Force flight
       nurses in Vietnam. The piece opens with a story
       of flight nurses working on the plane airlifting
       wounded out of Vietnam and, in coordination with
       Clark AFB, saving a young Marine's life. This
       incident illustrates the flight nurse's role:
       to be responsible for and to tend sick and

wounded men as they are evacuated from Vietnam
to other bases during trips which often take
from four to 24 hours. The average age of the
nurses is about 28, and between the two Air
Force teams involved, over 100 nurses serve on
flights. Drake covers thoroughly the types of
decisions these women make, the traumatic
medical experiences they endure, and the kind o
fortitude they develop to complete their jobs.

424. Lynn, Barbara. "Good Samaritans in Vietnam."
      Ebony 23, no. 12 (October 1968): 179-185.

      Lynn was a black Red Cross worker at Cam Ran
Bay and Cu Chi. She describes the extremely
positive reactions of black soldiers to her
presence in all the recreation centers she
worked and tells in general the highlights of
her year's experiences, experiences that
included a normal routine of work as well as th
shock of being mortared. She discusses, too,
how serving in Vietnam changed her views on
life.

425. Martin, Linda Grant. "Angels Of Vietnam."
      Today's Health 45 (August 1967): 16-22,
      60-62.

      Martin writes a tribute to the 754 military
nurses stationed in Vietnam. She begins
describing the nurses' lives through the eyes o
the women at Cu Chi, then moves on to picture
nurses working in a relatively secure area at
Cam Ranh Bay. She ends by covering the
experiences of nurses stationed on the U.S.S.
Repose and the U.S.S. Sanctuary, places
seemingly distant from combat zones, but which
receive extreme cases of wounded men, too.

426. Wald, Karen. "Vietnamese Women Fight Us."
      Guardian 22, no. 1 (October 4, 1969): 12.

      Wald reports on the presence of Vietnamese
women in Cuba on a tour there. The article
describes the combatant roles of three of the
women who take the tour.

1970-1979

427. Emerson, Gloria. "Hey Lady, What Are You Doing
        Here?" **McCall's** 98 (August 1971): 61.

        Emerson writes her response to the title's
        question which is that she does not understand
        the reasons why the war in Vietnam exists. She
        describes her feelings about being a woman in
        Vietnam.

428. Gehan, Jeanne. "One Woman's War." **Nursing
        Care** 6, no. 8 (August 1973): 15-19.

        Priscilla Gariepy, a nurse who lost her son
        in the Vietnam War in 1968, joined a Project
        Concern staff in a Vietnamese hospital at Lien
        Hiep. She spent a year on staff while training
        and assisting other Vietnamese medical
        personnel. Some of her hospital log entries are
        included in this story.

429. Kovacs, Joanne. "War Casualty: Gold Star Wife."
        Off Our Backs 1, no. 22 (May 27, 1971): 6-7.

        Kovacs interviewed Dava Ensell, a woman whose
        husband died in Vietnam. She explores Dava's
        feelings about her husband's enlistment, the
        American presence in Vietnam, and the government
        policies affecting widows. Dava admits her
        involvement as a woman in the May Vietnam
        Veterans Against the War protest in Washington,
        D.C.

430. Lang, Frances. "It's a Woman's War Too." **Off
        Our Backs** 3, no. 1 (September 1972): 26-27.

        The article is a retelling in her own words
        of a two-weekend trip to North Vietnam by Marge
        Tabankin, a past-president of the National
        Student Association. Her group's mission was to
        take testimony from civilians on the American
        violations of the Nuremberg Law. Tabankin
        describes the destruction they encountered, but
        basically her statement enlightens her readers
        about the generally good morale of the people
        and the Communists' social efforts. A section
        of her piece covers the status of women in North
        Vietnam. Tabankin comes away with decidedly

anti-war beliefs about the American military war
effort.

431. Lowes, Susan, comp. "Women At War." **Up From
      Under** 1, no. 2 (August/September 1970):
      50-54.

      Lowes uses autobiographical stories of
      Vietnamese women within her short history of the
      Vietnam War and its roots. Beginning with the
      French struggle to regain control of both North
      and South Vietnam in the 1940's and 50's, Lowes'
      women tell what it was like to work for the
      French. The stories continue, one on village
      changes by women inhabitants while cooperating
      with the NLF, and another by a woman who lived
      through a bombing assault by American forces.

432. Morris, Victoria, and Wilma Traker. "After the
      Battle." **American Journal of Nursing** 72, no.
      1 (January 1972): 97-9.

      The article is written from the point of view
      of a young Marine seriously wounded in combat in
      Vietnam and who is now a paraplegic on a ward.
      Told in his voice, it is a story of the power of
      one nurse's care which brought him along until
      he could take his place in the outside world.

433. Smith, Hilary. "What Do Nurses Do in America?"
      American Journal of Nursing 76, no. 2
      (February 1976): 278-80.

      Smith was a nurse at Minh-Quy Hospital, a
      medical unit serving Montagnards during the war.
      Recalling the freedom of judgment and autonomy
      she had there as a medical nurse, she contrasts
      that with the intensely bureaucratic methods of
      treating and curing patients in modern American
      hospitals. Smith echoes the experiences of many
      others as she describes the narrow duties that
      nurses retain once returning home from Vietnam.

434. Weiner, Lois. "Women and The War."
      International Socialist 20 (June 1970): 6.

      Weiner's article confronts women with the
      unfair effects of the war economy upon them as
      wage earners. She calls for women workers and

members of the Women's Liberation movement to
protest the war and thus end at least part of
the discrimination against women.

1980-1987

435. Alexander, Susan. "The Invisible Veterans:
        Nurses in the Vietnam War." **Women's Studies
        Quarterly** 12, no. 2 (Summer 1984): 16.

The article is about the military nurse
veterans of Vietnam. Alexander bemoans the
silence of women veterans and blames these
factors for it: (1) that the military treated
its women volunteers and those called to Vietnam
as virtually unimportant figures, and (2) that
women were subjected to a situation that
defeated their mythic view of "nurse as healer."
Thus, the Vietnam experience has become one that
encourages women to forget and be forgotten.

436. Allen, E. Ann. "The WAC Mission: The Testing
        Time from Korea to Vietnam." Ph.D. diss.,
        University of South Carolina, 1986.

In her history of the Women's Army Corps from
1948 to 1973, Allen explores how well the WAC
concept worked in both the Korean and Vietnam
wars. In particular, modern warfare in the
Vietnam War affected the role of WAC as did the
leadership of several strong women directors.

437. Enloe, Cynthia. "Black Women in the U.S.
        Military." **Sojourner: The Women's Forum** 10
        (November 1985): 16-17.

Enloe challenges her readers to examine the
relationships among sexism, racism, and
militarism, and states that one key to this
examination will be the experiences and insights
of young black women. Vietnam experiences are
seldom mentioned in this piece.

438. Holm, Maj. Gen. Jeanne. **Women in the
        Military: An Unfinished Revolution**. Novata,
        Calif.: Presidio Press, 1982. Rev. ed.,
        1986.

Holm writes a comprehensive history of women's involvement and changing roles in the military. Beginning with the story of Molly Pitcher in the American Revolution, the saga moves through the Vietnam War to contemporary times. One chapter covers women's military roles in Vietnam, while the succeeding one examines women during the Tet Offensive in Vietnam.

439.   Jezierski, Marlene. "Vietnam Women's Memorial Project: Donna Marie Boulay Highlights Women's Wartime Roles." **JEN: Journal of Emergency Nursing** 13, no. 2 (March/April 1987): 122-24.

Jezierski outlines briefly some of Donna-Marie Boulay's personal history, particularly the roots of her commitment to service to her country. Especially covered is her mission to correct the blank spot in the history of the Vietnam War which is that women, too, served in Vietnam.

440.   MacPherson, Myra. "Vietnam Nurses: These Are the Women Who Went to War." **Ms.** 12, no. 12 (June 1984): 52-56, 104-106.

In this excerpt from her **Long Time Passing**, MacPherson describes the experience of the nurse. Beginning by using the feelings and perceptions of one nurse, Saralee McGoran, MacPherson describes the traumas of saving severely wounded men, the nightmares and flashbacks experienced after their return from Vietnam, and the isolation of the female veteran at home. In the latter half of the article, Van Devanter's experiences and feelings appear as emblems of many nurses' experiences. MacPherson concludes with further statistics and general observations on nurses' roles.

441.   Marron, Judy. "A Woman Veteran Speaks: Don't Tell Me Women Don't Know About War...." **The Veteran** 12 (November-December 1982): n.p.

Written by a nurse veteran who later killed herself, the article is an angry letter to male combat veterans. Marron asserts that, because

of the nurse's grueling work, she, too,
experienced battle fatigue, fear of being hit,
despair over the dead, and stress disorder upon
her return to the States. Marron's anger
extends to her peacetime work in the Army where
she experienced sexual harassment. She
concludes her letter with a plea for the
acknowledgment of the woman veteran's problems.

442.   McRobbie, Joan. "The Unsung Heroines of
         Vietnam: Army Nurses." **McCall's** 114, no. 7
         (May 1987): 159.

        The brief article is a history of Diane
Evans' career as a Vietnam nurse, her subsequent
blocking of that experience, and, finally, how
she began the movement to erect a memorial
honoring all women Vietnam veterans.

443.   McVicker, Sara. "Invisible Veterans: The Women
         Who Served in Vietnam." **Journal of
         Psychosocial Nursing** 23, no. 10 (October
         1985): 13-19.

        McVicker attempts to describe an overview of
women's Vietnam experiences, an effort which
clearly shows that each one's experience was
particularly individual. For example, living
and working conditions varied dramatically for
women as did problems with social relationships
and types of experiences with casualties. In
spite of this, women were victims of the traumas
of war, she asserts, and suffer even now from
the effects. The rest of the article discusses
issues involved in the treatment of women
Vietnam veterans.

444.   Mithers, Carol Lynn. "Missing in Action: Women
         Warriors in Vietnam." **Cultural Critique**, no.
         3 (Spring 1986): 79-90.

        Mithers' point is that thousands of women who
went to war in Vietnám remain invisible in spite
of a national resurgence of interest in the
Vietnam War and the Vietnam veteran.
Characterizing those women as "sheltered good
girls," she uses numerous interviews and cites
several references to show the women's adverse
reactions to the war. Her central question,

since the war affected women, is "why the
relative silence in the literature?" Mithers
suggests an answer: women's war experiences are
not culturally valued, especially women's
Vietnam experiences which thrust them into roles
defying old stereotyped notions of women in war.

445.   Norman, Elizabeth M. "A Study of Female
        Nurses in Vietnam During the War Years,
        1965-73." **Journal of Nursing History** 2, no.1
        (November 1986): 43-60.

Norman's research posed the question: "What
were the nurses' professional and personal
experiences in Vietnam?" Fifty nurses were
interviewed according to pre-composed sets of
questions. She concludes that the experiences,
while being quite complex, do show that nurses
experienced the realities of war although very
differently from male combat veterans.
Stressors she found included the inability to
obtain further information on casualties after
they left the compound, triage decisions, deaths
of personal friends, and intense memories of the
casualties.

446.   Ortega, E. A. "Vietnam Nurses Speak Out on War,
        Coming Home--A Time of Elation and
        Confusion." **California Nurse** 79, no. 5
        (November 1983): 7-8.

Ortega joined the Army Nursing Corps in 1966
and was sent to Vietnam in 1967. In the
article, she tells why she joined the service
and describes her experiences at the 36th
Evacuation Hospital at Vung Tau.

447.   Saywell, Shelley. **Women in War**. New York:
        Viking Press, 1985. New York: Penguin Bks.,
        1986.

Saywell's book contains a chapter on women in
the Vietnam War. In it, she describes the
stories of two women, Donna-Marie Boulay and
Betty Stahl Doebbling. Periodically, she
intermixes the war stories of other women
veterans of this conflict. Each woman's
portrait extends from life before, during, then
after the return from Vietnam.

448. Spelts, Doreen. "Nurses Who Served--And Did Not Return." **American Journal of Nursing** 86, no. 9 (September 1986): 1037-38.

Spelts' short article describes the biographies of the ten nurses (eight women and two men) who were killed while serving in the Vietnam War. Beginning with Drazba's and Jones' stories (both were killed in the same helicopter crash) and ending with Mary Therese Klinker's death during the April, 1975 airlifts of children, Spelts tells the stories of these other heroes and heroines of the war.

449. _____. "Women Who Died in Vietnam." **Minerva: Quarterly Report of Women and the Military** 3, no. 4 (Winter 1985): 89-96.

Spelts shares a bit of the process of researching the lives of the eight women on the Wall, her current research project. The article ends with a call for information on any of the eight women.

450. Stremlow, Col. Mary V. **A History of the Women Marines, 1946-1977.** Washington, D.C.: U.S. Government Printing Office, 1986.

In this complete history of women in the Marine Corps, at least one section covers women's military assignments in Vietnam.

451. Tuxen, Peggy. "Vietnam Veteran Nurses Speak Out on the War: Helicopters, Heat, and Holding the Hands of the Dying." **California Nurse** 79, no. 5 (November 1983): 6-8.

Tuxen spent three years as an army nurse, and part of that time was spent in Vietnam. The article is her personal description of her experiences, thoughts, and feelings during her service in Vietnam.

452. Willenz, June A. **Women Veterans: America's Forgotten Heroines.** New York: Continuum, 1983.

Willenz' book tackles the issues of women in

American wars covering both history of
involvement, current concerns, and public
opinion on women's military service. Quite a
few of the profiles of women veterans used
(which make up half of the book) describe
Vietnam veterans.

1960-1969

453.   Higgins, Marguerite.   "No Club For Cookie
       Pushers."   **NEA Journal** 54 (March 1965): 15.

The article is a defense of the foreign
service and of American diplomats. Higgins
insists that their posts are not easy positions
to hold, and many face life-threatening risks.
She uses diplomats serving in South Vietnam to
prove her point.

454.   Trotta, Liz.   "Hey Fellows, Chet and David Have
       Sent a Woman."   **TV Guide** 17 (April 19-25,
       1969): 6-10.

Trotta describes one assignment when she
worked for NBC in Saigon. She covered an
Army-Navy operation in Kien Hoa Province.
Intermixed with her reporting on the combat
operations are incidents in which American
military men react to a woman journalist sent to
cover the story.

1970-1979

455.   Keylin, Arleen, and Suri Borangiu, eds.   **Front
       Page Vietnam--As Reported by the New York
       Times**. New York: Arno Press, 1979.

Through a chronological ordering of the **New
York Times'** front pages, the authors recreate
the history of the Vietnam War. They use, as
they allude to once, "the raw material of
history" to capture a sense of the people,
events, and emotions. The front pages appear,
interspersed with photographs of events
occurring during various phases of the war.

456.   Kilgore, Margaret.   "The Female War
       Correspondent in Vietnam."   **The Quill** 60 (May
       1972): 9-12.

Kilgore served as a war correspondent in

South Vietnam for 18 months beginning in 1970.
Her insights on reporting about the war include
the characteristics of a good war reporter: a
sound knowledge of political issues, military
knowledge, and linguistic and communication
abilities top her list. She shares, too, her
impressions of the women in the Vietnamese
culture and her insights about being one of a
handful of women reporters in the country during
that phase of the war.

457.   Murphy, Wanda Herndon. "A Comparison of Black
         and White Daily Newspapers' Editorial
         Opinions Regarding a Selected Set of Events
         Related to the U.S. Involvement in the
         Vietnam War: A Systematic Content Analysis."
         Masters thesis, Michigan State University,
         1978.

Murphy sampled the editorials on the Vietnam
War in four large American newspapers, the
Atlanta Daily World, the **Atlanta Constitution**,
the **Chicago Defender**, and the **Chicago Tribune**.
She drew the selected editorials from four time
periods between 1964 and 1970. All the papers
took similar stances on the war and no opinions
seemed to be affected by political, social, or
economic concerns.

458.   Turner, Kathleen. "The Effect of
         Presidential-Press Interaction on Lyndon B.
         Johnson's Vietnam War Rhetoric." Ph.D.
         diss., Purdue University, 1978.

Turner examines the kinds of strategies that
a media-wary Lyndon Johnson used to promote his
Vietnam War policies. In spite of his attempts
to couch his rhetoric in soothing terms,
Johnson's policies were met with antagonism by
many in control of the media. Turner argues
that these interactions influenced Johnson's
decision not to run for re-election in 1968.

459.   Welch, Susan. "The American Press and
         Indochina, 1950-56." Chapter 8 in
         Communication in International Politics,
         edited by Richard Merritt, 207-231. Urbana,
         Ill.: University of Illinois Press, 1972.

Welch analyzes aspects of American press coverage related to foreign policy decisions made by the U.S. in Indochina in the early to late 1950's. She discusses the quality of coverage and reasons for the press's views of the American presence there. Welch reveals that the press helped to fix the importance of this struggle in the American mind by supporting the American foreign policy of the early and mid-1950's. She also describes why, for most of the press, this support existed.

460. _____. "Vietnam: How the Press Went Along." **The Nation** 213, no. 11 (October 11, 1971): 327-330.

Welch declares that in the 1950's the press helped establish the importance of and rhetoric for support by Americans for Vietnam. Major newspapers helped establish the administration's notion that Vietnam's future held a showdown between Communists and non-Communists, that Ho Chi Minh was a Communist puppet, and that an American victory there was essential to a "free world." (Only the **Chicago Tribune**'s journalists remained skeptical of such rhetoric.) Welch cites four reasons why the press might not have challenged the 1950's administrative assumptions.

1980-1987

461. Adler, Renata. **Reckless Disregard: Westmoreland v. CBS, et al.; Sharon v. Time.** New York: Alfred A. Knopf, 1986.

The book is an expanded version of the two-part article appearing in the **New Yorker** on these two trials. In an extensive history of both trials, Adler unveils the errors behind the media's documentary, exposing its arrogance and power plays, as well as exposing the military's blunders during an unpopular war.

462. _____. "Two Trials-I." **New Yorker** 62 (June 16, 1986): 42-96.

In this first of two parts, Adler examines

the incidents which led to the two libel suits,
"Westmoreland v. CBS, et al." and "Sharon v.
Time." Both trials, to Adler, are significant
because they bring together four powerful,
modern institutions--the press, the courts, the
military, and the legal profession. In
particular, the Westmoreland trial became a
trial of the American involvement in the Vietnam
War, and a trial of the press's involvement in
the war as well.

463.   _____. "Two Trials-II." **New
        Yorker** 62 (June 23, 1986): 34-83.

    In this article, Adler continues her
description of the issues in the Westmoreland v
CBS, et al. trial. She succinctly describes
what was at stake for Westmoreland and for CBS;
the former needed to prove the documentary
factually false, while the latter needed to
defend press protections guaranteed by the First
Amendment. Adler concludes this piece with a
summation of what lessons about truth and the
mass media might be learned from the trial.
Adler's view obviously is anti-media.

464.   Castro, Janice. "Smoking Guns, Secret Tapes."
        Time 123, no. 21 (May 21, 1984): 86.

    Castro's story reports on an interview in
which the journalistic accuracy of the show "The
Uncounted Enemy: A Vietnam Deception" is
questioned. Castro suggests that the procedures
in obtaining and writing the story were somewhat
unethical.

465.   Elwood-Akers, Virginia. **Women War
        Correspondents in the Vietnam War, 1961-1975.**
        Metuchen, N.J.: Scarecrow Press, 1987.

    This is an extremely in-depth history of the
major women journalists writing about the
Vietnam War. Beginning with Chapelle and
Higgins, and ending with Emerson and Fitzgerald,
Elwood-Akers describes their experiences,
beliefs, and positions on the war, bringing out
the uniquenesses of their vision as women. Told
in eight chapters, the history is broken after
each chapter by an excerpt from a woman

journalist's book, article, or newspiece. A
very comprehensive bibliography completes the
book.

466. Fitzgerald, Frances. "The Vietnam Numbers
        Game." **The Nation** 234 (June 26, 1982):
        776-778.

        The article is about both the journalists'
failures to admit their own weaknesses in
reporting the war and about the enemy numbers
cover-up. Fitzgerald discusses the **TV Guide**
story about the poorly rated documentary "The
Uncounted Enemy: A Vietnam Deception" which
became the focus for the Westmoreland v. CBS,
et al. trial. Most of her article, however, is
an analysis of the facts portrayed in that
original broadcast. The article concludes as
she describes who the doctored numbers were
meant to fool; Congress, the media, and the
public are obvious, but she includes Johnson,
too. Fitzgerald also suggests that the MACV's
doctored figures may have affected the military
intelligence's ability to predict the Tet
Offensive in 1968.

467. Giesburg, Jean McClelland. "Star Spangled
        Banter: A Study of G.I. Humor in 'The Stars
        and Stripes' From World War I to Vietnam."
        Ph.D. diss., University of Houston, 1981.

        This study of American military humor covers
four major American wars in the 20th century
including the Vietnam War. Using the newspaper,
"The Stars and Stripes," Giesburg examines the
types of humor used by the soldiers in each war.

468. Gilbert, Dee. "Street Journalism." **Southern
        Exposure** 10 (March-April 1982): 17-20.

        The story covers the life and war protest
(including the Vietnam War during 1970-75) of
Elizabeth Rogers. Most of it is told, oral
history fashion, in her own voice, and she
spends much time discussing the anti-war
leaflets and brochures her husband and she
prepared and circulated on the streets in the
1970's.

469. Keeshen, Kathleen Kearney.   "Marguerite Higgins:
      Journalist, 1920-1960."   Ph.D. diss.,
      University of Maryland, 1983.

         This dissertation examines Higgins' career as
      a journalist from 1940 until 1966.   In
      particular, Higgins' contributions as a woman
      journalist are discussed.

470. Rothmyer, Karen.   "Retrial of History."   **New
      Statesman** 108 (December 21-28, 1984): 20.

         Rothmyer analyzes the Westmoreland v. CBS,
      et al. trial as a minor replaying of a war that
      was dominated by the media.   However, she finds
      that only one narrow aspect of the Vietnam War
      is really being brought up--not the entire war.
      She reviews pros and cons of Westmoreland's
      chances to win.

471. Schneir, Walter, and Miriam Schneir.   "The
      Uncounted Vietcong: How The Military Cooked
      the Books."   **The Nation** 238 (May 12, 1984):
      570-576.

         The article discusses the Westmoreland v.
      CBS, et al. case during the summer before it
      came to trial.   The Schneirs note that the
      pretrial deposition shows Westmoreland to be
      evasive about moral issues.   While evidence,
      they feel, shows that there was a conspiracy to
      cover up the actual numbers of enemy soldiers,
      the conspiracy seems to have gone beyond
      Westmoreland and involved a number of the
      President's advisors. The remainder of the
      article recounts the details of the cover-up as
      well as disclosing who may have been involved in
      it.

472. Springer, Claudia.   "Military Propaganda:
      Defense Department Films From WWII and
      Vietnam."   **Cultural Critique** 3 (Spring 1986):
      151-167.

         Springer analyzes the similarities and
      differences in the propaganda techniques used to
      make Capra's WWII films **Why We Fight** and the
      1965 military film, **Why Vietnam?** Springer

discusses the new use of ethnographic techniques
in the films about Vietnam.

473.   Turner, Kathleen. **Lyndon Johnson's Dual War:**
       Vietnam and the Press. Chicago: University
       of Chicago Press, 1985.

       Turner's analysis focuses on the
       interrelationships among Johnson, the members of
       the press, and the President's messages about
       the Vietnam War. Beginning with young Johnson's
       early development of a political style, Turner
       carefully recreates a portrait of a man whose
       political communications thrived in more
       informal settings than formal media coverage
       allowed for; thus, from the beginning, before
       his Presidency, the basis for conflict existed.
       Subsequent chapters trace his troubled
       relationship with the press, primarily about
       Vietnam, as Johnson assumed the Presidency. A
       special analysis of the importance of Johnson's
       Johns Hopkins speech on America's Vietnam policy
       underlines increasing tensions which boiled up
       and hastened Johnson's withdrawal from the race
       for office in 1968.

474.   Wilhelm, Maria. "An Angry Vietnam War
       Correspondent Charges That Black Combat
       Soldiers are Platoon's M.I.A.'s." **People**
       Weekly 27, no. 16 (April 20, 1987): 101-102,
       104.

       In this interview, Wallace Terry views the
       film **Platoon** as one misrepresenting black
       soldiers as lazy, inefficient, and lacking in
       leadership capability. Terry states that as a
       war correspondent for **Time** in Vietnam for two
       years, his own experiences revealed that black
       men served in leadership positions and with
       valor. Of interest is his account of the effect
       of the civil rights movement on the black
       soldier.

The American Society

1960-1969

475. Mydans, Carl, and Shelley Mydans. "Vietnam: The
        Continuing War." In their **The Violent Peace,**
        405-429. New York: Atheneum Pubs., 1968.

        The Mydans looked at the periods of peace
        after World War II and those small wars that
        have erupted since then, including America's
        Vietnam War. Using photographs and accounts by
        people there, this book demonstrates a peace
        period characterized by violence. One chapter
        is devoted to Vietnam.

476. Smith, Nelle Van D. **We Care.** New York:
        William Frederick Press, 1968.

        This is a sixteen page booklet of
        "inspirational messages" for soldiers in
        Vietnam. Many of the messages are quotations;
        some are government statements of support.

1970-1979

477. Arendt, Hannah. **Crisis of the Republic.** New
        York: Harcourt Brace Jovanovich, 1972.

        Arendt's book contains four essays which
        analyze the salient social and political issues
        of the 1960's and early 1970's. The first essay
        "Lying in Politics," specifically examines **The
        Pentagon Papers,** while the other three deal more
        generally with the legal and social upheavals
        related to both the Vietnam War and other
        critical human issues of the decade.

478. _____. "Home to Roost." In **The
        American Experiment,** edited by Sam Warner,
        61-88. Boston: Houghton Mifflin Co., 1976.

        Arendt's piece discusses the legacy of the

Vietnam War for American society in the context
of other social and political problems. Terming
the turbulent events of the 1960's and 70's as
problems caused by our politicians, Arendt
explicitly describes the Vietnam War as an
example. She analyzes it as a destructive event
aimed at not personal power, profit, or
idealistic concerns, but at maintaining the
American image as a world power. Arendt
believes that the war was a watershed point
during our history, albeit one Americans cannot
appreciate. She urges an acceptance of the past
and of political misdeeds as the only sure way
to recover.

479.   Barber, Sandra. "A Role Simulation: Escalation
        of U.S. Troop Commitment in Vietnam, October,
        1961." **Teaching Political Science** 5 (July
        1978): 405-420.

        The article describes a simulation designed
for undergraduates to help them understand
decisions, conflicts, and conflict resolution in
American foreign policy, specifically in the
Vietnam War. Roles include John F. Kennedy,
Lansdale, Taylor, and Rostow among others, and
the problem involves the continuation,
escalation, or withdrawal of America from
Vietnam. The method is fully described as are
the effects of simulation as a teaching tool.

480.   Baron, Virginia. "Voices of Vietnam-Era Women."
        Christian Century 93 (December 8, 1976):
        1092-93.

        Baron's quest to discover the legacies of the
Vietnam War for women led to discussions with
women vets, resisters, and wives or mothers of
soldiers both dead and alive. The collection of
war stories by women is part of a church Women
United Project, the "Vietnam Era Women's
Project." Women reported that contact with the
war often left them socially isolated; many
minority women experienced racism indirectly.
Most had never believed anyone cared about their
personal pain enough to ask them to talk, so
many women had not expressed their emotional
involvement with the war. Baron ends by

inviting people to respond to everyone's pain about Vietnam.

481. Crawford, Mary. "Peg Mullen and the Military: The Bureaucracy of Death." **Ms.** 5 (January 1977): 70-73, 95.

Crawford writes a portrait of Peg Mullen, one which counters her image of the paranoid mother in Bryan's **Friendly Fire**. In this article, Mullen talks about all her children and her husband, her feelings about the war and her objections to the apathy many Americans feel toward it. Although the image of a fighter remains, Crawford's statements reveal Mullen as a woman dedicated to principles and emotions, but not obsessed with them.

482. Fitzgerald, Frances. **Fire In the Lake: The Vietnamese and the Americans in Vietnam**. Boston: Little, Brown, and Co., 1972. London: Macmillan, 1972. New York: Vintage Press, 1973.

Fitzgerald writes perhaps one of the earliest and most comprehensive sociological, cultural, and political analyses of the American and Vietnamese involvement. By looking at questions about American involvement through the lens of the Vietnamese experience, Fitzgerald is able to cast light on problems with the American war effort. The Vietnamese perspective, recreated through the country's history, heroes, and culture, is first explored, then a history of American involvement, laid side by side with the first part, clearly shows that American aims and beliefs, so counter to Vietnamese reality, undermined prospects of success. The book is a readable, credible piece of cultural analysis.

483. Krich, Claudia. "Vietnam: The Sickness." **The Progressive** 38 (November 1974): 35-37.

Krich's article catalogues various examples of political and economic corruption operating in South Vietnam and clearly supported, however unknowingly, by the U.S. Examples include the increasing inability of people to buy food or to find any available while shop owners hoard

American donated rice hoping to sell at higher
prices, the bribery for false I.D. cards, and
the South Vietnamese military's abuses of
privileges. Krich concludes that such
corruption will continually weaken the country
even though the U.S. floods the country with
more money as time passes.

484.   Lake, Antonia, and Anthony Lake. "Coming of Age
        Through Vietnam." **New York Times Magazine,**
        section 6 (July 20, 1975): 9, 21-31.

        Both Lakes were in Vietnam during the early
        1960's; Antonia accompanied Anthony there on his
        assignment. In the piece, written as a dialogue
        between them, each shares the experiences of the
        past in Vietnam, revealing how each felt about
        the events there, and how the events impacted on
        their personal relationship. Antonia Lake
        reveals the "unliberated" view of herself as a
        professional women which she carried then, and
        her lack of role definition in Vietnam. She
        became further removed from politics and events
        while there, while Anthony became disillusioned
        with the American effort. Their separate
        journeys intersected again as they returned home
        and both developed strong anti-war sentiments
        based on their experiences in Vietnam.

1980-1987

485.   Amgott, Madeline. "Vietnam Nurse Veterans."
        American Journal of Nursing 85, no. 4 (April
        1985): 368-9.

        Amgott was assigned to produce a television
        piece based on some themes extending from Van
        Devanter's book, **Home Before Morning.** Appalled
        at being unable to find either hard data or
        sources for it, she calls for women nurses and
        other women veterans to begin to speak out. She
        also applauds those who have begun to voice
        their pasts.

486.   Blum, Shirley Neilson. "The National Vietnam
        War Memorial." **Arts Magazine** 59 (December
        1984): 124-128.

Blum relays the history behind the war memorial, retelling Scrugg's efforts and describing Maya Lin's design in great detail. In her description of the design, she compares it to other similar memorials in antiquity which honor the dead. Blum sees the Wall as a place of pilgrimage, a Wailing Wall for the American people.

487.   Brandon, Heather. "Death in Vietnam: Anguish and Survival in America." **Intervention: A Journal of War and Peace and the Vietnam Experience** 1, no. 2 (Winter 1985): 25-29.

This piece is an excerpt from Brandon's book, **Casualties**. The particular story is about Sam Cammarata, a young man who died in Vietnam. His wife, his medic-friend in Vietnam who came home to marry Sam's wife, and Sam's father all share their perspective on the war as it developed from the pain of Sam's death.

488.   Carter, Clare. "To Embody Peace: The Building of Peace Pagoda Around the World." In **Unwinding the Vietnam War: From War Into Peace**, edited by Reese Williams, 415-426. Seattle: Real Comet Press, 1987.

The author describes the various peace pagodas being established as reminders that the world should be at peace, not war. Carter notes the building of the Leverett Peace Pagoda in Western Massachusetts. At this point, plans for the building of a Peace Pagoda in Vietnam exist, too.

489.   Coburn, Judith. "Losing Vietnam, Finding Vietnam." **Mother Jones** 8, no. 9 (November 1983): 18-27.

Coburn retells experiences from one of her several trips back to Vietnam since the official end of the conflict in 1975. Going from Hanoi to Ho Chi Minh City, the sights and people trigger frequent comparisons to times she experienced from 1970-73. Coburn concludes that Americans must realize our common history with Vietnam if the U.S. is to heal itself from the wounds of that war.

490.   _____. "Terrorism in Saigontown, USA.
        Mother Jones 8, no. 2 (February-March 1983)
        15-22, 42-44.

        Coburn's article covers the murder of a
        Vietnamese living in San Francisco. In
        actuality, the article is also about the
        realities of "Saigontown, USA," an example of a
        mental state in which, for some, the war still
        rages. Coburn explains that within the
        refugees, there are divisive political
        philosophies which continue to cause dissention
        and bloodshed even on the soil of this country.
        The murdered man's personal history and views
        showed him to be a liberal thinker, someone
        dangerous to the anti-Communist thinking of man
        resettled Vietnamese.

491.   Davis, Lorraine. "And the Winner Is...: Young
        Woman Wins Design Competition for Vietnam
        Veterans Memorial." **Vogue** 171 (September
        1981): 115.

        This brief account is the story of Maya Ying
        Lin's win in the design contest for the Vietnam
        Veterans Memorial. In addition to a description
        of the design, Davis includes Lin's statements
        about prejudices against women that she
        experienced in her architecture classes.

492.   _____. "Their 'Platoon' Was Female:
        Activities of the Vietnam Women's Memorial
        Project, Inc." **Vogue** 177, no. 5 (May 1987):
        102, 106.

        This is a very brief feature story revealing
        the genesis of Diane Evans' idea for a memorial
        statue of a woman veteran at the Washington,
        D.C. site of the Vietnam Veterans Memorial.
        Davis' article also updates facts on the
        progress of the fund raising efforts for the
        project.

493.   Emerson, Gloria. "Vietnam Veterans Speak--An
        Introduction." In **Vietnam Reconsidered:
        Lessons from a War**, edited by Harrison
        Salisbury, 182-184. New York: Harper and Row
        Pubs., 1984.

Emerson's short piece gets to the bottom of America's avoidance of its Vietnam veterans. By concentrating on the stereotypes we have, Emerson thinks, Americans avoid confronting the issues of the war.

494. _____. **Winners and Losers: Battles, Retreats, Gains, Losses and Ruins from the Vietnam War**. New York: Harcourt Brace Jovanovich, 1978. New York: Penguin Bks., 1985.

Emerson interviewed American and Vietnamese people about the war and its effects on them personally as well as on the countries. Each portrait is developed carefully and with great empathy. Ultimately, the patterns of her comments reveal that everyone lost in the Vietnam War, even the "winners."

495. English, Deirdre. "Why Are We Still In Vietnam?" **Mother Jones** 8, no. 9 (November 1983): 5.

English states that as a nation, Americans cannot face our past in Vietnam, assume a moral responsibility for our actions, or come to terms with them. Yet, neither can we forget about the war. She suggests that until Americans resolve this national schizophrenia, the country will continue to repeat the destructive paths over and over.

496. Enloe, Cynthia. "Re-Imagining Vietnam." **Sojourner: The Women's Forum** 12, no. 10 (June 1987): 39, 40, 42.

Although the article is technically a book review, Enloe's perspective as a black woman and as a feminist is of interest. In reviewing **Shallow Graves** and **In the Combat Zone,** Enloe suggests new questions to be asked about women and war, especially minority women's involvement in the Vietnam War.

497. Fish, Lydia. **The Last Firebase: A Guide to the Vietnam Veterans Memorial.** Shippensburg, Pa.: White Mane Publishing Co., 1987.

The book gives a history of the origin of th
idea and design for the Wall itself. Pieces by
Hart (on the accompanying statue) and statement
by visitors punctuate this printed, guided tour
of the Wall. Fish describes the people who
visit, the surrounds of the Wall and how to bes
photograph it, make rubbings, or find a name.
Interesting also is her chapter on the women's
statue, and one on the collection of
memorabilia.

498. Fitzgerald, Frances. "Lessons From a War."
      **Intervention: A Journal of War and Peace and
      the Vietnam Experience** 1, no. 1 (Spring
      1984): 24-27.

      Fitzgerald concentrates on the avoidance of
      future "Vietnams." Contending that nothing
      could be simpler than to avoid creating another
      war like the U.S. created in Vietnam, she deftl
      describes the parallels between the Reagan
      administration's Central American policies and
      former Administrations' Vietnam decisions. Fro
      that point on, the article takes a close look a
      what can be learned about the current crises
      from the people, organizations, and events whic
      dominated the Vietnam War years.

499. Foss, Sonja K. "Ambiguity as Persuasion: The
      Vietnam Veterans Memorial." **Communication
      Quarterly** 34 (Summer 1986): 326-340.

      Using the principle that a visual image is a
      form of rhetoric, Foss analyzes the appeal that
      the Vietnam Veterans Memorial has for the
      American public. She isolates five features
      behind its emotional impact: (1) it violates
      conventional design; (2) its form invites the
      visitor to participate in the national mourning
      (3) it lacks information, thus allowing the
      viewer to bring meaning to it; (4) it does not
      focus on the war itself, but instead, on those
      who died; and (5) its form suggests multiple an
      ambiguous symbolic meanings.

500. Frey-Wouters, Ellen, and Robert Laufer, eds.
      **Legacy of a War: The American Soldier in
      Vietnam**. Armonk, N.Y.: M. E. Sharpe, 1986.

The lengthy study, while it admittedly
ignores women's perspectives on the war, does
indicate how young men, veterans and
non-veterans of the Vietnam era came to feel
about the war in the course of its long
evolution. The book is meant to be a study of
the war's effect on the society of the Vietnam
generation. The authors cover attitudes about
prisoners of war, the enemy, war crimes, and
anti-war activities. Charts of attitudinal data
conclude the book.

501. Greenfield, Meg. "Vietnam: Lessons Still
        Unlearned." **Newsweek** 105 (February 25,
        1985): 96.

Greenfield wrote this article on the eve of
the tenth anniversary of the American withdrawal
from Saigon. In it, she reminds the American
public that it has not found a way to come to
terms with the Vietnam experience nor to
understand it. Current attitudes are still
divided around "we could have won" vs. "we were
totally wrong to be there," and Greenfield
argues that neither attitude has helped
Americans learn better how to think about our
current and future involvements abroad. She
does not see hope for increased national
reflection or the country's ability to learn
from the past.

502. Hart, Lianne, and Jack Kelley. "The 25th
        Anniversary of the First U.S. Deaths in
        Vietnam Calls Up a Legacy of Loneliness and
        Pride." **People Weekly** 22, no. 2 (July 9,
        1984): 37-38.

The authors trace the lives of family members
of Chet Ovnard and Dale Buis, the first U.S.
soldiers to die in combat in Vietnam in July,
1959. Sketches of Ovnard's wife, Mildred, and
Buis's son, Kurt, reveal the scars which remain
after 25 years. Hart notes that Buis's and
Ovnard's names are the first two on the Wall.

503. Hess, Elizabeth. "Vietnam: Memorials of
        Misfortune." In **Unwinding the Vietnam War:
        From War Into Peace**, edited by Reese

Williams, 262-280. Seattle: Real Comet
Press, 1987.

This account describes the origins of the
Vietnam Veterans Memorial and the accompanying
statue. Hess describes Scrugg's initial idea,
Perot's original funding for the project, and
the decision of the VVMF to hold a competition
to select the design. When Lin's design was
selected, the attacks began--Perot's, Earhart's,
and Denton's--which were defeated although not
without adding Hart's more traditional
sculpture. The piece includes interviews with
Lin and Hart as well as a follow-up about
spin-off monuments built later around the
country.

504.   Howett, Catherine M. "The Vietnam Veterans
        Memorial: Public Art and Politics."
        Landscape 28 (1985): 1-9.

Howett discourses first on the problems of
creating public art, particularly monuments
which are not controversial but which truly
commemorate. The controversy surrounding the
acceptance of the design of the Wall both shows
the need for public memorials and the debates
that must emerge when design causes disagreement
on what styles our modern society determines and
accepts. Howett discloses the political causes
behind the controversy, admitting that these,
more than aesthetic concerns, embroiled people
in argument.

505.   Jacoby, Susan. "Women and the War." Chapter 12
        in **The Wounded Generation**, edited by A.D.
        Horne, 193-204. Englewood Cliffs, N.J.:
        Prentice-Hall, 1981.

Jacoby notes that during the Vietnam War, a
commonality between sexes existed unlike that in
previous wars. This commonality permanently
affected changes in male and female
relationships in politics, in economics, and in
society in general. Due to the civil rights,
anti-war, and feminist movements, women gained
and retained their statuses and opportunities
for roles outside the home. Jacoby also
discusses the issue of selective service,

women's obligatory military service, and the
sexism inherent in the anti-war ranks.

506. Knode, Helen. "'Nam' on the Rerun." **In These
      Times** 9, no. 29 (July 10-23, 1985): 24, 23.

      Knode's piece uses films of the past decade
to analyze the meaning of the Vietnam War for
American society. One point is that many films
have exploited the returned and deranged
veteran. Rambo, she finds, is the latest
version of this image. She laments that few of
the films have made political statements;
instead, most have not only created character
stereotypes, but have used Vietnam only as a
backdrop. Knode concludes that we may have
learned very little as a public from our
experiences in Vietnam.

507. MacPherson, Myra. **Long Time Passing: Vietnam
      and the Haunted Generation**. New York: New
      American Library, 1984. New York: Doubleday
      and Co., 1984.

      MacPherson's lengthy book captures the myriad
responses of the Vietnam generation to the war.
Opening with a tale of two brothers in combat,
each of whom embody opposing feelings about the
American roles in Vietnam as does the whole
generation, the book then unravels portrait by
portrait, the complexity of after-effects that
people experience. Sections are devoted to the
uniqueness of both the war and the generation
who fought it, the anti-war and peace movements
and those involved in them, and the bouts with
PTSD suffered by veterans. Special sections
cover "significant others" (in which the
problems of women companions are discussed), and
four chapters deal exclusively with the effects
of the war on women and women veterans.

508. Marling, Karal, and Robert Silberman. "The
      Statue Near the Wall: The Vietnam Veterans
      Memorial and the Art of Remembering."
      Smithsonian Studies in American Art 1, no. 1
      (Spring 1987): 5-29.

      Marling and Silberman's long excursive essay
on the Wall and the statue begins by showing the
influence of **The Deer Hunter** on veterans,

particularly on Scruggs. His battle to
establish a memorial is described, then the
essay, in a lengthy analysis, points up the
shortcomings of Lin's memorial design. The
statue and its symbolic message, on the other
hand, is extolled as a more fitting remembrance
of the war. The Wall's artistry and its effects
are compared and contrasted with Hart's statue,
and the statue definitely wins on all aesthetic
counts.

509.   Romo, Cheryl. "The War Away From Home." **In
       These Times** 7, no. 31 (August 10-23, 1983):
       12-13, 22.

The story covers the activity of the
Vietnamese Resistance Movement which exists
within the United States. One of the largest
resistance organizations actively promotes and
supports resistance against the current
Communist government in Vietnam. Romo gives
details on it and other groups' efforts to
demoralize Vietnamese Communists as well as
details on their efforts to weed out Communist
Vietnamese refugees in the U.S. One incident
spotlighted is the murder of Duong Trong Lam, a
California social worker and anti-war
activitist.

510.   Sevy, Grace. "Lessons of the War: The Effects
       of Disillusionment on the Consciousness and
       Political Thinking of Conservative Women
       Veterans." **Minerva: Quarterly Report on
       Women and The Military** 4, no. 2 (Summer
       1986): 96-132.

For her study on women volunteers and
supporters of the Vietnam War, Sevy chose
twenty-five women and interviewed each. Among
them were nurses and civilians, ranging from
journalists to entertainers, to other
specialists. Among the five areas concentrated
on during the interviews were motives for going
to Vietnam and the pre- and post-Vietnam
experience. A general profile emerged: (1)
most women who served there may have been
lower-middle or middle class; (2) over half were
Catholic; and (3) most had strong religious
backgrounds, a strong sense of duty and respect

for authority, yet were strong-willed. They
tended to be tomboys and disliked their mother's
roles. Most aimed for self-sufficiency. Most
women's motives for going to Vietnam were
idealistic; however, many went through major
shocks during the war and became disillusioned
with the effort quickly. While experiencing
exhilaration and vitality from doing their
tasks, confidence in ideals eroded. Many nurses
carried guilt home with them as a result of
exposure to violence, racism, and sexism. Upon
return to the United States, these women
reported feelings of alienation, the inability
to establish intimate relationships, and
political movement to anti-war, anti-draft
stances.

511.   Sporn, Pam. "Teaching the Vietnam War At a South
        Bronx Alternative High School." **Radical
        Teacher: A Socialist and Feminist Journal on
        the Theory and Practice of Teaching** 28 (May
        1985): 1-4.

        Sporn taught a social studies class on
        "Vietnam: What Happened" in an alternative high
        school for truants and dropouts. Using Kovic's
        book and Baker's **Nam** among others along with
        many films and veteran speakers, she and the
        students co-planned the course content and
        sequence. Sporn gives a nice perspective on
        this new generation of students who know little
        about Vietnam when she discusses why the course
        was successful.

512.   Stewart, Margaret. "Vietnam War Novels in the
        Classroom." **Teaching History** 6, no. 2 (Fall
        1981): 60-66.

        Stewart makes an argument for integrating
        fiction into courses on the war. Arguing that
        the use of fiction creates emotional involvement
        in the war, she discusses several useful works,
        including O'Brien's **Going After Cacciato,**
        Hasford's **The Short-Timers,** and Webb's **Fields of
        Fire**.

513.   Taylor, Sandra, and Rex Casillas. "Dealing with
        Defeat: Teaching the Vietnam War."
        Newsletter of the Society for the History of

American Foreign Relations 11 (December 1980): 9-16.

Taylor surveyed college instructors to see how much they were teaching about the Vietnam War. This first part discusses item by item her findings dealing with books used, learning approaches taken, and ideas espoused.

514.   Taylor, Sandra, and Rex Casillas. "Dealing with Defeat: Teaching the Vietnam War." **Newsletter of the Society for the History of American Foreign Relations** 12 (November 1981): 1-9.

This second part of a published study deals with an analysis of the lessons learned from the war as identified by college professors. The questionnaire used in the study is included.

515.   Tuchman, Barbara W. **The March of Folly: From Troy to Vietnam.** New York: Alfred A. Knopf, 1984.

The book contains a section on Vietnam in which Tuchman traces, decision by decision, the process of increasing American involvement in the Vietnam War. To Tuchman, this process led to the downfall of American self-esteem and public image.

516.   Wimbish, Eleanor. "Letters to Billy: Mother Leaves Letters to Dead Son at Vietnam Veterans Memorial." **McCall's** 112, no. 9 (June 1985): 87, 141.

Wimbish writes of one mother's way of grieving over her son's death in 1969 in Vietnam. After visiting the Wall in 1982, Bill Stocks' mother began writing letters and leaving them at the spot where his name is carved. Not only has this benefitted her, but according to letters received, other strangers in mourning also. Stocks' mother also discusses why she believes she and others leave the momentos.

517.   Young, Marilyn B. "Teaching the War." In

**Unwinding the Vietnam War: From War Into
Peace,** edited by Reese Williams, 356-362.
Seattle: Real Comet Press, 1987.

Young has been teaching about the war at the
college level since 1969. She describes how her
teaching of the war has changed radically over
the years as groups of students become younger
and enter the course with varied perceptions.

The Vietnamese Society

1954-1959

518. Durdin, Peggy. "Uncle Ho's Undisciplined Joy."
      New Yorker 31 (December 17, 1955): 140-147.

   In this feature article for the **New Yorker**,
   Durdin describes her purpose for writing it:
   "Having been acquainted with Hanoi...for fifteen
   years, I was curious to see what had happened to
   it under its new rulers...." Being one of the
   few Americans allowed to visit a week in Hanoi,
   she graphically describes its transformation
   from a somewhat colorful, delightful, and
   "sinful" place to an efficient, clean, yet,
   lifeless city. She compares the "new Hanoi" to
   the old French-influenced city. "Disciplined
   joy" describes the numerous demonstrations in
   which groups of citizens cheerfully chant
   Communist slogans.

519. Ortiz, Elizabeth. "The Mekong Project of
      Vietnam." **Far Eastern Economic Review** 25
      (November 6, 1958): 596-597.

   Ortiz reports on the U.N.'s plans for the
   taming of the Mekong River and the development
   of the land in that region. The project, slated
   for a 20 year period, was to increase the
   standard of living and prosperity through the
   extension of arable land, the use of irrigation
   techniques, the diversification of crop
   production, and the provision of cheap
   electricity. The major problem was locating
   money to pay for the project.

520. Thompson, Virginia, and Richard Adloff.
      Minority Problems in Southeast Asia.
      Stanford: Stanford University Press, 1955.

   The authors' study focuses on regional
   minorities in Southeast Asia, in particular,
   those which may influence the current course of
   events in that region. Not only do they examine
   Vietnam, Laos, and Cambodian minorities, but
   portions of the book discuss the roles of these

important groups. The Buddhist revolts, the
Vietminh, the Pathet Lao, and the Chinese in
each country are among those minorities
mentioned.

1960-1969

521.   Beechy, Atlee, and Winfred Beechy. **Vietnam:
       Who Cares?** Scottsdale, Pa.: Herald Press,
       1968.

       The Beechys describe the pain of the
Vietnamese people who suffer daily because of
the war. The book chronicles the growing
concern of the Mennonite Church for the refugee
situation in Vietnam.

522.   Bergquist, Laura. "Women of Vietnam." **Look**
       30, no. 26 (December 27, 1966): 17-21.

       Bergquist profiles three Vietnamese women,
each in a different place on the social
continuum. In doing so, she describes the
typical life of a woman in war-time Vietnam; fo
most, this means a life without men. Madame Ky
a war widow, and a Saigon bar girl appear as
examples of these women in war.

523.   Chapelle, Dickey. "The Fighting Priest of
       South Vietnam." **Reader's Digest** 83 (July
       1963): 194-200.

       The article features the work of Father Hoa,
a solder-priest of Chinese descent who, to
escape Communism in China, fled to Binh Hung in
South Vietnam in the late 1950's. Chapelle
tells the story of the growth of his village an
of the Diem-sanctioned vigilante army which
aggressively defends it. Her portrait derives
from her five weeks of living with the people
and accompanying the soldiers on raids against
the Viet Cong.

524.   Crawford, Ann. **Customs and Cultures of
       Vietnam**. Rutland, Vt.: Charles E. Tuttle Co.,
       1966.

       Crawford's book reviews the culture of

Vietnam, including the country's history and
involvement with the U.S. since 1954. She
describes the geography and customs, such as
festivals and holidays, as well as social
institutions like the educational systems and
various religions. The book, while not ignoring
the war, does not emphasize it either.

525.   DuBois, Coral. **Social Forces in Southeast
       Asia**. 1949. Reprint. Cambridge, Mass.:
       Harvard University Press, 1959.

DuBois' book contains three essays written on
Southeast Asia during the late 1940's. The
second and third essays discuss key factors
characterizing Southeast Asia as well as
suggestions about the region's future.
Subsequent reprintings of the book leave the
essays largely unchanged, but a lengthy
introduction discusses the actual changes in
Southeast Asia in intervening years in the 1959
printing.

526.   Fitzgerald, Frances. "Life and Death of a
       Vietnamese Village." **New York Times
       Magazine,** section 6 (September 4, 1966): 4,
       20-21, 23-24.

Fitzgerald profiles the village of Duc Lap,
unfortunately placed at the crossroads of a
major South Vietnam government highway and one
main Viet Cong supply trail from the North.
Centering on the people of the hamlet Ap Cha,
Fitzgerald lets the peoples' voices decry the
destruction of their homes, families, and
livelihoods over the course of recent wars which
involve three outside nations and Vietnamese
guerrillas. Fitzgerald's piece clearly
describes how comparatively radical the changes
brought about by Diem's regime and the American
involvement were to Duc Lap and other villages
similarly placed.

527.   _____. "The Power Set: The Fragil
       but Dominating Women of Vietnam." **Vogue** 149
       (February 1, 1967): 154-156, 204-205.

Fitzgerald makes the point early in this

article that Vietnamese women have a long
history of independence and of control of power
Madame Nhu, she contends, is an example in a
long history of delicate, yet ruthless women;
she, however, is far more blatant than most
Vietnamese women. Fitzgerald argues that
women's hidden power of the past (hidden within
families) has prepared them well for the
political upheavals of Saigon life. It also
prepared them for subtle management of an
economy, and women do deal much more in Saigon
business affairs than their Vietnamese husbands
Fitzgerald sees family life and the household as
one of the last cultural strongholds in Vietnam.

528.   Gregerson, Marylin. "Rengao Myths: A Window on
          the Culture." **Practical Anthropology** 16
          (September/October 1969): 216-227.

          Gregerson, a missionary linguist in South
          Vietnam, describes the mythology of the Rengao
          people there. As a Christian anthropologist,
          she views the knowledge of a people's belief
          system as a necessary pre-requisite to
          presenting the teachings of Christianity. Some
          brief mention is made of the Vietnam War's
          impact on the cultural changes within the tribe

529.   Hofman, Margrett. **Vietnamese Viewpoints: A
          Handbook for Concerned Citizens**. Austin,
          Tex.: Published by Author, 1968.

          Written in seven parts, the book covers
          history, debates about American aims in Vietnam,
          future concerns, and the effects of the war.
          Within each topic area, however, exist
          abstracts, statements, and paragraphs, all
          spoken or written by people concerned with the
          war. Hofman uses newspapers, government
          reports, magazines and books as major sources
          for these sections.

530.   Hoskins, Marilyn, and Eleanor Shepherd. **Life
          In a Vietnamese Urban Quarter**. Carbondale,
          Ill.: Center for Vietnamese Studies, Southern
          Illinois University, 1965.

          In an attempt to identify and understand

problems of family and social life in Vietnam,
the authors studied a site in Saigon, Xom Chua
Van Tho, a place of several hundred households.
The two authors taught and conversed with the
community for nine months. The data are
presented as descriptions of conditions,
services, and perspectives, along with case
studies of a cross-section of individuals. They
also develop excellent portraits of the
complicated governance structure and of
interesting recreation options for residents.
One section on economics speaks of opportunities
for women; women's roles are discussed in
sections on birth, marriage, and death.

531.   Louka, Kathryn. **The Role of Population in the
       Development of Southeast Asia**. Washington,
       D.C.: George Washington University, 1960.

       Louka's study includes Laos, Cambodia, and
Viet-Nam together. In her data reports, she
reports North and South production figures
separately. More data on mining, forestry,
agricultural, and rubber production is available
from the South than the North. Her conclusions
suggest that education and industrialization are
needed to buoy up the whole region's economy.

532.   Martin, Linda Grant. "The Thirty Seven Year War
       of the Village of Tananhoi." **The New York
       Times Magazine**, section 6 (October 29, 1967):
       30-31, 87-89, 92-102.

       Tananhoi, 20 miles north of Saigon, is
pictured as a battleground for 30 years before
the American involvement in the Vietnam War.
Described as non-Communist by day and
Vietcong-dominated by night, the town exists as
an example of the schizophrenic existence with
which most Vietnamese citizens must cope. Its
center houses American and South Vietnamese
soldiers and their families, along with
brothels. Its fringes boast huts, gardens, and
businesses of the regular citizenry. A great
deal of Martin's description depicts present
living conditions as well as some historical
perspective on the city, all of which is
sprinkled with cameo portraits of local people.

533. McElroy, Marjorie. "Household Expenditure
         Patterns in Rural South Vietnam." Ph.D.
         diss., Evanston, Ill.: Northwestern
         University, 1969.

         McElroy uses a comprehensive income and
      expenditure survey of rural households in South
      Vietnam to describe expenditure patterns and to
      project future income and demand forecasts. The
      investigation suggests that, while the war may
      impact heavily on the nature of the results of
      the data collection, budget studies of rural
      areas in underdeveloped nations are essential.

534. Sheehan, Susan. "Reporter At Large: LeQuang."
         New Yorker 42 (November 5, 1966): 137-149.

         Sheehan writes a portrait of a 13-year-old
      orphaned South Vietnamese boy making his own way
      in DaNang. Both his parents were killed in the
      war in the early 1960's. Eventually separated
      from his brothers and sisters, too, he migrated
      with neighbors to DaNang where he now survives
      as a seller of ice cream sticks. Sheehan
      describes his daily routines, his methods of
      coping with his homelessness and his survival
      strategies. Poignant, in particular, are his
      dreams for his own future.

535. Starner, Frances. "A Real New Life?" **Far
         Eastern Economic Review** 57 (September 7,
         1967): 456-60.

         Starner's article was the result of a visit
      to Vinh My, a hamlet in the Revolutionary
      Development program labeled a "real new life
      hamlet." These were the 1967 versions of
      "strategic hamlets." The new buildings were
      present, but so were the remains of older
      programs and attempts to free the hamlet from
      Vietcong influence and control. The article
      continues by describing the difficulties of
      developing and maintaining such programs
      throughout the region.

536. Ward, Barbara, ed. **Women in the New Asia: The
         Changing Social Role of Men and Women in
         South and Southeast Asia**. Lanham, Md.:
         UNESCO, 1965.

The book attempts to look at the actual
public status of women in countries in Asia and
Southeast Asia. Ward discusses women's roles in
Viet-Nam in the first section, and issues such
as equal pay, educational access, political
status, and changing family infrastructures
follow in her subsequent chapters.

1970-1979

537. Adams, John, and Nancy Hancock. "Land Economy
      in Traditional Vietnam." **Journal of
      Southeast Asian Studies** 1, no. 2 (September
      1970): 90-98.

The authors argue that Vietnamese society
evolved into a well-functioning social and
economic society before the French and other
Western influences intruded upon the culture.
They maintain that the resistance to the Western
encroachment on the society and the intensity of
it suggest that a healthy progress and growth
continued to occur and that the Vietnamese in no
way wished to see this compromised.

538. Betz, Christiaan. "Vietnam: Social
      Transformation from Confucianism to
      Communism". Ph.D. diss., California
      Institute of Asian Studies, 1977.

Betz analyzes how the Vietnamese society
could be transformed within one century from a
Confucian society to a Communist one. Claiming
that the French domination of Vietnam opened the
way for the shift to Communism, Betz details how
French occupation set up centralized rule in
rural areas while imparting the Western ideas
which undermined the Confucian ethic. The
growth of Communism thus played off the
remaining ideals of both Confucian and French
heritages.

539. Bunch-Weeks, Charlotte. "Asian Women in
      Revolution." **Women** 1, no. 4 (1970): 2-9.

The author describes the complex situation of
women's liberation for Chinese and Vietnamese
women. The section on Vietnamese women is based

on a trip that Bunch-Weeks took to Hanoi in
1970. She notes the close relationship between
both the country's move to socialism and the
defeat of the U.S. with movement towards women's
equality. She analyzes the growth of each
aspect of women's equality and discusses the
role of the Women's Union of North Vietnam in
perpetuating women's equality. A final section
contrasts the women of the south with the
northern women.

540. Eisen-Bergman, Arlene. **Women of Vietnam**. San
      Francisco: People's Press, 1975.

      Eisen-Bergman studies the effects of French
colonialism and U.S. involvement on women in
Vietnamese society. Discussion also includes an
analysis of the effects of the war on American
women. The nature of the Vietnamese resistance
and its identification with women's liberation
provides another interesting facet of women's
lives in this country.

541. _____. "Women's Work in
      Vietnam." **Science for the People** 7, no. 4
      (July 1975): 24.

      Bergman reports on her visit to Vietnam for
three and one half weeks at the invitation of
the Viet Nam Women's Union. She describes the
essential role of women in this people's war.
Part of her tour included areas nearly destroyed
by U.S. bombing, but mostly, she describes the
collective solidarity of women in the DRV, women
who comprise the main force of reconstruction
workers. Strides made for women's identity,
health, and physical needs dominate the report
as do admonishments of Western people for
continued rebuilding.

542. Fitzgerald, Frances. "Annals of War:
      Survivors." **New Yorker** 48 (July 29, 1972):
      56-69.

      In the last of a five part series based on
her book, **Fire in the Lake**, Fitzgerald explores
why the war expanded under Nixon's Presidency
even though he had promised to end it before his

election to office. Extensively analyzed is the
"Vietnamization" of the war.

543. _____. "Journey to North
       Vietnam." **New Yorker** 51 (April 28, 1975):
       96-119.

     Fitzgerald visited North Vietnam, stopping
first in Hanoi where she found buildings similar
to Saigon's, but a lifestyle much different--one
slower, more ordered, and with little threat of
war imposing on the people's daily lives. In
the 19 days she was there, she spoke with
politicians, intellectuals, artists, saw two
more provinces, and engaged in various planned
recreations. Fitzgerald concentrates on
descriptions of the people she met to portray
the intellectual, economic, and industrial
situation in the North. The article ends with
an assessment of the future military movements
by the North in the South.

544. Froines, Ann. "Know Your Enemy." **Liberation**
       15, no. 9 (November 1970): 20, 21, 40.

     The article begins with a lengthy series of
quotes from a DRV cadre in Hanoi. Froines then
counters with ploys she feels Nixon will use to
sway American public opinion to his position and
to debilitate the left wing opposition to his
tactics.

545. _____. "What We'll Leave Behind in
       Saigon." **Women's Press** 2, no. 3 (May 1972):
       13.

     Froines describes the negative legacy left by
Americans for the Vietnamese cities, peasants,
culture and lifestyles. Centering particularly
on women, Froines offers statistics on the
numbers of women forced into prostitution by the
war and those forced into unequal marriages to
Americans out of necessity for survival. She
concludes by restating the nature of the
psychological and cultural violence the U.S.
perpetrates constantly on South Vietnam.

546. Garrett, Banning, and Katherine Barkley, comps.

Two, Three, Many Vietnams. San Francisco:
Canfield Press, 1971.

Garrett and Barkley compiled others' writings
on the wars in Vietnam, Cambodia, and Laos and
on the American protest both in the universities
and within the American public. The book is a
continuation of the **Ramparts** editors' challenge
to the morality of the American war effort.
Many articles cover the Vietnamese experience of
the war as well as the Americans' reactions to
Vietnam both there and in the U.S.

547.   Gough, Kathleen. **Ten Times More Beautiful:**
        The Rebuilding of Vietnam. New York: Monthly
        Review Press, 1978.

Gough visited North Vietnam for 10 days in
1976. Her account includes descriptions of the
economics (including agricultural and industrial
sites), some history of Vietnam, and discussions
of the current life and thoughts of the
Vietnamese. Two chapters are devoted to the
women's role during the conflict and in the
post-American Vietnam war.

548.   Hoskins, Marilyn, and Eleanor Shepherd.
        Building Rapport with the Vietnamese.
        Washington, D.C.: Department of the Navy,
        1971.

Hoskin's report offers advice for
establishing rapport with the Vietnamese. She
outlines several key perceptions which may aid
Westerners: (1) the personal basis of Vietnamese
social life which dictates how one communicates
or acts; (2) the distrust of outsiders; (3) the
importance of traditional beliefs in daily life;
and (4) the perceptions of Americans as people
of unlimited wealth. The rest of the document
offers tips on ways to establish contact without
insulting the Vietnamese.

549.   Ilyama, Patti. "Indochinese Women Discuss
        Struggle." **Militant** 35, no. 17 (May 7,
        1971): 9.

Based on the April, 1971, conference held in

Toronto, Ilyama covers stories by women
prisoners and others on their wartime
experiences and on their present and future
roles as women in a society now dominated by
war.

550.   Lifton, Betty Jean, and Thomas Fox. **Children
       of Vietnam**. New York: Atheneum Pubs., 1972.

       The book compiles a cross-section of
       children. The authors describe the physical
       situation for those who are wealthy and
       sheltered, those in refugee camps, the homeless,
       and those in prison camps. Another group of
       portraits reveals the value shifts that young
       Vietnamese experience because of the pervasive
       American influence. Not forgotten are Amerasian
       and Montagnard children, who are outcasts from
       the other groups. The book concludes with
       stories from the child victims of My Lai who
       retell their versions of what happened there.

551.   Nakahara, Liz. "Vietnamese Women and Culture."
       Gidra 5, no. 9 (September 1973): 18-21.

       The article begins with a history of Vietnam
       from its beginnings through the intrusions of
       Western culture when the French and the
       Americans arrived. As each age is discussed,
       Nakahara brings in contemporary views and
       statuses of Vietnamese women. World War II is a
       turning point in the social history of women
       since the Northern women developed more
       independent roles than Southern women from that
       time on.

552.   Peck, Gerri. "Meeting With Vietnamese Women."
       Willamette Bridge 3, no. 51 (December 17-31,
       1970): 18.

       Peck's article announces plans for three
       conferences to be held in Canada for American
       women, primarily feminists, and Vietnamese
       women. She also reflects on the July, 1969,
       conference with American and Vietnamese women
       and calls for an American women's campaign
       against the war.

553.   Randall, Margaret. **Spirit of the People: The**

Role of Vietnamese Women in the Revolution.
Vancouver, B.C.: New Star Bks., 1975.

This is a book describing the journeys in
North and South Vietnam in the fall of 1974 of a
woman who is extremely pro-North Vietnamese.
She traveled with Arlene Eisen-Bergman gathering
details and forming portraits, in particular of
the women's changing roles during the war years
in both North and South Vietnam.   Her journey
begins in the North and works southward. She
reports her conversations, interviews, and
places visited, noting in particular Vietnamese
women's perspectives on marriage, children,
prison situations, and the war in general.

554.   Shaker, Peggy, and Holmes Brown. **Indochina Is
       People.** Philadelphia: United Church Press,
       1973.

This text covers important aspects--military,
political, social, and historical--of Vietnam.
Summing up each section are suggested plans for
teaching about Vietnam. The last of the five
sections deals with the American involvement in
the war.

555.   Starner, Frances. "South Vietnam: A Need to
       Devalue." **Far Eastern Economic Review** 69
       (July 16, 1970): 22-23.

Starner notes that South Vietnam enjoys the
fruits of a peacetime economy in the midst of a
war economy. However, "Vietnamization" does
affect the economy, and President Thieu
stabilized the piastre by taxation, by cutting
off illegal transactions, and by conceiving
other measures. Starner suggests that Vietnam
needs a long-range plan for economic
development.

556.   _____. "South Vietnam Land Reform:
       Bowing to Revolution." **Far Eastern Economic
       Review** 69, no. 27 (July 2, 1970): 75-77.

Starner analyzes the problems that President
Thieu's government may have as he attempts to
implement a new land reform program. Termed the
"Land-to-the-Tiller" program, the plan takes all

land not directly cultivated and redistributes
it to anyone who farms it. Thus, thousands
should receive title to land they have been
working. Landowners are to be compensated. The
problem is the cost, which many assume will be
taken care of by the U.S. In actuality, the
plan appears to Starner to be another attempt to
counter Vietcong tactics and another way to "win
hearts and minds."

557.   Steinberg, Marsha. "Women of the South."
        Great Speckled Bird 6, no. 2 (January 15,
        1973): 14.

        This is a series of interviews with two women
in the PRG who were in Paris when Steinberg
talked with them. Both Vietnamese women share
in the telling about women's historical roles.
Steinberg points out the disparity between the
sexual equity that Vietnamese men espouse and
their sexist behavior in the home as well as the
negative effect on women caused by the American
presence in Vietnam.

558.   Swerdlow, Amy. "Up from the Mud." **Win**
        Magazine 7, no. 20 (December 15, 1971): 6-10.

        Swerdlow writes of her visit to Hanoi as part
of the Women Strike For Peace group. In this
article, she hails the great strides for women
made since the 1946 DRV constitution which
granted women many rights. Swerdlow examines
the possibility that women's liberation in
Vietnam may be a temporary exploitation, but
concludes that since the consciousness of sex
equity has been raised, this is not a likely
occurrence. In her view, the social changes for
women strike too deeply. Swerdlow concludes
with interesting comparisons of Vietnamese
women's liberation goals vs. those of American
women.

559.   Werner, Jayne. "Cao Dai: The Politics of a
        Vietnamese Syncretic Religious Movement."
        Ph.D. diss., Cornell University, 1977.

        Werner examines the Cao Dai religion in
Vietnam, exploring fully its characteristics,
its historical roots, and the probable social

and political causes for its widespread appeal
to the peasants. She details the status of the
Cao Dai during WWII and during the subsequent
French occupation, outlining the various shifts
in the sect's political alliances during this
war period. She concludes with its absorption
into the NLF in 1960.

560.   _____. "Women, Socialism, and the
        Economy of Wartime North Vietnam, 1960-1975."
        Studies in Comparative Communism 14
        (Summer-Autumn 1971): 165-190.

        Werner discusses the relationship of women's
liberation to socialist doctrine and analyzes
Vietnam as a case in which women's positions
changed as a result of ideology, wartime
conditions, and societal growth. She assesses
the changes in women's roles during the
resistance, noting that women's equality has not
been achieved although women's participation in
society and politics has increased.

561.   White, Christine. **Land Reform in North
        Vietnam**. Washington, D.C.: Agency for
        International Development, 1970.

        White analyzes the agricultural reforms
implemented by the North Vietnamese since the
late 1950's. She describes the two major land
reforms: (1) the abolition of landlord controls
and the establishment of private ownership; and
(2) the abolition of private ownership of land
and the creation of cooperatives (collective
ownership).

562.   Wiegersma, Nancy. "Land Tenure and Land Reform:
        A History of Property and Power in Vietnam."
        Ph.D. diss., University of Maryland, 1976.

        The author's study is an examination of the
process by which the traditional Vietnamese
economy was transformed by French colonialism
into a market economy. The furthering of this
transformation by the Americans, who brought
technological innovations in agriculture to the
Vietnamese society and economy, heightened the
stressful transition. Wiegersma links these

shifts to the continuing political strife during
the Vietnamese wars.

1980-1987

563. Borton, Lady, and Asia Bennet. "American
        Friends Service Committee Group Visits
        Indochinese Women." **Minerva: Quarterly
        Report on Women and the Military** 3, no. 3
        (Fall 1985): 43-48.

        This article is a brief report on a recent
visit by American Friends Service Committee
women to Vietnam and Kampuchea. They made
contact with the members of the Vietnamese
Women's Union and others in order to correspond
about women's situations in Indochina. The
delegates found some evidence of decline in
women's roles in leadership capacities since the
war, but also found the Union actively engaged
in trying to preserve women's rights and in
fighting trends requiring women to play
conservative, traditional female roles.

564. Cooper, Nancy. "Vietnam's Awkward Drill: 10th
        Anniversary Celebrations." **Newsweek** 105 (May
        13, 1985): 48-49.

        Cooper reports on Vietnam's celebration of 10
years of reunification, a celebration which was
a thin veneer over the real problems which still
plague the country. Hints of many
still-confined prisoners exist, and evidence
that many groups are mistreated surfaced.

565. Eisen, Arlene. **Women and Revolution in
        Vietnam.** London: Zed Bks., 1984.

        Eisen writes this book to examine what
happened to the liberated Vietnamese woman after
1975. The book separates into three sections:
(1) a historical background revealing women's
roles of the past and present; (2) several
chapters describing how women's liberation
became a possibility in Vietnamese society; and
(3) a description of the current condition for
women in politics, education, and the family.
Several interesting chapters exist; one is a

section on violence against Vietnamese women,
and another is her description of the work of
the Vietnam Women's Union.

566.   Ferringer, Natalie Jean.   "Crimes Against
         Humanity: A Legal Problem in War and Peace."
         Ph.D. diss., University of Virginia, 1980.

The dissertation looks at the Nuremberg Law
which defines crimes against humanity. As part
of the examination, one chapter discusses the
claims by North Vietnam against the U.S.
Specifically focused on are the problems dealt
with because civilians and combatants were often
not distinct entities.

567.   Gough, Kathleen.   "The Hoa in Vietnam."
         Contemporary Marxism 12 (Spring 1986): 81-91.

Gough writes an update on the condition of
the Hoa in post-war Vietnam. While blaming
their recent misfortunes on both Chinese and
American exploitation, she nevertheless finds
them surviving under the new Vietnam government.

568.   _____.   "The War Against Women."
         Manushi, no. 21 (March 1984): 29-32.

Gough's article describes the treatment of
Vietnamese women by American troops during the
war, specifically identifying prostitution as
the result of the American presence in Vietnam.
The widespread social effects of prostitution
are described as are the new re-education
programs mandated for the rehabilitation of
these women after 1975.

569.   O'Hair, Madalyn Murray.   **War in Vietnam: The
         Religious Connection**.   Austin: American
         Atheist Press, 1982.

O'Hair argues that the war in Vietnam is a
semi-religious one. Beginning with a religious
history, one of dominance and conflict over
Vietnam, she describes the role of religion in
the causes of each Vietnamese factions'
conflicts with the other. Diem's destruction of
the Hao Hoa and Cao Dai are examples. O'Hair,
too, sees the Dulles/McCarthy pursuit of war on

"godless" Communism as a misguided religio-capitalist notion which kept America in the war.

570.   Werner, Jayne. **Peasant Politics and Religious Sectarianism: Peasant and Priest in the Cao Dai in Viet Nam.** Series No. 23. New Haven, Conn.: Yale University Southeast Asia Studies, 1981.

This pamphlet is a complete history of the Cao Dai peasant movement. Werner discusses the sect's economic and social origins as well as the reasons for its success as a political group. Having established that its widespread adoption occurred in part due to social changes under French colonialism, she describes how the Cao Dai sect fared with the Viet Minh and with increased Communist influence at that time.

571.   _____. "Socialist Development: The Political Economy of Agrarian Reform in Vietnam." **Bulletin of Concerned Asian Scholars** 16, no. 2 (April-June 1984): 48-55.

Werner describes both the severe agricultural and economic losses in Vietnam and the reasons for them after the war ended in 1975. She describes, too, the government's decentralized economic reforms, attempts beginning in 1979 to revive the economy after 45 years of war. Werner questions if these are not counter to the socialist vision. Finally, she examines the two forms of decentraliziang production: the family economy, and sub-contracting, noting how each may have significant impact on the Vietnamese society in the years to come. In part of her article, she analyzes the negative effects of the new economic policies on the women's equality movement.

572.   _____. "Women and Revolution: China and Vietnam." **Problems of Communism** 31, no. 1 (1982): 51-55.

Werner argues that Socialist movements, particularly those in the Soviet Union, China, and Vietnam, have supported the notion of women's equality primarily for party advancement

or for mobilization for war, not from a solid
dedication to the ideals of women's liberation.
Werner reviews several studies which analyze the
reasons why women have not achieved full
equality in China or Vietnam in spite of both
ideology and war.

573.   White, Christine.   "Agrarian Reform and National
        Liberation in the Vietnamese Revolution:
        1920-1957."   Ph.D. diss., Cornell University,
        1981.

        White analyzes the relationship between
national liberation and social revolution in the
Democratic Republic of Vietnam from the 1920's
to the 1950's.   In particular, she looks at the
periods of resistance against the French and the
Americans.   Although these times include
extremist and often harmful policies of land
reform, by the 1950's, the DRV had completed
both a social revolution and achieved
independence.

574.   White, Christine.   "Women's Double Day in
        Vietnam."   **Sojourner: The Women's Forum** 12,
        no. 8 (April 1987): 17-18.

        White probes the reasons for the continuing
economic and social inequality between men and
women in Vietnam today.   While comparing this
problem with other situations of inequity, the
author also analyzes how the images shown in
America of Vietnamese women forced American
women of the time to question their own societal
roles.   The relationships among feminism, the
American anti-war movement, and the Vietnamese
woman are discussed, and White suggests that
western feminism may now be able to give back
some inspiration to the Vietnamese woman.

1960-1969

575.   Adler, Renata.   "The Price of Peace is
       Confusion."   **New Yorker** 41, no. 43 (December
       11, 1965): 195-202.

       Adler identifies three phases of 1960's
       social criticism, all taken up by student
       revolutionaries. One of them is the Peace
       Movement which aims to influence political
       leaders to end the war in Vietnam and ultimately
       to change the aggressive tactics of American
       foreign policy. Adler very copiously describes
       the Washington Convention held by various peace
       group delegates located at the city's Harrington
       Hotel. Included too is a description of an
       accompanying peace march. Adler suggests that
       the peace groups were riddled with disagreement
       about how to proceed among the various factions.

576.   _____.   "Letter From the Palmer House."
       New Yorker 43, no. 31 (September 23, 1967):
       56-88.

       Adler describes the failure of the New
       Politics Convention in Chicago to attract
       radical delegates opposed to the American
       involvement in Vietnam. Her extensive article
       proposes reasons why the convention failed: (1)
       the failure to find a common language and
       vocabulary; and (2) the failure of many factions
       to communicate and reach consensus on views
       about important issues.

577.   Gray, Francine du Plessix.   "The
       Ultra-Resistance."   **New York Review of Books**
       13 (September 25, 1969): 11-22.

       Gray describes what she terms the "radical
       core of the peace movement." She opens by
       describing several incidents of destruction of
       draft records in protest of the Vietnam War,
       including one by an all-woman band of draft
       board resisters, the Women Against Daddy
       Warbucks (Manhattan). This "ultra-resistance"
       used tactics of violence and sacrifice to

instigate more militant reactions. The
evolution of this resistance from older to
younger resisters is traced; she showcases the
Milwaukee Twelve as an example of the new
ultra-resistance tactics. At less length Gray
covers the Pasadena 3, the Chicago 15, and a
women's resistance group.

578. Long, Margaret. "The Movement." **New South**
     21, no. 1 (Winter 1966): 1, 94-103.

     The article is actually about the civil
rights movement in America, but in it, Long does
discuss the civil rights activists' involvement
with the peace movement and the stance of many
black leaders against the Vietnam War.

579. Morris, Marjorie. **And/Or: Antonyms for Our
     Age**. New York: Harper and Row Pubs., 1967.

     This is a collection of quotations and
photographs, which juxtapose scenes of the
Vietnam War and violence with scenes of human
love and compassion. The book is meant as a war
protest publication.

580. Woodward, Beverly. "Vietnam and the Law: The
     Theory and Practice of Civil Challenge."
     Commentary 46, no. 5 (November 1968): 75-86.

     Woodward analyzes issues involved in the
civil disobedience cases of the Boston Five
(Spock, Coffin, Goodman, Raskin, and Ferber) who
were found guilty of counseling young men to
violate the draft laws during the Vietnam War.
She draws vital distinctions among "civil
challenge" (protesting the draft with the intent
of changing the law), and "draft evasion,"
"draft refusal," or "draft challenge." Examined
closely is the Supreme Court's refusal to settle
cases of a similar nature to the Boston Five,
the issue of Congressional powers vs. executive
powers to declare war, and the reasons for the
confusions involved in this particular case.
Woodward argues for more avenues of bringing
issues to the higher courts without breaking the
law.

1970-1979

581.   Agnew, Kim, and Marty Mitchell. "What Would
          Madame Binh Think?" **Off Our Backs** 1, no. 22
          (May 27, 1971): 2.

          The short article is a story on the Vietnam
       veterans who were in Washington, D.C. to protest
       the war. The authors mingled with the veterans
       on the Mall, interviewing several. Their
       descriptions leave a clearly unromantic picture
       of the American G.I., one which shows young men
       both victimized and settled in a prolonged
       adolescence.

582.   Aldous, Joan, and Irving Tallman. "Immediacy of
          Situation and Conventionality as Influences
          on Attitudes Toward War." **Sociology and
          Social Research** 56, no. 3 (April 1972):
          356-367.

          Noting the general student hostility toward
       the Vietnam War in the early 1970's, the authors
       set about to study whether or not people were
       hostile to war in general or toward this
       specific war. Findings revealed several
       insights: (1) those with higher educational
       levels advocated more military restraints in any
       situation; (2) men and women who were more
       inner-oriented and self-conscious rather than
       vocation-oriented tended to advocate more
       pacifism; (3) women tended to be more pacifistic
       than men; and (4) attitudes did not favor
       anti-war methods for every threatening situation
       or every possible war.

583.   Bannon, John, and Rosemary Bannon, eds. **Law,
          Morality and Vietnam: The Peace Militants and
          the Courts**. Bloomington, Ind.: Indiana
          University Press, 1974.

          The authors' exploration centers around the
       conflicts between law and morality relating to
       the Vietnam War. Acknowledging the overt
       efforts of the peace movement to involve the
       judicial system in the struggle to end the war,
       they then examine several landmark trials
       including those of the Fort Hood Three and the
       conspiracy trials of Dr. Spock and the

Catonsville Nine. The book concludes with
various views presented on the nature of civil
disobedience.

584.   Bell, Bruce, and Beverly Bell. "Desertion and
        Anti-War Protest: Findings from the Ford
        Clemency Program." **Armed Forces and Society**
        3 (Spring 1977): 433-443.

        The authors conducted this study in order to
determine the relationship between a deserter's
ideas and attitudes toward the war and the act
of desertion itself. The subjects were army men
participating in President Ford's Clemency
Program. They discovered that the profile of
these deserters merged with that of deserters of
other wars; they were less well-educated, were
trouble-makers, and tended to not be a part of
any resistance to the Vietnam War.

585.   Butwin, Miriam, and Pat Pirmantgen, eds.
        **Protest II: Civil Rights and Black
        Liberation. The Anti-War Movement New
        Directions in Protest**. Minneapolis, Minn.:
        Lerner Pubns., Co., 1972.

        The book contains three sections, all
delineated by the title of the book. Section II
deals with the protest of the Vietnam War.
Beginning with a brief history of the wars in
Vietnam before American involvement, various
forms of American war protest are then
developed; demonstrations, teach-ins, rallies,
and marches are among them. They include a
large section focusing on student protest and
mention is made of the women's peace efforts
also.

586.   Connally, Orabelle. "Anti-War Work by
        Discouragement of Warriors: A Critique of
        Anti-War Tactics Used Among Naval Personnel
        in the Vietnam War." **Journal of Sociological
        and Social Welfare** 4 (January-March 1977):
        626-638.

        Connally examines competing and erosive
structures of authority within the Navy while
anti-war fervor was at its height in military
men. Even though the anti-war movement shook

these authority structures and used its flaws
against the Navy, the movement failed to
diminish Navy participation in Vietnam.
Connally surveys methods of anti-war protest
fostered by these groups.

587.   Crowell, Joan. **Fort Dix Stockade: Riot and
       Demonstration**. New York: Link Bks., 1974.

   Crowell, a free-lance writer, decided to
locate and interview young draft resisters and
record their experiences and reasons for
protesting the Vietnam War. She was able to
visit and interview imprisoned resisters at Ft.
Dix after a major riot there. The book brings
out war issues, the treatment and abuse of
prisoners, and follows up on the trials of some
resisters.

588.   Erskine, Hazel. "The Polls: Is War a Mistake?"
       Public Opinion Quarterly 34 (Spring 1970):
       134-150.

   Erskine's poll reveals that opposition to the
Vietnam War in America was more widespread among
the general public than among young people as a
sub-group. In fact, some evidence showed more
positive backing of the war among the youth.
However, in comparison to dissent about World
War I and the Korean War, anti-war sentiment
about Vietnam appeared lower overall.

589.   Field, Martha. "Problems of Proof in
       Conscientious Objector Cases." **University of
       Pennsylvania Law Review** 120 (May 1972):
       870-940.

   Field's long paper is, in part, a history of
the draft in the United States. She explains
the normal process of applying for conscientious
objector status and the decision-making and
appeal processes involved in some cases. Field
offers a proposal for changing the
administration of the draft to insure a more
equitable selection process. While not totally
focused on the Vietnam War, the lengthy analysis
and proposal are occasioned by it, and the cases
quoted stem from it.

590.   Fonda, Jane. "We Have Never Built So Many
           Roads." **Freedom News** 6, no. 9 (September
           1972): 2.

        Fonda witnessed and now describes American
        bombing of non-industrial targets in North
        Vietnam while she visited. Specifically, she
        questions the bombing of dikes that the North
        Vietnamese have built. She also refutes Nixon's
        denials that civilian targets were being hit.

591.   _____. "Who's Really Being Brainwashed?"
           Great Speckled Bird 6, no. 20 (May 28, 1973):
           14-15.

        Fonda asks why the POW's reports of
        atrocities are unquestionably believed while
        Americans immediately doubt the stories of
        American-inflicted atrocities revealed by
        veterans during the Winter Soldier
        investigations. She fails to condone the effort
        of the American government to make heroes of the
        POW's, noting that only those who speak the
        current government line are accorded hero status
        anyway. Fonda's points all lead to this
        conclusion: that the American public, not the
        American POW's, have been brainwashed, not by
        Vietnamese, but by our own government.

592.   Fox, Tina. "Was Feminist for the FBI."
           Majority Report 4, no. 25 (May 3, 1975): 11.

        The brief story replays the time that Mary Jo
        Cook, an undercover agent for the FBI, spent
        with various anti-war, peace, and feminist
        groups. One of the groups she spent a good deal
        of time with was the VVAW.

593.   Gray, Francine du Plessix. **Divine
           Disobedience: Profiles in Catholic
           Radicalism.** New York: Alfred A. Knopf, 1970.

        Gray examines the lives and the dissent of
        several men, including the Berrigans and the
        Catonsville Nine, whose dissent involved
        opposing the Vietnam War. Her focus is the
        radical element of the Catholic Church.

594.   Gross, Harriet Engel. "Jane Kennedy: Making

History Through Moral Protest." **Frontiers** 2, no. 2 (1977): 73-81.

Gross writes a case study of one woman's contribution to the protest movement against the Vietnam War. Kennedy, a Chicago nurse and anti-war activist, spent time in prison because of her moral protest. Gross traces the growth of Kennedy's commitment to her stand on the war. Beginning with involvement in the civil rights movement in the 1960's, Kennedy soon began attending peace activities and meeting others who protested the war. Gross speculates that personal concern grew to public commitment when protest activity became a group concern. Kennedy herself believes that her longterm irritations over constraints forced on women in our society also played a significant role in her protest.

595. _____. "Micro and Macro Level Implications for a Sociology of Virtue: The Case of Draft Protesters to the Vietnam War." **Sociological Quarterly** 18 (Summer 1977): 319-339.

Gross asserts that identity formation based on self-directed acts of virtue exist more commonly than thought. She studied types of Vietnam war protestors in order to describe this phenomenon.

596. Harris, Janet. **Students In Revolt**. New York: McGraw-Hill Bks., 1970.

Harris looks at key universities and student groups whose protests in the early and mid-1960's bespoke a general national and global unrest among young people. Although issues of protest extend well beyond antagonism toward America's role in the Vietnam War, Harris' accounts detail the protestors' antagonism toward that phenomenon often. Even her accounts of student protest in Czechoslovakia, France, and Germany reveal the international student concern about the war. While, of all the issues, race is focused on more than the war, the book offers good insight into the anti-war sentiments of young people.

597. Horan, Jean. "Jane Fonda: Women, War and
          Politics." **Off Our Backs** 4, no. 4 (March
          1974): 4-5.

      The article is really a narrative by Jane
      Fonda resulting from an interview with her.
      Fonda discusses both the status of women in
      North Vietnam and efforts by the Vietnamese
      Women's Union to insure women's rights. She
      also analyzes why American women might have left
      the male-dominated anti-war movement, and
      suggests that American women, like Vietnamese
      women, ought to have formed a politically based
      and independent movement.

598. Kasinsky, Renee. **Refugees From Militarism:
      Draft-Age Americans in Canada.** New
          Brunswick, N.J.: Transaction Bks., 1976.

      Kasinsky discusses the American men who
      resisted the draft and fled to Canada. Using
      some examples, she talks about who came and why,
      the careers available to them, and the reactions
      of the Canadian people and government. The
      exiles' adjustments are also examined.

599. Miller, Judith. "Amnesty: Eddie McNally Comes
          Home." **The Progressive** 38 (February 1974):
          17-21.

      Miller, putting at 39,000 the number of
      American deserters during the Vietnam War, tells
      of the surrender of two men, Eddie McNally and
      Lew Simon. McNally, who went underground in
      this country for four years, worked through the
      amnesty group, Safe Return, to obtain his
      discharge from the army and to avoid a prison
      sentence. Miller uses his story as a case
      example not only of the deserter (Eddie did
      serve in Vietnam), but as a way to spotlight the
      numbers, types, and goals of the amnesty
      organizations which try to negotiate the return
      of other deserters.

600. Paley, Grace. "I Guess It Must Have Been
          Someone." **Win Magazine** 7, no. 9 (May 15,
          1971): 30-35.

      Paley, in reaction to this edition's

publication of a serviceman's diary, publishes a
piece in which accounts by POW American pilots
are described. Each describes his capture and
captivity as satisfactory. Interspersed with
these stories are scenes of the devastation of
civilian life and property wrought by the
bombing missions. The message seems to lead to
the conclusion that the American pilots are
evil, while the Vietnamese are totally virtuous.

601. Parmalee, Patty Lee. "Vietnam Vets Charge U.S.
     with War Crimes." **Guardian** 23, no. 20 (May
     13, 1971): 7.

Parmalee describes the three-day testimony
against the war by over 100 Vietnam veterans in
the Winter Soldier investigations. Supported by
the VVAW, the three days of testimony indicted
the U.S. military for war crimes, testifying
that atrocities were not isolated cases. The
report details parts of the stories revealed by
veterans and points out that most veterans
participated in the crimes because they had been
taught to think of the Vietnamese as less than
human.

602. Potts, Linda. "The Conscientious Objector:
     From the Pearly Gates to Walden." **Tennessee
     Law Review** 37 (Spring 1970): 595-697.

Potts examines current legal issues relating
to the status of the conscientious objector.
Although not directly about the Vietnam War, the
subject refers to issues and cases brought up by
this war (its "undeclared" status caused
questions about the legitimacy of conscription).
Cases involving conscientious objectors to the
Vietnam War are also cited.

603. Shaffer, Helen. "Amnesty Question."
     Editorial Research Reports 2 (August 9,
     1972): 603-620.

Arguments for and against amnesty by American
leaders are included as is a history of amnesty
in the United States. One issue Shaffer tackles
is the unwillingness of Vietnam War resisters to
accept "forgiveness" for taking what they
considered to be moral actions.

604.   Silva, Ruth.   "The Constitution, The
        Conscientious Objector, and the 'Just' War."
        Dickinson Law Review 75, no. 1 (Fall 1970):
        1-61.

        Silva defines four types of conscientious
        objectors, and concentrates on an analysis of
        the fourth category, "religious objectors to a
        particular war," since this group dominated the
        courts since 1969.   She illustrates the problems
        with the court's deciding on conscientious
        objector status by illustrating cases; for
        example, in United States v. Bowen and United
        States v. McFadden, both were Roman Catholics
        who objected to serving in Vietnam because the
        war did not fit the religious characteristics of
        a "just war."   The Supreme Court also heard
        several other cases illustrating the "Nuremberg"
        objections.   Silva discusses problems in
        defining "religion," "religious establishment,"
        "free exercise (of beliefs)," and "equal
        protection" rights as they relate to
        conscientious objector status.

605.   Thorne, Barrie.   "Protest and the Problem of
        Credibility: Uses of Knowledge and
        Risk-Taking in the Draft Resistance Movement
        of the 1960's." **Social Problems** 23, no. 2
        (Winter 1975): 111-123.

        Thorne examines how protest movements
        establish authority and win supporters.   Two
        strategies seem implicit: (1) draft counseling
        by resistance groups; and (2) encouraging
        non-cooperation of those receiving draft
        notices.   Thorne concludes that non-cooperation
        was more visible during the war, yet, each
        method incurred some backlash.

606.   _____.   "Women in the Draft Resistance
        Movement: A Case Study of Sex Roles and
        Social Movements." **Sex Roles** 1, no. 2 (June
        1975): 179-195.

        Thorne studies the role of women involved in
        the Resistance movement in America during the
        Vietnam War.   She describes the increasing
        disillusionment of women within this movement to
        the strong bias against women and links this

frustration to the eventual formation of a
women's resistance and to the embracing of
feminism. The formation of a new social cause
follows from classical conditions that usually
cause such new movements to arise.

607. Vogelgesang, Sandy. **The Long Dark Night of
the Soul: The American Intellectual Left and
the Vietnam War**. New York: Harper and Row
Pubs., 1974.

Vogelgesang writes about the shift in
intellectuals' viewpoints on the Vietnam War
from the Kennedy to the Nixon eras. She finds
three basic perspectives on the war through
which many American intellectuals of the Left
developed: (1) the war was a product of poor
judgment, a mistake; (2) the war was an immoral
crusade; and (3) the war was a criminal
endeavor. The leftists and what they wrote
comprise the first part of the book, then
Vogelgesang traces many of their political
responses through Nixon's election.

608. _____. "The Long Dark Night of
the Soul": American Intellectual Left versus
Johnson's Vietnam Policy, 1964-1968." Ph.D.
diss., Tufts University: Fletcher School of
Law and Diplomacy, 1971.

In a thorough review of American
intellectuals and the Vietnam War, Vogelgesang
delves into historical influences on
mid-twentieth century intellectuals, their
relationships to American youth, and government
policies that generated friction in these
groups. Problems and issues are discussed
within the framework of the various roles that
intellectuals experienced: (1) as moral
guardians of society; (2) as alienated people;
(3) as powerful/powerless people; and (4) as war
critics. She mentions a few women intellectuals
and their work, among them Grace Paley and Mary
McCarthy.

609. Waters, Mary A. **G.I.'s and Their Fight
Against the War**. New York: Pathfinder Press,
1971.

Waters examines the anti-war sentiment of
Vietnam generation G.I.'s by citing one of the
first troop supported anti-military
protests--the "Bring the Troops Home" movement
immediately following WWII, a protest by
America's and other country's G.I.'s against
occupation of other countries. The Vietnam War
protest by both civilians and soldiers is seen
in the context of a history of steadily arising
protest against unpopular causes.

610.   Wickes, Mariette.   "Here We Are We've Been
       Detained." **Off Our Backs** 1, no. 22 (May 27,
       1971): 4-5.

The author took part in the May, 1971
anti-war protests in Washington, D.C. Detained
in a camp for several days, she describes the
protestors, who they are, their protest ideals,
and subsequent events during the several days of
protest. Her account humanizes the crowds of
protestors.

611.   Woodstone, Norma Sue.   **Up Against the War**.
       New York: Tower Publications, 1970.

Woodstone focuses on young Americans'
resistance to the Vietnam War. Opening sections
characterize the resisters, also probing reasons
for widespread American dissent. Relying on
case studies of resisters who chose to defy the
draft rather than go, Woodstone's book
chronicles the rise of protest from the early to
late 1960's. Also analyzed are the lives of
those resisters who choose exile and those who
support them.

612.   Wright, Laurie.   "WSP/Women Strike for Peace."
       Off Our Backs 1, no. 16 (January 21, 1971):
       9.

This brief article reports on the Women
Strike for Peace Workshops in Milwaukee. The
emerging focus at the meeting was "setting the
date for withdrawal of all U.S. troops from
Vietnam."

1980-1987

613. Bradley, Anna. "A Nation of Heroes." **Win**
      Magazine 18, no. 5 (March 15, 1982): 14-15.

      Bradley writes of her interview with Ngo Ba
      Thanh, currently the vice-president of the
      Vietnam Women's Union, and a woman who staunchly
      agitated for peace and helped lead the South
      Vietnamese peace movement in the 1970's. She
      addresses reasons why women may have lost some
      presence in the government, noting that women's
      political power is actually unchanged.

614. Darby, Henry E., and Margaret Rowley. "King on
      Vietnam and Beyond." **Phylon** 47 (March,
      1986): 43-50.

      The two authors investigated and describe
      here King's opposition to the war in Vietnam.
      Drawn primarily from King's 1967 "Beyond
      Vietnam" speech, they review King's seven
      reasons why he opposed the war. They further
      recount the stands he took against the war
      before his assassination, finally making the
      point that King's thoughts on the war were
      prophetic.

615. Jackson, Miriam Ruth. "We Shall Not Be Moved: A
      Study of the May 4th Coalition and the Kent
      State University Gymnasium Controversy of
      1977." Ph.D. diss., Purdue University, 1982.

      This study probes the causes for the defeat
      of the Kent State May 4th Coalition in its
      effort to persuade the Board of Trustees to
      preserve a national symbol to student opposition
      of the Vietnam War. The study also examines the
      role played by groups of people who had come to
      terms with the war and the Kent State slayings
      as opposed to the American public which, Jackson
      postulates, has not. This work is also a
      thoughtful examination of the Coalition itself.

616. Klejment, Anne. "In the Lions' Den: The Social
      Catholicism of Daniel and Philip Berrigan,
      1955-1965." Ph.D. diss., State University of
      New York at Binghamton, 1981.

This study examines the social welfare
commitments of both Daniel and Philip Berrigan
from their early ideas through their expanding
commitment to anti-war resistance. The two
men's ideological stances are discussed in the
context of family, religious upbringing, and th
social milieu of the 1960's.

617.   Linder, Patricia Lofton. "World-View and
       Rhetorical Choice: The Ideology and Tactics
       of Selected Antiwar Protest Groups in the
       Vietnam Era." Ph.D. diss., Northwestern
       University, 1980.

       Linder defines the idea of "world-view" and
       explains the methodology involved in linking it
       to rhetorical choices as overt expressions of
       world views. Two groups analyzed are The
       Resistance and the Vietnam Veterans Against the
       War. Each is distinctive in its rhetoric and
       world view.

618.   Miller, Melissa, and Phil Shenk, eds. **The
       Path of Most Resistance: Stories of Mennonit
       Conscientious Objectors Who Did Not Cooperat
       With the Vietnam War Draft**. Scottsdale, Pa.
       Herald Press, 1982.

       The book is about 10 young Mennonite men who
       chose to resist the draft rather than serve in
       the usual alternative service capacity for
       C.O.'s. Miller and Shenk introduce each man's
       circumstance and narrate his experience while
       examining the motives behind each person's
       decision to resist.

619.   Zaroulis, Nancy, and Gerald Sullivan, eds.
       **Who Spoke Up? American Protest Against the
       War in Vietnam, 1963-75**. Garden City, N.Y.:
       Doubleday and Co., 1984.

       The co-authors chronicle the beginnings of
       the American anti-war movement. Because this
       Vietnam War protest was an American born and
       bred movement, the authors begin with Norman
       Morrison's self-immolation in protest in 1965,
       then explore the build-up of protest in 1963-64
       through the Winter Soldier hearings in 1971.
       The book concludes with the dedication of the

Wall. Key people covered include the Berrigans,
Tom Hayden, and Wayne Morse, but the entire text
is peopled with well-known protestors.

The Psychological and Human Impact of the War

Returning Veterans: Men and Women

1970-1979

620. Granberg, Donald and Gail Corrigan.
"Authoritarianism, Dogmatism and Orientations
Toward the Vietnam War." **Sociometry** 35, no.
3 (September 1972): 468-476.

The authors studied the relationships among
authoritarianism, dogmatism and attitudes toward
the Vietnam War. The study reveals, among other
results, a strong relationship between hawkish
attitudes and authoritarianism.

621. Haley, Sarah. "When the Patient Reports
Atrocities." **Archives of General Psychiatry**
30 (1974): 191-196.

Haley studied the mental psychological status
of 40 male veterans who were responsible for
acts of atrocity during the war. A major
question of the study, however, is to not only
describe various states associated with the
confessions, but to probe how a therapist might
best react to such occasions in order to better
assist the veteran's adjustment. Haley
concludes that the establishment of a trusting
relationship between client and counselor is
itself the treatment needed to help this
veteran.

622. Holden, Constance. "Agent Orange Furor
Continues to Build." **Science** 205 (August 24,
1979): 770-772.

Holden's report describes the result of
outcries by veterans which is the reluctant
agreement on the part of the U.S. government and
military to undertake some studies on the
possible links between herbicide warfare (Agent
Orange) and veteran health problems. Holden
describes such efforts and their possible impact
which is likely to be minimal as the cynical

veteran groups realize. She suggests that Agent
Orange has become a symbol for the aftereffects
of the war.

623.   Kuhn, Mary Ann. "War Casualty: Verdict for a
         Troubled Vet." **Time** 113, no. 8 (February 19,
         1979): 23.

         This short account describes the incident
         that brought Vietnam vet John Coughlin into
         court. The court's decision to treat him as a
         victim of "traumatic war neurosis" and not hold
         him criminally responsible for his actions is
         precedent-setting; i.e., Vietnam-caused
         disorders can be taken into account in criminal
         charges. Kuhn points out the difference in
         American attitudes that this decision reflects;
         veterans no longer exist as scapegoats, and the
         Coughlin case is, to her, a recognition of the
         public neglect and blame that returning veterans
         received upon their re-entry into the States.

624.   Martindale, Melanie, and Dudley Posten.
         "Variations in Veteran/Nonveteran Earning
         Patterns Among World War II, Korea and
         Vietnam War Cohorts." **Armed Forces and
         Society** 5, no. 2 (Winter 1979): 219-243.

         The authors set out to test the assumption
         that military service provides a bridge between
         a low-skill, low-income background and a better
         economic situation, especially for black and
         Mexican-American minorities. They found that,
         in general, black and Mexican-American veterans
         were better able to make better earnings than
         their non-veteran cohorts. This finding proved
         true for groups related to all three wars, but
         were not as strong for the Vietnam War era
         group.

625.   Michelotti, Kopp, and Kathryn Gover. "The
         Employment Situation of Vietnam Era
         Veterans." **Monthly Labor Review** 95 (December
         1972): 7-15.

         Gover and Michelotti report that the jobless
         rate for veterans in 1972 dropped from past
         years due to both upswings in the economy and
         fewer discharges from the military. Other

factors are race differences, participation in special benefits, and the continually unemployed.

626. Norman, Liane Ellison.   "The Spell of the War."
The Center Magazine 12 (March-April 1979):
72-78.

Norman discourses on the emotions and perceptions about war that characterize soldiers' attitudes toward combat. Drawing on the writing in a Vietnamese soldier's diary and Caputo's and Herr's memoirs, she probes the curious mixture of emotions experienced by troops. Her article concludes with a description of the negative impact of war on the human psyche, especially on the American one.

627. Waldman, Elizabeth.   "Vietnam War Veterans
Transition to Civilian Life." **Monthly Labor
Review** 93 (November 1970): 21-29.

Waldman's study focuses on the impact of a reduction of personnel in the Armed Forces on civilian and veteran job-seekers in 1969 and 1970. Findings include: (1) a lack of participation by veterans in education benefits (G.I. Bill); (2) limited participation in reemployment rights; and (3) comparative unemployment rates for veterans and non-veterans.

1980-1987

628. Adams, Margaret.   "An Inpatient Treatment Unit."
American Journal of Nursing 82, no. 11
(November 1982): 1704-1705.

Adams describes the problems treatment teams encounter when assisting Vietnam veterans with PTSD; bearing the brunt of anger and not being trusted are two examples. She also describes the particular differences between veteran responses to female therapists vs. their male therapists, and finds that women therapists quickly came to feel alienated by their male clients. One solution evolved to overcome this

isolation of women therapists, and Adams
outlines it.

629.   Attebury, Maj. Mary A. "Women Vets Gather in
        Washington, D.C. To Kick Off Vietnam Women's
        Memorial Fund-raising Drive." **Minerva:
        Quarterly Report on Women and the Military** 4,
        no. 4 (Winter 1986): 32-35.

        Attebury describes the organizational efforts
        to raise money for the Vietnam Women's Memorial
        by the Vietnam Women's Memorial Project. The
        fund is aimed at adding a monument to the
        present Vietnam Veterans Memorial, a statue of
        a woman in fatigues who will symbolize both
        military and civilian women who served.

630.   Bagnatoria, Lisa. "Where Are They Now? J.
        Farley's Current Life and Experiences as a
        Marine in 1965." **People Weekly** 23, no. 11
        (March 18, 1985): 98-101.

        The story is about doorgunner James Farley's
        experiences in Vietnam in 1965. Since then, he
        has married and lost that marriage, failed to
        complete his education, and suffered through the
        failure of a business.

631.   Boulanger, Ghislane. "Post-Traumatic Stress
        Disorder: An Old Problem with a New Name."
        In **The Trauma of War: Stress and Recovery in
        the Vietnam Veteran**, edited by Stephen
        Sonnenberg, Arthur Blank, John Talbott,
        13-29. Washington, D.C.: American
        Psychiatric Press, 1985.

        Boulanger traces the history of the
        psychological disorder PTSD, revealing her
        profession's reluctance to accept it as a
        psychological problem. She analyzes the
        characteristics of PTSD as well as the
        prevalence of it among Vietnam veterans.
        Boulanger also discusses the issues surrounding
        predisposition for PTSD, finding that although
        men from less stable families tended to develop
        symptoms of PTSD most often, men from stable
        backgrounds did also depending on the
        stressfulness of their combat tours.

632.   Boulanger, Ghislane, and Charles Kadushkin, eds.

The Vietnam Vet Redefined: Fact and Fiction.
Hillsdale, N.J.: Lawrence Erlbaum Assocs.,
1986.

The book is a compilation of papers presented
on the theme "Further Legacies of Vietnam." The
editors contribute articles on Post Traumatic
Stress Disorder while five other women
contribute other chapters dealing with the theme
of the aftermath of the war. One chapter by
Sheryl Canter deals specifically with women
friends of men who were in Vietnam.

633.   Bupp, Cheryl Sorensen. "An Examination of Shame
and Guilt Among the American Veterans of the
Vietnam Conflict." Ph.D. diss., University
of Minnesota, 1983.

In this study on the nature of shame and
guilt experienced by Vietnam era veterans, Bupp
finds that her data does not support the notion
that service experience is a major contributor
to levels of shame and guilt now experienced by
these veterans. She finds a relationship
between guilt and receiving psychiatric care,
and with low guilt and receiving treatment for
drug dependency, however.

634.   Carney, Caren Marie. "Perceived Symptoms among
U. S. Army Nurses: The Effects of Combat
Environment, Gender, Control, and Social
Support." Ph.D. diss., The George Washington
University, 1985.

Carney compares the health status of Army
Nurse Corps Vietnam veterans with veterans of
the same time period who were assigned
elsewhere. Because nurses served in
"psychological" combat zones, many developed
stress symptoms which may put them at a greater
health risk in later life. Carney's study also
suggests certain military changes for nurses
which might benefit nurses in similar future
assignments.

635.   Chandler, Mary. "Where Are They Now?
Recollections of Charter Pilot R.D. Hedrix."
People Weekly 23, no. 16 (April 22, 1985):
63-64.

As part of its search for people involved in Vietnam, **People Weekly**'s Mary Chandler interviews Robert Hedrix, a civilian pilot and veteran who was in Southeast Asia from 1955-70. Hedrix describes the final days of April, 1975, as the last Americans and Vietnamese were being evacuated. He himself was one of the helicopter pilots during those evacuations. Hedrix also explains his continued pro-military, pro-Vietnam involvement views.

636.   Corbit, Irene Elizabeth. "Veterans' Nightmares: Trauma, Treatment, Truce." Ph.D. diss., The Union for Experimenting Colleges and Universities, 1985.

The study follows a seven month project, a dream group composed of Vietnam Veterans attempting to deal with their reoccurring nightmares of the war. Corbit discovered that veterans experiencing dream therapy could transform their nightmares into spiritual dreams with a healing power.

637.   Denzler, Brenda. "Acceptance and Avoidance: The Woman Vietnam Vet." **Minerva: Quarterly Report on Women and the Military** 5, no. 2 (Summer 1987): 72-96.

Denzler addresses the problem of male Vietnam veterans not giving credence to the female Vietnam veteran's needs. The article speculates on this tension as a possible reason why women veterans fail to avail themselves of self-help rap groups. Part of the article outlines a history of nursing in the military and addresses the gender issues implicit in a female's military experience. Denzler sees the veterans' groups, composed of men and women alike, as potentially powerful tools to reshape our cultural images of war, masculinity, and women's roles.

638.   Dewane, Claudia. "Posttraumatic Stress Disorder in Medical Personnel in Vietnam." **Hospital and Community Psychiatry** 35, no. 12 (December 1984): 1232-1234.

Dewane examines the incidence of PTSD among

medical personnel who served in Vietnam during
the war. While many medical personnel she
studied show the classic symptoms of PTSD, those
symptoms often take on special forms. For
example, "survivor guilt" is extremely
heightened because many medical people have a
high sensitivity to human suffering. Special
methods of treating medical personnel are
discussed.

639. Fish, Lydia. "Nurses At the Wall." **American
      Association for the History of Nursing
      Bulletin** 12 (Fall 1986): 3-4.

      Fish overviews the situation of women Vietnam
      veterans both during and after the war. She
      describes statistics on women who served and
      points out the particular traumas of these
      women's homecomings and adjustments.

640. Furey, J.A. "For Some, The War Rages On."
      American Journal of Nursing 82, no. 11
      (November 1982): 1695-1696.

      Furey spent a year in Vietnam as a nurse and
      recalls in this article her initial anger at
      seeing a belated interest spring up about PTSD
      in the early 1980's. Realizing that more needed
      to be done, she describes turning from negative
      anger to productive program development
      involving inservice education about PTSD. The
      article describes the nature of this program.
      Most references are to men veteran's problems.

641. Goun, Barbara Diana. "A Case Control Mortality
      Study on the Association of Soft Tissue
      Sarcomas, Non-Hodgkin's Lymphomas, and Other
      Selected Cancers and Vietnam Military Service
      in Pennsylvania Males." Ph.D. diss.,
      University of Pittsburgh, 1986.

      Goun's study aimed to test the assertion that
      Vietnam military service could be connected to
      selected cancers. Her study included 349 men
      who served in Vietnam and who had died of the
      selected cancers between 1969 and 1983, and 349
      men who did not serve in Vietnam, but who also
      died in the same time frame of the same cancer
      types. The results of the study did not support

a link between the cancers and Vietnam military service given her study's parameters.

642. Gulzow, Monte, and Carol Mitchell. "Vagina Dentata and Incurable Venereal Disease from the Viet Nam War." **Western Folklore** 39 (October 1980): 306-316.

The authors collected stories from American Viet Nam veterans about two legends: (1) the prostitute with razors inside her; and (2) the soldier with incurable V.D. The article reports the various versions they collected from interviews. Reasons for the persistence of such stories are also discussed.

643. Hart, Lianne. "Where Are They Now? B. Masoti, Catholic Battlefield Chaplain." **People Weekly** 23, no. 13 (April 1, 1985): 109-110.

Hart's story describes Bruno Masotti's Vietnam experience in 1965. Masotti, a Catholic chaplain assigned to the 101st Airborne Division, gave masses, travelled with troops, wrote the parents of dead soldiers, and administered comfort where he could. Masotti also shares his views of Vietnam and how they have changed since his service there.

644. Hendin, Herbert, and Ann Pollinger Haas. "Combat Adaptations of Vietnam Veterans Without Posttraumatic Stress Disorders." **The American Journal of Psychiatry** 141, no. 8 (August 1984): 956-60.

The authors try to isolate characteristics that might prevent the development of PTSD in soldiers. Using 10 American Vietnam veterans who did not develop PTSD during this violent war, they determined that a cluster of traits may indicate emotional stability under similar combat conditions: (1) calmness; (2) being mentally in control; (3) self-structuring abilities; (4) acceptance of human limitations; and (5) lack of excessive guilt feelings.

645. _____. **Wounds of War: The Psychological Aftermath of Combat in Vietnam.** New York: Basic Bks., 1984

Hendin and Haas worked with over 100 combat veterans with PTSD. Their evaluations seek to clarify the continued meaning of combat experiences for the veteran as a way to help find more effective ways to treat PTSD. They discuss various themes such as suicidal tendencies and guilt. Case descriptions of combat veterans elucidate both their findings and the process of working with Vietnam veterans.

646.   Hodge, Margaret. "Civilian Veterans Should Not Be Overlooked by Women Veterans Memorial." **Minerva: Quarterly Report on Women and the Military** 4, no. 1 (Spring 1986): 108-114.

Hodge's piece is an excerpt from a statement given to the Senate. As a former SRAO (Red Cross) employee, she served in Vietnam. Her article argues that a women's memorial should not overlook the service of women volunteers in organizations like the Red Cross, the USO, or U.S. AID. In the course of her argument she describes the Red Cross worker's tasks.

647.   Huppenbauer, Sandra. "PTSD: A Portrait of the Problem." **American Journal of Nursing** 82, no. 1 (November 1982): 1699-1703.

Huppenbauer's article describes the unique characteristics of the Vietnam War (type of combat, individual DEROS's, etc.) as part of the problem which causes some veterans' bouts with PTSD. A catalogue of PTSD symptoms is also included along with techniques for assistance.

648.   Jackson, Helene. "The Impact of Combat Stress of Adolescent Moral Development in Vietnam Veterans." Ph.D. diss., The Smith College School for Social Work, 1982.

Jackson theorizes that the psychological problems many Vietnam veterans grapple with after returning home may be related to their being arrested in a psychological state of moral development akin to nihilism. After reviewing theories of moral development and defining both nihilism and adolescence, she reports on four cases, noting that each experienced a phase of moral nihilism stemming from combat experience and associated with adolescent development. No subject had been able to develop a higher level of moral thinking since those years in Vietnam. She concludes by suggesting some therapeutic methods to assist these veterans in resuming a normal development.

649. Karrgeski, Gregory, and Gloria Leon.
      "Correlates of Self-Reported and Objectively Determined Exposure to Agent Orange." **The American Journal of Psychiatry** 140 (November 1983): 1443-49.

      The authors compare male Viet Nam veterans who may have been exposed to Agent Orange. In particular, they wanted to see if the veterans' beliefs about exposure was related to particular symptoms and what psychological and neuropsychological damages are indicative of contamination by Agent Orange. The study does not support the notion that Agent Orange causes psychological problems.

650. Kinney, Lois. "A Laboratory Investigation of the Changes in the Sleep Physiology of the Dream-Disturbed." Ph.D. diss., University of Cincinnati, 1983.

      The study examines veterans who experienced night terrors, and Kinney finds that these veterans did show a physiological hyperreactivity during sleep. Other factors are identified which characterize the group that experienced night terrors.

651. Kulp, Denise. "Women Vets Health Problems Ignored." **Off Our Backs** 13, no. 6 (June 1983): 16.

      The article describes the current inequities in women veterans' health benefits. Women cannot receive gynecological care from the VA, mental health care has been virtually non-existent, and women have not been included in studies of the effects of Agent Orange on veterans in Vietnam.

652. Laufer, Robert, Thomas Yager, Ellen

Frey-Wouters, and Joan Donellan. **Post-War Trauma: Social and Psychological Problems of Vietnam Veterans in the Aftermath of the Vietnam War.** Vol. 3 of **Legacies of Vietnam: Comparative Adjustment of Veterans and Their Peers.** Springfield, Va.: National Technical Information Service, U.S. Department of Commerce for the Veteran's Administration, 1981.

Composed of three major chapters, the report first surveys and discusses veterans' attitudes toward military service and the war, followed by, in Chapter 2, descriptions of the returning veterans' readjustment problems. Chapter 3 covers current problems, including psychological and drug abuse situations. The study covers, primarily, if not solely, men veterans' experiences. A number of data tables are included in the last half of the book along with appendices presenting various scales used in the study.

653. MacPherson, Myra. "Long Time Passing: Eddie's Lasting Nightmare of Vietnam." **The Progressive** 48 (June 1984): 30-5.

Before profiling Vietnam veteran Eddie Coyle, MacPherson describes the part of Boston (Southie) that he comes from, and the honor the community now pays to these veterans. Most of the article, however, recounts Eddie's wounds and loss of his leg in combat as well as his slow, painful readjustment to coming home. Eddie reveals the motivation behind joining the Marines, stories of his combat days in Vietnam, of his days at Brandeis University, and his early jobs. In the final parts of the article, Eddie reflects on the war's legacy for the country and for the young men who may be called to serve.

654. _____. "The Private War of Eldson McGhee." **Essence** 15 (November 1984): 96-98, 146, 148, 151-52.

This portrait describes Eldson McGhee, a black Vietnam veteran from Atlanta, Georgia. Beginning with his drafting, McGhee describes

his metamorphosis in Vietnam from a young black
man with ideals and dreams of the future into a
disenchanted, angry, and finally drug-stupored
killer. Blaming his subsequent stateside crimes
on his combat experiences and drug addiction,
McGhee nevertheless struggled while in prison to
attain the academic degrees necessary to attain
his goals. Emerging as a socially committed
individual, he exemplifies the individual whose
fall during the war and later triumph have left
him a scarred but determined pacifist.

655. McGoran, Saralee. "Vietnam Veterans of America
     Show Respect for Women at Funding
     Convention." **Minerva: Quarterly Report on
     Women and the Military** 2, no. 1 (Spring
     1984): 8-13.

     This is a description of the VVA's founding
convention, during which a number of resolutions
were drafted. Among them were several
supportive of women, including pledges to use
non-gender related language, to initiate a
women's column in **VVA Veteran,** and promises to
highlight women's interests in recruitment
literature.

656. Norman, Elizabeth M. "Nurses in War: A Study of
     Female Military Nurses Who Served in Vietnam
     During the War Years 1965-1973." Ph.D.
     diss., New York University, 1986.

     Norman's dissertation includes fifty women
who served in the military services during
Vietnam. She focuses on four areas: (1) the
experience of the individual in Vietnam; (2) the
patterns among those individuals' experiences;
(3) the lasting effect of the war on the nurses
after returning home; and (4) the prevalence of
PTSD among nurse veterans. Results showed that
nurses with strong social support tended to have
lower incidences of PTSD, and that service in
Vietnam did affect many nurses' career paths
after the war.

657. _____. "PTSD: The Victims Who
     Survived." **American Journal of Nursing** 82,
     no. 11 (November 1982): 1696-98.

Norman describes some general themes characterizing PTSD symptoms: nightmares, depression, guilt, inability to keep jobs, anxiety, and alienation among others. Interesting, too, is her discussion of theories of causation. Only male veterans are considered.

658. Ott, Janet. "Women Vietnam Veterans." In **The Trauma of War: Stress and Recovery in the Vietnam Veteran**, edited by Stephen Sonnenbaum, Arthur Blank, and John Talbott, 309-319. Washington, D.C.: American Psychiatric Press, 1985.

Ott was herself a nurse in Vietnam for 12 months, and since her return, has become involved with therapy groups and therapy for women Vietnam veterans. From the perspectives of experience and clinical knowledge, she attempts to create a sense of the types of reactions and problems a nurse veteran might experience, even years later. After detailing the conditions nurses were subjected to, and the kinds of problems many report, she outlines ideas for therapy. A final suggestion encourages further research on women Vietnam veterans.

659. Parent, Norbert R., and Hazel Magaziner. "Vocational Adjustment of Vietnam Era Veterans." **Journal of Rehabilitation** 49 (January-March 1983): 24-28.

After reviewing the research on the uniqueness (or lack of it) of adjustment problems for Vietnam era veterans, the authors reveal the nature and results of their study on the comparative difficulty of rehabilitating non-Vietnam veterans with problems as opposed to Vietnam veterans with problems. Citing at least five major factors working against successful rehabilitation of Vietnam veterans, the study nonetheless reveals that more of the Vietnam veterans were successfully rehabilitated. They probe several key reasons for this finding.

660. Paul, Elizabeth A., and Jacquelyn O'Neill.

"American Nurses in Vietnam: Stresses and
After-Effects." **American Journal of Nursing**
86, no. 5 (May 1986): 526.

The authors summarize their data on female
nurse Vietnam veterans suffering from PTSD. The
stressors for women were noted, among them
survivor guilt, lack of experience with the
military, and sexual harassment. Paul and
O'Neill also break down the types of
aftereffects some nurses suffer from;
physiological problems, emotional problems,
relationship problems, alcohol abuse, and
depression are among the many aftereffects
bothering some nurse veterans still.

661.   _____. "Wounded Healers: A Summary
of the Vietnam Nurse Veteran Project."
Military Medicine 150, no. 11 (November
1985): 571-76.

Paul's study identifies eight stressors that
nurses in Vietnam experienced. Included are
sexual harassment and two that overlap with
stressors for combat veterans: threat to life,
and survivor guilt. Other than these two, types
of stressors differ greatly for female nurses
and male combat veterans. The study also
identifies common aftereffects that women
experience including nightmares, flashbacks,
emotional disturbances, and career failures.

662.   Podesta, Jane Sims. "The Other Vietnam Vets."
Ms. 10 (June 1982): 23.

Using Lynda Van Devanter's memories, Podesta
describes the traumatic experiences of women
during the war. The article encourages women
veterans to contact Van Devanter, Director of
the Vietnam Veterans of America, in order to
find out helpful information.

663.   Rinne, Rudi. "Vietnam Vets 'Welcome Home'
Features Women's Symposium." **Minerva: The
Quarterly Report on Women and the Military** 3,
no. 4 (Winter 1985): 18-21.

This is a description of the eight hour

symposium planned as part of the Firebase
Colorado LZ85 Welcome Home for Vietnam Veterans
Weekend. The weekend's events served as a time
of healing for women and also as a beginning to
networking among themselves.

664. Rothblum, Esther, and Ellen Cole, eds.
**Another Silenced Trauma: Twelve Feminist
Therapists and Activists Respond to One
Woman's Recovery from War.** New York:
Harrington Park Press, 1986. Originally
published in **Women and Therapy** 5, no. 1
(Spring, 1986).

The 12 articles compiled here concern the
case of Ruth, a 39-year-old Vietnam War Navy
veteran and nurse who was treated for
alcoholism. The book begins with a five page
case description of Ruth's problems as they
related to her Vietnam experience. Following
this, each of the 12 therapists describes a
method of treatment. These approaches reveal a
diversity of therapeutic methods, but each is
feminist in orientation.

665. Schnaier, Jenny. "Women Vietnam Veterans and
Mental Health Adjustment: A Study of Their
Experiences and Post-Traumatic Stress."
Master's Thesis, University of Maryland,
1982.

Schnaier proposed to investigate the presence
or lack of presence of PTSD in women Vietnam
veterans. She surveyed, by mail, 89 female
veterans, asking for reports of their
experiences and reactions to the war. Her
findings indicate that these women veterans were
very different as a population from male
veterans, yet these women, too, suffered from
mental health distress, specifically certain
symptoms of PTSD. The open-ended section of her
instrument yielded the insight that many women
found positive and growth-producing aspects to
their experiences in Vietnam.

666. Schwartz, Linda Spoonster. "Women and the
Vietnam Experience." **Image: Journal of
Nursing Scholarship** 19 (Winter 1987): 168-73.

This is a good, concise summary of data and consistent themes that have come out of the many recent accounts of nurses' experiences in Vietnam. Covering the military, combat, actual nursing and returning home experiences, Schwartz intersperses these accounts of common experiences with many statistics. The article is informative, but brief.

667.   Shea, Frances. "Stress of Caring for Combat Casualties." **U.S. Navy Medicine** 74 (January-February 1983): 4-7.

The text of the article is a speech given by Shea in 1983. Admitting that she speaks only from personal experience, Shea graphically describes her role as operating room supervisor in Vietnam. She openly shares her own guilt about not being able to console patients or their families, but also unlocks a secret to many nurses' problems once they had returned from Vietnam. She pinpoints the lack of outlets for grief for nurses as a major stressor.

668.   Stroud, Julia. "Adjustment Difficulties of Women Vietnam Veterans." Ph.D. diss., University of Montana, 1984.

Stroud studied 15 female Vietnam women veterans, comparing them against 15 male Vietnam combat veterans and an equal group of female non-veterans. Female veterans report significant differences from the other groups of women on their abilities to deal with personal relationships and other psychological problems.

669.   Theiler, Patricia. "The Untold Story of Women and Agent Orange." **Common Cause Magazine** 10 (November-December 1984): 29-34.

Theiler's article points out that there were about 17,000 women in Vietnam during the war, and many may have been exposed to Agent Orange. Unfortunately, women will not be included in the government's $73 million epidemiological study. Theiler continues by citing several cases in particular, that of Lily Adams, Saralee McGoran, Joan Maimon, Kammy Malloy, and Becky Pietz, who

either their families or themselves have had
significant health problems. Both military and
civilian women veterans' recognition problems
are discussed.

670. Thienes-Hontos, Patricia, Charles Watson, and
      Teresa Kucala. "Stress-disorder Symptoms in
      Vietnam and Korean War Veterans." **Journal of
      Consulting and Clinical Psychology** 50, no. 4
      (August 1982): 558-61.

The authors compare cases of stress disorder
using records of Vietnam and Korean war veterans
hospitalized for psychiatric problems within
three years after each war. The researchers
conclude from their results that stress
disorders are not unique to Vietnam veterans.

671. Trifoli, Laura Catherine. "Vietnam Veterans:
      Post Traumatic Stress In Relation to
      Situational Reactions." Ph.D. diss., Hofstra
      University, 1986.

The dissertation compares several groups of
people (those Vietnam veterans displaying
stress, those not, Vietnam era veterans, and
non-veterans) and analyzes responses to various
stress symptoms. Vietnam veterans experiencing
combat showed more stress symptoms, and, in
particular, more socially unacceptable reactions
to emotional situations.

672. Tutelian, Louise. "Vietnam Veteran." **Glamour**
      79 (July 1981): 73.

This is a very brief piece on Lynda Van
Devanter and her efforts to raise funding to
study the problems of Vietnam women veterans.

673. Van Devanter, Lynda. "The Unknown Warriors:
      Implications of the Experience of Women in
      Vietnam." In **Post-Traumatic Stress Disorder
      and the War Veteran Patient**. Psychosocial
      Stress Series, No. 5. Edited by William
      Kelly, 148-169. New York: Brunner/Mazel,
      1985.

Van Devanter states that little is known

about the pre-, post-, and during-the-war
experiences of women Vietnam veterans. Citing
Jenny Schnaier's 1982 study examining the
readjustment of women Vietnam vets, she reports
some of its major findings. Van Devanter then
summarizes the typical in-country experiences of
women medical personnel and their homecoming
experiences. She also poses a myriad of
research questions which need to be explored
about the effects on women of serving in
Vietnam.

674. _____. "VVA's Women Veterans
      Project Carries Issues to Congress and
      Public." **Minerva: Quarterly Report on Women
      and the Military** 1, no. 1 (Spring 1983):
      14-25.

      In this report, Van Devanter describes the
purposes of the Women Veterans Project and the
reasons for its existence. Because of the
important and unacknowledged roles women played
in Vietnam, the Project seeks to make women
veterans visible by encouraging publicity of
women's roles and research on the demographics
of women's involvement.

675. West, Andrea, and Cheryl Leon. "Health Needs of
      the Vietnam Veteran Exposed to Agent Orange."
      Nurse Practitioner 11, no. 11 (November
      1986): 33, 37-40.

      The authors describe the deadly effects of
dioxin, a substance associated with the Agent
Orange used in defoliation during the Vietnam
War. They document several studies on these
effects, the VA's slow adaptation to its
existence, and the needed treatments for
veterans. The authors conclude with suggestions
for assisting veterans suspected of suffering
from Agent Orange.

676. Wikler, Norma. "Hidden Injuries of War."
      Chapter 5 in **Strangers At Home: Vietnam
      Veterans Since the War**, edited by Charles
      Figley and Seymour Leventman, 87-106. New
      York: Praeger Pubs., 1980.

      Wikler's thesis is that some veterans suffer

from identity problems and the inability to
establish intimate adult relationships because
of the personal trauma occasioned by their
violent actions during the course of war. These
acts damaged the sense of self irreparably. She
discusses possible reasons for such a high rate
of veteran maladjustment upon returning to this
country: (1) the year rotation system; (2) the
inability to identify the enemy; (3) the
unwelcome home; and (4) the poor economy and
lack of jobs in the United States.

1960-1969

677.   Martin, Linda Grant. "When Crisis is a Way of
          Life." **Mademoiselle** 64 (November 1966):
          172-173, 214-215, 223.

Martin writes of the character and social
position of the contemporary Vietnamese woman.
Labeling her "tough-willed" and strong, Martin
describes the economic, social, and emotional
controls women evidence in this culture in
turmoil. Her examples are numerous--from women
Buddhists, to wives, female warriors, business
owners, and interpreters. Particularly poignant
are her in-depth profiles of several women--a
young journalist, a wife, and an ex-Viet Cong
soldier all caught up in the war's beginning
momentum.

1970-1979

678.   Bey, Douglas, and Jean Lange. "Waiting Wives:
          Women Under Stress." **American Journal of
          Psychiatry** 131, no. 3 (March 1974): 283-286.

The authors examined 40 wives who each had
non-career military husbands serving one-year
tours of duty in Vietnam. Results show that
most wives wavered between despair and
depression and superficial euphoria at the time
their husbands received orders. During
separation, many wives felt abandoned and angry;
others felt estranged and isolated from social
contacts. Upon the husband's return, many felt
tensions with the reality of return because they
had over-idealized it. Communication between
husband and wife was often disrupted and often
months passed before adjustments to living
together again occurred.

679.   McCubbin, Hamilton, Edna Hunter, and Barbara
          Dahl. "Residuals of War: Families of POW's
          and Servicemen MIA's." **Journal of Social
          Issues** 31, no. 4 (Fall 1975): 95-109.

Noting how little work has been done on family adjustments to the POW or MIA status of husbands, the authors describe a study they performed with 215 families of Army, Navy, and Marine men POW's or MIA's. The results show that normal patterns of coping were disturbed because of the length of absence, and major role adjustments probably would permanently affect family dynamics even upon the partner's return. The authors thus predict even longer re-adjustment phases for reunited families.

680.   Murphy, Jane M.   "War Stress and Civilian
        Vietnamese: A Study of Psychological
        Effects."   **Acta Psychiatrica Scandinavica** 56,
        no. 2 (1977): 92-108.

Murphy tries to determine the level of psychological disturbance for civilian Vietnamese, who in the midst of war (1972), were subject to high levels of stress. Her sample consists of 102 civilians evacuated from the Iron Triangle in South Vietnam to Bien Hoa village. The study indicates that a very high and lasting degree of psychological disturbance characterizes most of the people. Especially susceptible were women who lost a husband or son and who suffered an economic downfall as a result.

681.   Price-Bonham, Sharon.   "Missing in Action Men: A
        Study of Their Wives."   **International Journal
        of Sociology of the Family** 2, no. 2
        (September 1972): 202-211.

Price-Bonham studied 32 wives of MIA men who were classified as MIA in 1969-70. Looked at were variables associated with the wife's belief of whether her husband was dead or alive. Major variables relating to assumptions of his being alive or dead were: (1) age of the children; (2) length of time the husband had been MIA; and (3) living arrangement of the family.

682.   Stratton, Alice.   "The Stress of Separation."
        U. S. Naval Institutional Proceedings 104
        (July 1978): 52-58.

Stratton is the POW wife of a Navy officer

captured in 1967 in the Vietnam War. In the
article, Stratton uses her own experiences,
analyzed within the framework of the
Kuebler-Ross stages of acceptance of death, to
articulate the psychological norms determining a
woman's coping ability in such an ordeal. She
collapses numerous experiences into the five
categories of acceptance: denial, anger,
bargaining, depression, and acceptance.
Finally, she examines each stage in light of the
POW's experience, then the wife's and family's.

1980-1987

683.   Brown, Patti Coleen. "Legacies of a War:
       Treatment Considerations with Vietnam
       Veterans and Their Families." **Social Work**
       29, no. 4 (July-August 1984): 372-379.

       Brown focuses on the problems that the
veteran's family faces because of his or her
PTSD problems. Brown covers carefully the
various perceptions veterans and families may
carry about the war and lays out the myriad
kinds of problems, experiences, and feelings
exhibited by the female partner of the veteran.
Suggestions for therapeutic intervention are
given including providing the partner (usually a
woman) with information and with group therapy.

684.   Card, Josefina J. **Lives After Vietnam: The
       Personal Impact of Military Service**.
       Lexington, Mass.: D.C. Heath and Co., 1983.

       Card's study, completed in 1981, included men
of the high school graduating class of 1963 who
were non-veterans, non-Vietnam veterans, and
Vietnam veterans. The study sought to determine
if combat experience and military service
affected the veterans, now in their 30's, and if
either affected the current lives of various
sub-groups of men. Indeed, a major part of the
research sought to determine who served and who
saw combat. Each question is considered in a
separate section and summarized there. A
general summary of important findings concludes
the volume. The study considers only male
veterans.

685.   Haley, Sarah. "The Vietnam Veteran and His
          Pre-School Child: Child Rearing as a Delayed
          Stress in Combat Veterans." **Journal of
          Contemporary Psychotherapy** 14 (Spring/Summer
          1984): 114-121.

          Haley reveals two cases of Vietnam veterans
          whose problems with PTSD hampered a healthy
          involvement with their own young children. Each
          case demonstrates that children's developmental
          stages often trigger delayed stress syndrome in
          veterans.

686.   Harris, Martha J., and Bari Fisher. "Group
          Therapy in the Treatment of Female Partners
          of Vietnam Veterans." **Journal for
          Specialists in Group Work** 10, no. 1 (March
          1985): 44-50.

          Both authors note the need for special
          treatment and therapy for the woman partner of
          the troubled Vietnam War veteran. They describe
          the type of therapy developed and used at the
          Portland, Oregon Vet Center for women partners.
          Covered are issues of group leadership, group
          processes, and special problems arising for
          group members because of a veteran partner's
          behaviors.

687.   Shehan, Constance. "Spouse Support and Vietnam
          Veterans' Adjustment to Post-Traumatic Stress
          Disorder." **Family Relations** 36 (January
          1987): 55-60.

          Shehan maintains that Vietnam veterans having
          positive relationships with their spouses suffer
          from less negative effects of combat, and have
          come through a recovery and healing process more
          efficiently than other veterans. To better
          define the nature of spouse support, Shehan
          describes a model which could affect therapy
          sessions. The model is based on communication,
          including the ability for self-disclosure,
          defensive communication, and communication
          apprehension. Shehan finally offers nine
          suggestions for wives to create better
          communication channels through therapy.

688.   Smith-Schubert, Sharon C. "The Relationship of

Sex Role Orientation to Anxiety, Depression
and Marital Adjustment Among Women Who Are
Wives or Partners of Vietnam Veterans
Identified as Suffering Delayed Stress."
Ph.D. diss., University of Denver, 1984.

The author's premise is that various,
distinct sex-role orientations characterizing
the women wives or partners of Vietnam veterans
suffering from delayed stress make a difference
in how well the women handle the stresses of
that marital relationship. In general, women of
all sex role orientations in this relationship
report some depression, anxiety, and low marital
adjustment. Also, women with either masculine
or androgynous orientations suffer less anxiety
and depression than women identified as feminine
or undifferentiated.

689.   Stringer, Jeri. "Learning to Be a 'Significant
        Other' to a Combat Veteran." **Minerva:
        Quarterly Report on Women and the Military** 1,
        no. 4 (Winter 1983): 91-95.

Stringer opens her article by describing her
own lack of appreciation for her returning
veteran husband. Over a period of years, she
began to appreciate the painful process of
adjustment that many veterans coped with and
began to see how she too could help ease this
process.

690.   Weisman, Joan. "The Effects of Exposure to
        Agent Orange on the Intellectual Functioning,
        Academic Achievement, Visual-Motor Skill, and
        Activity Level of the Offspring of Vietnam
        War Veterans." Ph.D. diss., Hofstra
        University, 1985.

Weisman studied the effects that veterans'
exposures to Agent Orange had on their children.
Her data indicate a probable relationship
between the parent's exposure to dioxin and
learning deficiencies of elementary-aged
children. Of the 54 children in the study,
those within the "exposed" group (parents having
physical evidence of their exposure to Agent
Orange) scored less well on tests for
intellectual functioning, academic achievement,

1954-1959

691. Samuels, Gertrude. "Passage to Freedom in
     Vietnam." **National Geographic** 107, no. 6
     (June 1955): 857-874.

   Samuels' article covers the migration of the
over 700,000 people from North Vietnam to South
Vietnam. She probes, through interviews, why
the mostly Roman Catholic migrants fled the
North, noting that suppression of religious
freedom and incidents of terrorism against their
families motivated many. The mechanics of the
migration are described as is the reception of
refugees in Saigon, where many disembarked from
American ships. Samuels also witnessed the
reception center camps, but spends more time
describing the rise of new villages built by
incoming peasants.

1960-1969

692. Gellhorn, Martha. "Suffer the Little Children."
     Ladies Home Journal 84 (January 1967): 57,
     107-109.

   Gellhorn chastises Americans for ignoring the
plight of civilian children in Vietnam who are
caught up in the war and maimed, abandoned, or
killed. Using the provincial hospitals at My
Tho and Quinhon, Gellhorn graphically describes
the tragedies suffered by Vietnam's children.
She proposes near the conclusion of her article
that we bring maimed children to America, but
notes that the American government seems very
unresponsive to this idea.

1970-1979

693. Crist, Evamae Barton. **Take This House**.
     Scottsdale, Pa.: Herald Press, 1977.

   Crist and her husband took in nine refugees

after the exodus of people from Vietnam in April, 1975. Crist worked with refugees as a volunteer at a resettlement house where she was able to locate a family of nine to sponsor. She describes their adjustments, the reactions of outsiders to her plan, and her own family's changed lifestyles while they waited for the Vietnamese family to find its own home.

694.   Fitzgerald, Frances. "Punch In! Punch Out! Eat Quick!" **New York Times Magazine**, section 6 (December 28, 1975): 8-10, 32-35, 38.

Fitzgerald's article describes the progress made in the relocation in the U.S. of over 130,000 mostly Vietnamese refugees after the war. Fitzgerald reports on Fort Chaffee where many Vietnamese cling to the camp because it is composed of familiar Vietnamese faces and customs. Her article brings out the problems with these centers, which according to Americans working there, recapture all the old problems with all former American aid projects in Vietnam. Fitzgerald presses forward to examine how the integrated refugees are adapting, using case studies of specific families.

695.   Jenkins, Loren. "Vietnam's War-Torn Children." **Newsweek** 81, no. 22 (May 28, 1973): 52-61.

Jenkins describes the plight of Vietnam's children. Most are scarred by the war in some way; either they have lost parents, siblings, homes, are orphaned, or maimed themselves. Few services to help them are made available by the Americans or Vietnamese governments. Interspersed within the commentary are the frequent portraits of these forgotten children.

696.   Kasinsky, Renee. "The Continental Channeling of American Vietnam War Refugees." **Crime and Social Justice** 6 (Fall-Winter 1976): 28-40.

The article is based on her book, **Refugees from Militarism: Draft-Age Americans in Canada**. The focus is again on the men draft resisters and the aid groups in Canada which helped channel them and adjust them to economic and social life there. As part of this assimilation process, Kasinsky details the assistance efforts in stages: 1966-68, and 1968-75, comparing and contrasting earlier and later efforts according to the emerging consciousness of war resistance efforts on the part of Canadian support groups.

697.   Kelly, Gail. **From Vietnam to America: A Chronicle of the Vietnamese Immigration to the United States.** Boulder, Colo.: Westview Press, 1977.

Kelly's book examines the Vietnamese refugees in America. Beginning with a description of typical refugees, the common reasons for leaving and details of the escape, Kelly then profiles the refugee camps in the U.S. She describes preparation for entry into American culture, and finalizes her account with reports of Vietnamese adaptations within American society. Kelly's work at the Ft. Indian Town Gap refugee camp, reports, documents, and interviews fuel the basis for the book.

698.   _____. "Schooling, Gender and the Reshaping of Occupational and Social Expectations: The Case of Vietnamese Immigrants to the United States." **International Journal of Women's Studies** 1, no. 4 (1978): 323-335.

In order to examine her main point, Kelly analyzes the re-education of Vietnamese women entering the United States after the war. Using educational programs at Ft. Indian Town Gap, Kelly assesses the differences between the treatment of women and men in the educational process. While most programs and publications reinforce a subservient role for women, Kelly describes one alternative, "Women in America," which presents liberated images of women in society. Kelly concludes that the sexism inherent in the preparation of male and female immigrants did little to help prepare females to enter the workforce and only prepared men for jobs usually held by women here. Thus, not only were expectations different, but they were lower for everyone.

699.   Marti, Jill. "Mascots of War." **Ramparts** 10

(January 1972): 52-53.

The story is about "Bobby," a Vietnamese
youth who for two years served as an
interpreter-scout for the American military in
Vietnam. After he lost his legs to a land mine
on a scouting mission, he was abandoned by the
military, but now intends to return to his
village. Marti's story points up the cruel
usage of people during the war.

700.   Myerhoff, Barbara, R.   "The Revolution as a
           Trip: Symbol and Paradox."   Chapter 13 in **The
           New Pilgrims: Youth Protest in Transition**,
           edited by Phillip Altbach and Robert Laufer,
           251-266.   New York: David McKay, Co., 1972.

Myerhoff examines the congruence between
behavior and belief systems of a small group of
student radicals during a week-long campus
strike during the Vietnam War.   She discovered
that paradoxes existed caused by inconsistency
of political and cultural goals, and that where
a preference emerged, cultural goals usually won
out.

701.   Plank, Jane.   **An Organization and Welcome
           Guide for Groups Sponsoring Indochinese
           Refugees**.   Washington, D.C.: Interagency Task
           Force for Indochina Refugees, 1975.

This is a brochure designed to assist
individuals or groups with sponsorship of
Vietnamese as they resettle in the United
States.   The brochure outlines a plan for
organizing all the details of the sponsorship.

1980-1987

702.   Baer, Florence E.   "'Give Me ... Your huddled
           masses': Anti-Vietnamese Refugee Lore and the
           'Image of Limited Good'."   **Western Folklore**
           41 (October 1982): 275-291.

Baer analyzes negative legends circulating
orally about recently immigrated Vietnamese.
She traces the evolution of one story, that of
the Vietnamese stealing and eating a pet.   The
effects of such lore include threats against

local Vietnamese, which cause many to move to
other locales and cause many prejudiced feelings
among ethnic/racial groups.

703. Beck, Melinda. "Where is my Father?: Legacy of
      U.S. Presence in Vietnam." **Newsweek** 105
      (April 15, 1985): 54-57.

      The article concerns the plight of Amerasian
children whose American fathers remain unknown
to them. Of the 8,000 to 15,000 such children,
most live in Vietnam where they remain outcasts
from that society. Unfortunately, the United
States' efforts to bring these children to this
country remain mired in bureaucratic and
political tangles. Beck describes various
immigration and settlement arrangements.

704. Calhoun, Mary Atchity. "The Vietnamese Woman:
      Health/Illness Attitudes and Behaviors."
      Health Care Women International 6 (1985):
      61-72.

      Calhoun maintains that nurses must understand
the whole person, including attitudes and
cultural beliefs, when treating people of
differing cultures. Her descriptions of
Vietnamese women's attitudes toward health is
designed to assist in providing this background.
Recent female immigrants supported treatments by
physicians, good health, cleanliness, and health
education; however, a high percentage of females
believed in folk and home cures, too. She
discusses other attitudes toward pregnancy and
the family's role in treatment.

705. Horell, Jeanette. "A South Vietnamese Woman's
      Story." **Big Mama Rag** 9, no. 3 (March 1981):
      22.

      Horrell tells the story of Tuyet, a
Vietnamese woman who married an American soldier
and emigrated to the United States 10 years ago.
The story reveals Tuyet's problems adjusting to
American life both before and after her divorce.

706. Kelly, Gail. "The Schooling of Vietnamese
      Immigrants: Internal Colonialism and Its
      Impact on Women." In **Comparative**

Perspectives of Third World Women: The Impact of Race, Sex, and Class, edited by Beverly Lindsay, 276-296. New York: Praeger Pubs., 1980.

Kelly describes the kind of education Vietnamese refugees received in 1975 in the four camps available for resettlement. Her concern was internal colonialism, of which education was an instrument, and how these two activities affected women. Kelly reports that, at first, women were not admitted to English language classes (Fort Indian Town Gap). When women were in class, they were taught using materials which clearly locked them into traditional roles. Even the written newspapers of the camp differentiated between men and women audiences, denying women the same opportunities as men were receiving.

707. Matthews, Ellen. **Culture Clash.** Chicago: Intercultural Press, 1982.

The book is written by the sponsor of two Vietnamese refugees from Saigon and reveals all of their experiences between 1975 and 1979. The book is revealingly honest, describing in detail the problems caused by ungratified and false expectations of the Vietnamese family and the American one and the pain caused by the American family due to misunderstandings about the Vietnamese. The ups and downs of living together, of the Vietnamese family's move into their own first apartment, and the gradual move of the two families from child-parent relation to independent friendship dominate the rest of the book. Matthews concludes wishing that the American sponsors had been counseled about the cultural realities they were to encounter.

708. O'Brien, Colleen. "The Children that Americans Left Behind (Vietnam)." **Scholastic Update** (Teachers' Edition) 117, no. 15 (March 29, 1985): 13-14.

Written for high school students, the piece discusses the plight of Amerasian children left behind in Vietnam. O'Brien describes the kinds of problems these children face while living in

Other Resources

1960-1969

715. "A Salute to Our Chief Nurse in Viet
Nam--Colonel Althea E. Williams." **Washington
State Journal of Nursing** 40, no. 2 (March
1968): 4, 33.

This piece is a brief biographical glance at
the military career of Colonel Althea E.
Williams, Chief Nurse of the U.S. Army, Viet
Nam. Williams describes her job: placing
military nurses assigned to Viet Nam, and
coordinating hospital support of military
action. Much of the article relates her past
history of nursing assignments.

716. "Victoria Charlenes." **Time** 89 (June 23,
1967): 28.

The brief article discusses some of the roles
women play in the Viet Cong forces. Aside from
soldiering, women serve in troop support roles
and in the Viet Cong recruitment efforts.

1970-1979

717. D.C. Conference Committee. "Indochinese
Sisters." **Off Our Backs** 1, no. 22 (May 27,
1971): 14-15.

This series of mini-articles covers the 1971
Toronto Conference for American, Canadian, and
Southeast Asian women. The reports focus on the
stories of revolution and American aggression
told by the Vietnamese and Laotian women. A
definite anti-American tone pervades the
reporting.

718. "Jane Fonda on Vietnamese Prisoners." **Women's
Press** 3, no. 6 (September 1973): 4.

The article summarizes the gist of a Fonda
speech on the status of American abuse of the
Vietnamese woman during the war. Cited are
examples of U.S.-sponsored torture of Vietnamese

women and the results of sexist attitudes
imported by American soldiers.

719.   "Sisterhood/Revolution and Wonder." **Great
       Speckled Bird** 5, no. 21 (May 29, 1972): 3.

       In this brief piece, an American woman
       celebrates her spiritual union with Vietnamese
       women. She condemns American values, while
       extolling revolution as the ultimate act of
       love.

720.   "Twelve-Year Summary of the Women's Movement in
       the Democratic Republic of Vietnam."
       Bulletin of Concerned Asian Scholars 7, no. 4
       (October-December 1975): 61.

       This is an unauthored one page series of
       tables showing the number of women in various
       military and civilian roles in North Vietnam.

721.   "Viet Women From Slave to Revolution." **Seed**
       7, no. 10 (November 1971): 16.

       This is a story, told in a cartoon format, of
       the typical life of a Vietnamese woman. From
       birth to death, the common fears, hopes, and
       social realities are described within the
       context of the traditional expectations and the
       more modern era expectations for the liberated
       Vietnamese woman.

722.   "Vietnam/Feminist View." **Gay Sunshine**, no.13
       (June 1972): 6.

       The thesis of the article is that American
       imperialism in Vietnam is a re-creation of the
       act of rape. The authors contend that the
       formal rationales for this war given by other
       anti-war activitists (e.g., the war promotes the
       economy) do not go far enough in explaining the
       inhuman violence of the war. The particular
       sadism of the war is, they maintain, a product
       of socialization of male sexual violence in the
       American culture. They call for a feminist
       analysis of the motivation to fight wars.

723.   "Women in Vietnam." **Goodbye to All That** 39
       (April 1973): 9.

The article describes the content of Jane
Fonda's slide show on Vietnamese women, a show
presented in San Diego at the Indochina Peace
campaign. The slides and narration include
Vietnamese women's history, their contributions
to society both present and past, and their
abuse by the Americans currently in their
country.

724.   "Women in Vietnam." **Guild Notes** 8, no. 6
         (November 1979): 5.

The article examines the reasons why
Vietnamese women have made greater strides
toward independence and social equality than
American women. The reasons include the 30
years of contributions in war by women, both as
combatants and as people in service to the war
effort. Also important to the preservation of
gains made during wartime is the Vietnam Women's
Union, a political force extending beyond the
war.

725.   "Women Prisoners in South Vietnam." **Up From
         Under** 1, no. 3 (January/February 1971):
         43-44.

The brief article is actually a letter from a
group of women political prisoners held in Chi
Hoa prison. The piece was translated by Don
Luce, and sent to the U.S. The women expose the
use of tiger cages at Con Son prison, the
frequency of torture, the lack of food and
medical care, and the filthy, crowded cells.
The women are imprisoned primarily for actively
seeking the release of political prisoners or
for protesting the war and the American presence
in Vietnam.

726.   Women's International Democratic Federation.
         **The Situation in the Countries of Indochina.
         And Solidarity with Their Peoples**. Berlin:
         Women's International Democratic Federation,
         1970.

After the WIDF meeting in Budapest in
October, 1970, this report was issued supporting
the struggle against the Americans, especially
that by women and children in South Viet Nam.

Five messages or reports from women in women's
unions are recorded, all supportive of the
struggle for independence.

1980-1987

727. "Vietnam Women's Memorial Project." **JEN:
     Journal of Emergency Nursing** 12, no. 1
     (January-February 1986): 22A-23A.

     The article covers the history of the
     inception of the Women's Memorial, concluding
     with short biographical pieces on Donna-Marie
     Boulay and Diane Evans, co-founders of the
     project.

WOMEN OF OTHER NATIONALITIES WRITING ABOUT
THE AMERICAN EXPERIENCE IN VIETNAM

Imaginative Works

1954-1959

728. Bertrand, Gabrielle. **The Jungle People**.
      London: Robert Hale, 1959.

      This is a book illustrating the retelling of
      the legends and songs of various people of the
      Moi dialects. The stories are framed by
      Bertrand's travels through Vietnam.

729. Ekert-Rotholz, Alice. **The Time of the
      Dragons**. Translated by Richard and Clara
      Winston. New York: Viking Press, 1958. New
      York: The New American Library, 1958.

      The book is a romantic thriller, spy, and war
      story rolled into one, told against the backdrop
      of pre- and post-WWII Asia. The complicated
      plot spans the 1920's through 1955 and crosses
      one family for two generations. The character
      thread binding these two is Helen Weigeland, the
      Norwegian sister of Knut Weigeland, Consul of
      the Far East, whose three daughters and their
      exploits constitute most of the plot and
      relationships from birth to middle age. The
      novel offers an interesting view of Japan's
      Southeast Asian occupation before and during
      World War II. Vietnam is not a central setting
      but major characters often go in and out of
      Dalat and Saigon.

1960-1969

730. Elliott, Ellen. **Vietnam Nurse**. New York:
      Arcadia House, 1968. Sydney: Calvert
      Publishing, n.d.

      Elliott is an Australian writer; consequently
      her main character is Joanna Shelton, an
      Australian nurse, who is summoned to Vietnam by
      the American military. She learns that her

father, a missionary who had been working on an important plot to help establish negotiations between Americans and North Vietnamese, has been captured by the enemy and is rumored to be ill. She undertakes a dangerous journey with the special forces to save her father. The eventual release of them all, including her father, concludes the book. Throughout the plot, she and the Captain of the Special Forces grow to love each other and plan a marriage upon their return.

731. Morris, Edita. **Love to Vietnam**. New York: Monthly Review Press, 1968. Published as **The Seeds of Hiroshima**. New York: George Braziller, 1966.

The novel concerns the lives of two war victims: Shinzo, a burn victim from the atomic bombing of Nagasaki, who writes to Dan Thanh, a young woman napalm victim of the Vietnam War. The book is a series of letters from him to her until they are united in Part II of the novel. The book is also a spiritual record of his transformation from the passive acceptance of his condition to an active hatred for those who create such human destruction.

732. Nguyen Sang. "The Ivory Comb." In **The Ivory Comb**, 103-124. South Viet Nam: Giai Phong Publishing House, 1967. 2nd ed. Hanoi: Phong Publishing House, 1968. Also in **Phoenix Country** (a **Fireweed** Special Issue). **Fireweed** 6 (September 1976): 2-15.

This story is a relatively sophisticated narrative. The narrator, an old soldier, tells a war story to a group of listeners while waiting for his next orders. He remembers meeting the daughter of an old companion years after his friend died, and, after discovering her identity, gives her an ivory comb her father had meant to bring her. The story forsakes combat, and, instead, draws upon the effect of the war on families and friends.

733. Sun, Ruth. **The Land of Seagull and Fox**. Rutland, Vt.: Charles E. Tuttle Co., 1967.

Sun, while lecturing at the University of
Saigon in 1964-65, translated these 31 stories
or legends of the Vietnamese into English.

1970-1979

734. Brooke, Dinah. **Games of Love and War**.
      London: Jonathan Cape, 1976. Published as
      Death Games. New York: Harcourt Brace
      Jovanovich, 1976.

      Elspeth, a young English woman who is
      suicidal, and her American boyfriend, Alfred who
      is a Vietnam veteran, both aimlessly travel in
      Southeast Asia. Separated from Alfred, she
      continues to follow her father and his mistress
      from place to place. At one point, she finds
      herself with a journalist covering the war in
      Cambodia, then in Saigon where the war fails to
      stop her quest for self-destruction. The book
      is punctuated with flashbacks to Alfred, who
      himself, is torn by his destruction of others in
      the war and by the deaths of his friends in
      Vietnam. The book ends as Elspeth's destructive
      search, comparable to the war's destruction,
      kills her father.

735. Cass, Shirley, Ros Cheney, David Malouf, and
      Michael Wilding, eds. **We Took Their Orders
      and Are Dead: An Anti-war Anthology**. Sydney:
      Ure Smith, 1971.

      This anthology of poetry and stories,
      contains literature written by at least five
      women; most are anti-war.

736. **Distant Stars**. Hanoi: Foreign Language
      Publishing House, 1976.

      The book is a collection of eleven short
      stories, some by female authors. The theme of
      the anthology, which characterizes the content
      of each selection, is the resistance of foreign
      aggression, specifically American intervention
      in Vietnam. The stories often center on key
      women characters.

737. Gibson, Margaret. "All Over Now." In her

Considering Her Condition, 53-67. New York: Vanguard Press, 1978.

The story is a series of letters, written by a young woman named Clare to a young soldier in Vietnam named Calvin. Some letters are from him. The final letter to Calvin is completed after Clare knows he has been killed.

738. **The Mountain Trail**. Hanoi: Viet Nam Women's Union, 1970.

This book contains seven stories about women's lives in North Vietnam in the late 60's, early 70's. Many are written by women. The book's purpose is to portray the military and social struggles that women endured then as well as their roles in the war.

1980-1987

739. D'Alpuget, Blanche. **Turtle Beach**. New York: Simon and Schuster, 1981. New York, Ballantine Bks., 1984.

This novel is set partly in Australia and Southeast Asia where the main character, a woman war correspondent, covers the story of Vietnamese refugees attempting to emigrate through Malaysia to other parts of the world. Other plot threads surround this theme making the novel more a book of romance and intrigue than any record of the war.

740. **Vietnam Poetry**. Fullerton, Calif.: Union of Vietnamese in the United States, 1980.

This collection of poems, mostly in English, gives insight into Vietnamese thoughts and customs. The authors are both men and women.

Accounts Of Personal Experiences

1960-1969

741. Briand, Rena. **No Tears to Flow: A Woman at War**. Melbourne: Heinemann, 1969.

The story covers this journalist's three year stay as a free-lance writer in Vietnam. While there, her husband, and later, another lover both desert her. Briand's personal tragedies are woven into her tale of the war's tragedies.

742. Evans, Barbara. **Caduceus in Saigon: A Medical Mission to South Vietnam**. London: Hutchinson, 1968.

Evans is a British woman who was in Vietnam from August 1966-67. She was part of the first medical team to the Children's Hospital in Saigon. In addition to sharing her experiences at the hospital, she discusses what life is like living amongst the Vietnamese in Saigon.

743. Leroy, Catherine. "A Tense Interlude with the Enemy in Hue." **Life** 64 (February 16, 1968): 22-29.

Leroy and another French correspondent describe their capture by Viet Cong and NVA regulars while trying to cover the action in Hue in 1968. Held overnight at a captured villa, the Communist forces bound them, but treated them well and allowed them to photograph the scene. Within one day they were released and then joined the American Marines who led them to safety.

744. Ray, Michelle. **The Two Shores of Hell**. Translated by Elizabeth Abbott. New York: David McKay Co., 1968.

Ray writes this book as a portrait of day-to-day war experiences of American military men that she observed. But she also spends time with the Vietnamese peasants as well as with the Viet Cong. Many of her descriptions are about the frustrations and pain experienced by those on each side of the war.

745.   Stafford, Ann. **Saigon Journey**. London:
       Campion Press, 1960. New York: Taplinger
       Publishing Co., 1960.

       This British woman's goal was to meet the
       women of the East. To travel in Southeast Asia
       and other countries nearby, she signed on for a
       mission with the Catholic International Union
       for Social Service and accepted a lecture tour
       from the British Council. Ultimately, her
       destination was Saigon, but her tours took her
       to Bangkok, Angkor, Phnom Penh, Dalat, Burma,
       and Calcutta among others. Four weeks were
       spent in Saigon, where she visited and described
       an orphanage for refugee children. Interesting,
       too, is her account of a talk with a woman
       deputy who explains to her the independence of
       Vietnamese women.

746.   Terry, Susan. **House of Love: Life in a
       Vietnamese Hospital**. London: Newnes Bks.,
       1967.

       Terry, an Australian nurse, was a member of a
       small medical team sent to Vietnam under the
       auspices of the USOM. She describes her
       decision to go to Vietnam, her arrival, her
       growing friendships and love for the beleaguered
       Vietnamese people as well as life during the war
       in Saigon.

747.   Weatherly, Marjorie [Salmon, Lorraine]. **Pig
       Follows Dog**. Hanoi: Foreign Language
       Publishing House, 1960.

       Weatherly lived in the DRV during the year of
       the Dog and the Pig, (1958-59), a time of
       economic transference from capitalism to
       socialism. She writes of the humanity of the
       people she knows and works with: Ba, her
       housekeeper; Du, her driver; and a host of
       others equally appealing. Her image of the life
       there is relatively non-political as the book
       describes the people's daily routines, the
       country's geography, its customs, and its
       reverence for its leaders. In the midst of
       reported horrors of economic readjustment, her
       book counters negative prevailing images with
       scenes of the humanity of the North Vietnamese.

1970-1979

748.   Briand, Rena. **The Waifs**. Melbourne:
       Phuong/Hoang Press, 1973.

       This is a book about interracial and
international adoption. Briand adopted a
Vietnamese orphan girl, Tuyen, and the book
begins with her struggle to get Tuyen into
Australia as a single parent. Once there, she
and others launch a campaign to get five more
Vietnamese children adopted by foster parents
outside Vietnam. She discovers that the South
Vietnamese government allows few adoptions in
order to cover up most homeless children's
extremely poor living conditions. Her main
points seem to be humanitarian, and she does a
thorough job of muckracking relief agencies.

749.   Fallaci, Oriana. **Nothing and So Be It: A
       Personal Search for Meaning In War**.
       Translated by Isobel Quigley. New York:
       Doubleday and Co., 1972.

       This autobiography is a personal search for
the reasons why humans make war at all. Central
to Fallaci's time covering the Vietnam War and
to this book is the question: "What is life?," a
question whose answer is much colored by her
search through war-torn Vietnam for the answers.

750.   Nguyen Thi Dinh. **No Other Road to Take:
       Memoir of Mrs. Nguyen Thi Dinh**. Translated
       by Mai Elliott. Ithaca, N.Y.: Southeast Asia
       Program, Department of Asian Studies, Cornell
       University, 1976.

       After a lengthy introduction covering the
history of Vietnam's recent struggles for
independence, Elliott presents the memoirs of
Nguyen Thi Dinh, one of Vietnam's honored woman
generals. Beginning with her childhood,
marriage, and involvement in the Communist
movement as a young mother, Nguyen Thi Dinh
writes an autobiography of a dedicated woman
leader of the Front.

751.   Schwinn, Monika, and Bernhard Diehl. **We Came**

to Help. Translated by Jan Van Heurch. New
York: Harcourt Brace Jovanovich, 1976.

This is the story of two German nurses
working in DaNang who were captured and held
prisoner in North Vietnam. Much of the
description of their experiences comes from
Schwinn's journal and both of their
recollections, but the narration is shared from
chapter to chapter.

752.   Webb, Kate. **On the Other Side: 23 Days With
the Viet Cong**. New York: Quadrangle Bks.,
1972.

Webb, a British subject, worked as a UPI
reporter at the time of her capture by the
Laotians on Highway 4 roughly 50 miles from
Phnom Penh. The book is an account of her 23
days of captivity. Her first person story
recreates the fears, the weariness, the scenes
of hardship and comic relief. The impression
she leaves about her captors is not that they
are faceless enemies, but are only other humans
with their own fears, pain, and thoughts.

1980-1987

753.   Hawthorne, Lesleyanne, ed. **Refugee: The
Vietnamese Experience**. New York: Oxford
University Press, 1982.

Hawthorne, an Australian woman, edits this
book of first-hand accounts by refugees from
Vietnam. Twenty Vietnamese and Chinese people
are represented. She organizes their stories
into three parts: (1) life before the end of the
war (1954-75); (2) life in Vietnam after 1975;
and (3) current conditions in Australia. In all
parts, men and women tell brief autobiographical
sketches which include the events of the war as
they affected each individual.

1954-1959

754. Fischer, Ruth. "Ho Chi Minh: Disciplined
Communist." **Foreign Affairs** 33 (October
1954): 88-97.

   Written by a European Communist, the article
is a brief history of Ho Chi Minh's life and
influences on his political and social
development. The author concludes by predicting
that Ho will move his country gradually away
from alignment with Moscow and Peking, and
gravitate instead toward a coalition of
independent nations free from both the West and
the major Communist powers.

755. Kahn, Alice. "Journey to the 17th Parallel."
Viet-Nam Advances 3, no. 7 (July 1958):
11-14.

   Kahn journeys to the 17th parallel,
describing the small tragedies caused by the new
line of demarcation around Vin-Linh and the
demilitarized zone. Her descriptions are
pro-North and anti-Diem.

756. Sergeyeva, Natalia. "Glimpses of the New Life."
Soviet Woman 11 (September 1955): 31-32.

   Sergeyeva, a Soviet journalist, writes about
the post-Geneva Conference North Viet-Nam. She
attends a festival for North Vietnamese children
on International Children's Day, and compares
their spirit and energy to the renewed
beginnings of the post-colonial country. One of
the features of the new country is the **Viet-Nam
Woman** magazine, which Sergeyeva praises highly
as a sign of the society's belief in the
equality of men and women.

1960-1969

757. Arora, Gloria. **Vietnam Under the Shadows: A**

Chronological and Factual Book That Records the Tragedy of Vietnam. Bombay: Jaico Publishing House, 1965.

This fairly straightforward chronology of political and historical events leading to the Vietnam war is told by an East Indian author. The first three chapters are highly critical of Diem's handling of the Buddhist crisis in the summer of 1963. In subsequent chapters, Arora criticizes the U.S.'s role in the Diem coup. The last half of the book describes Johnson's escalation of the war after the "Maddox" incident, and the rise and fall of several "puppet" governments. Of more interest are her reports of the reactions against U.S. war escalation among the populations of Russia and China.

758. Brittain, Victoria. "GI's Fight for Peace." **New Statesman** 77 (May 9, 1969): 643-644.

Brittain describes the widespread numbers of anti-military newspapers published by underground presses on American military posts. These are becoming vehicles for uniting radicals within the American services.

759. _____. "Nixon's Non-Strategy for Peace." **New Statesman** 78 (September 26, 1969): 401-402.

Here, Brittain analyzes Nixon's policy of troop withdrawal and draft cuts as simple placation of anti-war sentiment. His stand on the war actually remains the same so that the peace negotiations can proceed from a basis of strength. She further analyzes the confounding of problems by the Thieu government in Saigon.

760. _____. "Unmaking of a President?" **New Statesman** 78 (October 24, 1969): 556.

Brittain describes October 15, 1969, and the Vietnam Moratorium. The large peace demonstration turnout raises, to her, the issue of the limits of a president's political power in carrying out his own policies.

761. Cook, Freda. "A Film Industry Is Born in

Hanoi." **Eastern Horizon** 3 (July, 1964):
42-49.

Cook chronicles the beginnings of film-making
in North Vietnam. Beginning with a first
documentary in 1946, she details the development
of documentaries and newreels until 1959 when
feature films began to be produced. Cook
reports that even the Vietnamese are critical of
the feature films. Her article concludes with
descriptions of actors and actresses, directors,
and summaries of several of the more prominent
feature films.

762. Fallaci, Oriana. "From North Vietnam: Two
American POW's." **Look** 33 (July 15, 1969):
30-35.

Fallaci was allowed to interview two American
POW's while in Hanoi--Lt. Frishman and Major
Ingvalson. The former, a talkative young man,
reveals certain details about his capture, his
prison life, and his response to his captivity;
the latter, a more silent interviewee, is less
responsive to Fallaci's questions.

763. _____. "An Interview with a Vietcong
Terrorist." **Look** 32 (April 16, 1968): 36-42.

Fallaci interviews a captured Vietcong man
imprisoned in the South. The interview reveals
methods of psychological torture used on
prisoners as well as the personal background of
the Vietcong terrorist himself.

764. _____. "Nguyen Cao Ky." In **The
Egotists: Sixteen Surprising Interviews**,
63-80. Chicago: Henry Regnery Co., 1968.

Fallaci opens with an essay describing Ky's
life and his current personal situation--all
necessary background to her subsequent
interview. In the interview she presses him on
issues about his views on the North Vietnamese,
about his aims for the revolution and its
future, and about his place in Vietnam now and
in the future.

765. Hunebelle, Danielle. "North Vietnam's Most

Disquieting Experiment." **Realites,** no. 150
(May 1963): 66-73.

Hunebelle reports on the economic aspects of
North Vietnam based on her firsthand experiences
during a visit there. She finds, nine years
after French withdrawal, that people in Hanoi
are healthier, more well-off than before, and
extremely tough and purposeful. However, she
does find flaws in the system: the civilian
bureaucratic offices are inefficient, and the
hotels, food, roads, and telephone service are
obviously those of an underdeveloped country.
But these flaws, she maintains, are not
indicative of the great agricultural, economic,
social, and health strides made in those nine
years. Hunebelle concludes that the concrete
policies of the leaders have produced these
gains, aided by the country's unusual autonomy
and lack of internal struggle.

766.   Labin, Suzanne. "Killing Our Ally: A Disclosure
       of Communist Methods Used to Discredit and
       Undermine the Government of South Vietnam."
       Military Review 42 (May 1962): 28-38.

In a highly pro-Diem, pro-American government
piece, Labin describes the tactics used by
Communists to undermine the South Vietnamese
government which include: (1) unpopular press
about Diem; (2) artificial guerrilla soldiers;
and (3) the calls for a "neutralist" government.
All of these are part of her list of weapons
used by the enemy to win control over the South.

767.   _____. **Sellout in Vietnam?**
       Springfield, Va.: Crestwood Bks., 1966.

Labin writes about another of her visits to
Vietnam, again attempting to defend the American
role there. Her arguments for U.S. involvement
are based on the "domino theory."

768.   _____. **Vietnam: An Eyewitness
       Account.** Springfield, Va.: Crestwood Bks.,
       1964.

Labin is an extreme anti-Communist who sees

the American involvement in Vietnam in the early
1960's as an apathetic series of attempts to
assist a tiny struggling country retain its
freedom against encroaching Communism. In the
book's first section, Labin defends Diem,
denying his persecution of the Buddhists and
offering evidence to place the blame for the
problems on Communist secret manipulations.
Major sections of the book are spent describing
the American complicity in Diem's overthrow.
Labin blames the world press and these liberals
as well for betraying Diem, and thus, the cause
of freedom. To her, these groups are enemies of
freedom just as the Communists are.

769. Levchenko, Irina. **Land Aflame**. Moscow:
        Progress Pubs., 1969.

      Russian-born Levchenko visited North Vietnam
during the war and writes a very sympathetic
view of the lives, problems, and events of the
people she came to know while she lived there.
The book also includes a visit she paid to the
United States as part of the Soviet War Veterans
Committee. No translator is listed although the
work is published in English.

770. Salmon, Lorraine [pseud.] "Down Mandarin Road."
        Viet-nam Advances 5, no. 8 (1960): 25-27.

      Salmon (a pseudonym for Marjorie Weatherly)
and her husband took a trip from Hanoi down
Mandarin Road (Highway 1) to Vin Linh. In a
very pro-North Vietnamese article, Salmon
describes the scenery, the peasants at work, and
the rebuilding of destroyed areas. She adds a
few of the Southern refugee's tales of Diem's
terrorism.

771. Vernon, Hilda. "North Vietnam's Achievements."
        Eastern World 18, no. 12 (December 1964):
        7-8.

      Vernon vouches for the industrial progress
she saw on a visit to North Vietnam in the
summer of 1964. In the production of electrical
plants, potential chemical plants, building
materials, and communications, the 1950's and

60's Three and Five Year Plans seem to her to be successes.

772.   _____. **Vietnam: The War and Its Background**. London: British Vietnam Committee, 1965.

This is an anti-American account of the less than idealistic U.S. motives for intervening in Vietnam. The author chronologically describes a brief history of the Vietnamese struggle for independence and condemns Britain also for its occasional support of the American war plans. The book concludes as Vernon warns that increased involvement by Britain, and especially America, will threaten world peace.

1970-1979

773.   Brittain, Victoria. "Vietnam's New Economic War." **New Statesman** 86 (July 13, 1973): 42.

This piece describes the economic woes of Thieu's government and suggests that they will be helpful to the PRG.

774.   Culhane, Claire. "How Canada Torpedoed the Peace in Vietnam." **Canadian Dimension** 9 (July, 1973): 6-7.

Culhane writes a scathing description of Canada's troops and diplomats at the ICCS headquarters in South Vietnam. Her article clearly points out that Canadians do not maintain impartial stances as required on issues of peace negotiations. She cites various instances in which Canada's anti-Communist leanings prompted actions. Culhane views history as repeating itself; as in 1955, she sees Canada playing an obstructionist role in the possible reunification of Vietnam in 1973.

775.   _____. "Women and Vietnam." **Canadian Dimension** 10, no. 8 (1975): 4-8.

Culhane uses the year 1975 and its celebration of International Women's Year along with the victories in Vietnam and Cambodia, to

reflect on her memories of trips she made to
Vietnam. She describes the liberated life that
women lead in the North and liberated parts of
the South, and discusses the issues concerning
refugee movement adoptions.

776.   Fallaci,   Oriana.   "General Giap." Chapter 3 in
       her **Interview With History**. Translated by
       John Shepley, 74-87. Boston: Houghton Mifflin
       Co., 1976. New York: Liveright Publishing
       Corp., 1976.

       In her usual style of prefacing an interview,
Fallaci sets the tone of this piece by
describing Giap's mystique, his aura of the
menacing warrior. She describes the
circumstances of her interview with him,
beginning with the appointment, her first
impressions of him in person at their
introduction, and the attempt by Giap to force
her to publish a version of her interview typed
by him. Refusing to withhold her own notes of
the interview, Fallaci finishes the piece with
the true transcript of a dialogue in which Giap
analyzes the political and military reasons for
the impending American defeat in Vietnam.

777.   _____. "Nguyen Van Thieu." Chapter 2
       in her **Interview with History**. Translated by
       John Shepley, 45-73. Boston: Houghton
       Mifflin Co., 1976. New York: Liveright
       Publishing Corp., 1976.

       In 1973, Fallaci held this interview with
Nguyen Van Thieu in which she explores Thieu's
disagreements with the U.S. while negotiations
with North Vietnam progressed. Thieu reveals
his disagreements with the U.S. and his
assessments of North Vietnamese aims should a
cease-fire and total American withdrawal occur.
He also responds to both Fallaci's questions
about the future place of the NLF in South
Vietnamese politics as well as to accusations of
his dishonesty.

778.   _____. "Working UP to Killing."
       Washington Monthly 3, no. 12 (February 1972):
       39-46.

       Fallaci, under the escort of a French priest,

works her way through Hue after its liberation
from the Vietcong. Described are scenes of mass
destruction, death, and the horror of clearing
away the human debris in Hue after the battles.
Fallaci's central question haunts her: "Why do
men become soldiers and kill each other?" In
trying to answer this question, the article
shifts to two meetings with two very different
men. In one, Fallaci interviews a Vietcong
terrorist, and in the other, she talks with an
American pilot.

779.   Ross, Jane. "The Conscript Experience in
         Vietnam." **Australian Outlook** 29 (December
         1975): 315-322.

         Ross interviewed Australian soldiers at two
bases in Vietnam in 1971. Her findings point to
the fact that soldiers in this war, unlike those
in WWI and WWII, were highly uncommitted.
Ross's analysis of this leads to points about
the purposelessness of Australia's presence in
Vietnam, and the inactivity and boredom
characterizing the kind of combat in the war.
She concludes by discussing the effects of this
attitude toward soldiering on the Australian
military.

780.   Thomas, Liz. **Dust of Life: Children of the
         Saigon Streets**. London: Hamilton, 1977. New
         York: E.P. Dutton, 1978.

         Thomas is a British woman, a young nurse who
wanted to serve in Vietnam since she was 14.
She first works with orphanages, where she
closely views what life is like for the children
of Vietnam. She stayed until after the
Communist takeover, attempting to help the
Vietnamese people.

1980-1987

781.   Jacobus, Helen. "Operation Propaganda." **New
         Statesman** 107 (May 11, 1984): 8-10.

         This account is written by a British woman
who volunteered to assist with the Vietnamese
refugees airlifted to Britain (sponsored by the

Daily Mail). She attempts to locate now those orphans that were brought to Britain in the 1970's. Jacobus found that those adopted had very little recollection of their lives in Vietnam, and that occasionally, these children were not really orphans. Jacobus also speculates that there may have been very little danger after April, 1975, and that these children were uprooted largely to promote world-wide sympathy for South Vietnam's plight, not because their own safety demanded it.

Author Index